CONTESTED NATIONALISM

Ethnopolitics

General Editors: **Stefan Wolff**, Department of European Studies, University of Bath, and **Timothy D. Sisk**, University of Denver

Focussing on the ethnopolitical dimensions of the security and stability of states and regions, this series addresses theoretical and practical issues relating to the management, settlement and prevention of ethnic conflicts.

Volume 1
Disputed Territories: The Transnational
Dynamics of Ethnic Conflict Settlement
Stefan Wolff

Volume 2
Peace at Last? The Impact of the Good Friday
Agreement on Northern Ireland
Edited by **Jörg Neuheiser** and **Stefan Wolff**

Volume 3
Radical Ethnic Movements in Contemporary Europe
Edited by **Farimah Daftary** and **Stefan Troebst**

Volume 4
The Romani Movement: Minority Politics and
Ethnic Mobilization in Contemporary Central Europe
Peter Vermeersch

Volume 5
Modernity and Secession: The Social Sciences and
the Political Discourse of the lega nord in Italy
Michel Huysseune

Volume 6
Contested Nationalism: Serb Elite Rivalry in
Croatia and Bosnia in the 1990s
Nina Caspersen

Contested Nationalism

Serb Elite Rivalry in Croatia and Bosnia in the 1990s

Nina Caspersen

Berghahn Books
New York • Oxford

First published in 2010 by

Berghahn Books

www.BerghahnBooks.com

©2010 Nina Caspersen

Library of Congress Cataloging-in-Publication Data

A C.I.P. record for this book is available from
the Library of Congress

British Library Cataloguing in Publication Data

A catalogue record for this book is available from the British Library

Printed in the United States on acid-free paper.

ISBN: 978-1-84545-726-6 (hardback)

CONTENTS

LIST OF FIGURES AND TABLES

Figures

Tables

LIST OF ABBREVIATIONS

DPB: Democratic Patriotic Bloc (Demokratski patriotski blok)
DS: Democratic Party (Demokratska stranka)
DSS: Democratic Alliance of Socialists (Demokratski socijalistički savez)
DSS: Democratic Party of Serbia (Demokratska stranka Srbije)
FRY: Federal Republic of Yugoslavia
HDZ: Croatian Democratic Community (Hrvatska demokratska zajednica)
HSP: Croat Party of Right (Hrvatska stranka prava)
HVO: Croat Defence Council (Hrvatsko vijeće odbrane)
ICTY: International Criminal Tribunal for the former Yugoslavia
JNA: Yugoslav People's Army (Jugoslovenska narodna armija)
JSDS: Yugoslav Independent Democratic Party (Jugoslavenska samostalna demokratska stranka)
JUL: Yugoslav United Left (Jugoslovenska ujedinjena levica)
LS: Liberal Party (Liberalna stranka)
NDH: Independent State of Croatia (Nezavisna država Hrvatska)
RS: Serb Republic (Republika Srpska)
RSK: Republic of Serb Krajina (Republika Srpska Krajina)
SAO: Serb Autonomous Region (Srpska autonomna oblast)
SDA: Party of Democratic Action (Stranka demokratske akcije)
SDP: Social Democratic Party (Socijaldemokratska partija), earlier SKH-SDP/SK-SDP
SDF: Serb Democratic Forum (Srpski demokratski forum)
SDS: Serb Democratic Party (Srpska demokratska stranka)
SDSS: Independent Democratic Serb Party (Samostalna demokratska srpska stranka)
SFOR: Stabilization Force, in Bosnia and Herzegovina
SK-SDP: League of Communists – Party for Democratic Change (Savez komunista – Stranka demokratske promjene)
SKH-SDP: League of Communists of Croatia – Party for Democratic Changes (Savez komunista Hrvatske – Stranka demokratskih promjena)
SK-PZJ: League of Communists – Movement for Yugoslavia (Savez komunista – Pokret za Jugoslaviju)
SNS: Serb National Party (Srpska narodna stranka)
SNS: Serb National Alliance (Srpski narodni savez)
SNSD: Alliance of Independent Social Democrats (Saves nezavisnih socijaldemokrata)
SNV: Serb National Council (Srpko nacionalno vijeće)

SPO: Serb Renewal Movement (Srpski pokret obnove)
SPRS: Socialist Party of Republika Srpska (Socijalistička partija Republike Srpske)
SPS: Socialist Party of Serbia (Socijalistička partija Srbije)
SPS: Serb Party of Socialists (Srpska partija socijalista)
SRS: Serb Radical Party (Srpska radikalna stranka)
SRSJ: League of Reform Forces of Yugoslavia (Savez reformskih snaga Jugoslavije)
SSS: Independent Serb Party (Samostalna srpska stranka)

ACKNOWLEDGEMENTS

This book has been six years in the making and over the years I have become indebted to a large number of people and institutions without whose support it would have remained but an interesting idea.

The project had its beginnings as a PhD thesis at the London School of Economics and benefited immensely from lengthy discussions with friends and colleagues who would gladly spend their free hours dwelling over the intricacies of the Yugoslav disintegration. I would like to thank the Danish Research Council for supporting me with the very generous grant which made this research possible. The book was further developed at my new intellectual home at Lancaster University, where the Richardson Institute for Peace and Conflict Research provided an intellectually stimulating environment and gave me the opportunity to delve more deeply into the world of contested nationalisms.

I am grateful to all the colleagues who have commented on the project at various stages and helped me refine my ideas. Special thanks are owed to Florian Bieber, Sumantra Bose, Feargal Cochrane, Jasna Dragović-Soso, Chip Gagnon, Eric Gordy, Peter Viggo Jakobsen and Dejan Jović. Also thanks to Ayse Kaya, Camille Monteux and Indraneel Sircar for their invaluable friendship, encouragement, dark sense of humour and late-night discussions throughout our years at the LSE.

During my fieldwork, I would often have been at a loss had it not been for the considerable support I received. Thanks, in particular, to Sanja Janjatović, Milorad Pupovac, Ivan Šiber, Nenad Zakošek and Vojislav Vukćević. Many hours were also spent going through newspapers and archives at the Bosniak Institute in Sarajevo, the National and University Library in Zagreb and the University Library in Belgrade. Thanks to the staff for their assistance. I am also immensely grateful to all the people I interviewed in Croatia, Bosnia and Serbia. This book would not have been possible without the information and insights that they provided me with.

Finally, thanks to the editors of the Studies in EthnoPolitics series, Timothy Sisk and Stefan Wolff. And most importantly, thanks to Keith for his love and support and for reminding me that there are other things in life than academia.

Introduction

'Only unity saves the Serbs' is the famous call for unity in the Serb nationalist doctrine.[1] But even though this doctrine was ideologically adhered to by most of the Serb leaders in Croatia and Bosnia, disunity characterized Serb politics during the Yugoslav disintegration and war: divisions between leaders, between competing Serb parties and eventually also between leaders in the Serb statelets and in Belgrade. Nationalism was, thus, contested and nationalist claims to homogeneity did not reflect the reality of Serb politics.

The call for unity is not only found in Serb nationalist discourse, but is an integral part of nationalist ideology: the claim that the nation is, or should be, a unitary actor with a single goal. However, the reality in situations of national and ethnic conflict is often contrary to such claims: it is not a question of unitary nations in a conflict solely spurred by conflicting group needs and interests. As Milton J. Esman argues, 'Factional conflict is inherent in ethnic politics'.[2] Intra-ethnic leadership rivalry should be expected and this not only contradicts the nationalist claim to homogeneity and unity, but also affects the political positions adopted by leaders and thereby the development of the conflict. Examples of such internal leadership rivalry are plentiful and by no means confined to the former Yugoslavia. The conflict in Israel/Palestine has not only been influenced by Israeli–Palestinian relations but also by internal politics, by the changing balance of power between Hamas and Fatah on the Palestinian side and between Likud and the Labour Party on the Israeli side, as well as by intra-party struggles. Similarly, in the case of Northern Ireland, the Ulster Unionist Party faced continuous outbidding from the more radical Democratic Unionist Party, while the rapprochement between Sinn Fein and the Social Democratic and Labour Party helped the movement towards peace in the 1990s.

Without the recognition of such divisions there is no understanding of more moderate voices, of hardliners breathing down the neck of incumbent leaders, of processes of outbidding. Intra-Serb rivalry was pervasive in both Croatia and Bosnia and this significantly affected the positions adopted by

1. 'Samo Sloga Srbina Spasava': the so-called *ocila* can be traced to St Sava who, in the twelfth century, called for Serb unity in an independent Orthodox Church.
2. M.J. Esman. 1994, *Ethnic Politics*, Ithaca: Cornell University Press, 248.

the victorious Serb leaders and parties. This intra-Serb competition constituted an important dynamic in the Yugoslav conflict but it has, nevertheless, been afforded little attention in existing literature. The same lack of attention is characteristic of the theoretical literature on ethnic conflicts: while intra-ethnic elite rivalry may be recognized, it is very rarely made the object of analysis and the effect of divisions *within* groups on the relations *between* groups is genuinely under-analysed. The decisive role of elites in national and ethnic conflicts has, on the other hand, long been acknowledged: they are the sine qua non of conflict resolution and will, furthermore, often have had more than a little to do with causing the conflict in the first place. But, however powerful these elites may be, they will rarely be monoliths: competition is the norm and this can either emanate from within the leader's own ranks or from competing political parties and movements. Such competition, or even the anticipation of its potential emergence, will significantly affect the positions in the conflict that a leader is willing and able to take. The dynamics of internal competition, therefore, ought to be an integral part of the study of ethnic conflict but, in reality, very little theorizing exists. Nevertheless, one theoretical assumption is often adhered to: intra-ethnic competition will foster radicalization based on elite appeals to mass extremism. But this assumption requires further analysis: how will leaders react to challengers? Are popular attitudes decisive in internal competition?

This book undertakes an in-depth analysis of Serb elite rivalry in Croatia and Bosnia with a view to improving theorizing in this relatively undeveloped area of conflict studies;[3] it presents fresh, primary research in a new conceptual framework. The book is not primarily focused on *why* elites choose a certain position but analyses *how* the political positions adopted by Serb leaders were affected by internal rivalry. The analysis, moreover, asks how more moderate forces were marginalized and why hardliners proved victorious. Serb leadership rivalry in Croatia and Bosnia represents an underdeveloped, but important, aspect of the Yugoslav disintegration that should be included in order to fully understand the development of the conflict, the outbreak of war and the persistent rejection of peace settlements. The increasingly strenuous relations between local Serb leaders and the Serbian president, Slobodan Milošević, are frequently cited in the literature and conflicts among local Serb leaders are also mentioned, but mostly in passing. Actual analysis of the effect of intra-Serb rivalry is decidedly lacking. This book analyses

---

3. Or, in the words of Arend Lijphart, to 'develop theoretical generalizations in areas where no theory exists yet'. A. Lijphart. 1971. 'Comparative Politics and the Comparative Method', *American Political Science Review* 65(3), 692.

the extent of Serb disunity and its impact on the positions adopted by Serb leaders, their acceptance or rejection of compromise solutions and the use of peaceful or violent means. It also critically assesses the widely held assumption that Milošević was always able to control Serb leaders in Croatia and Bosnia. The empirical findings depart from existing theoretical assumptions of outbidding and they are used to suggest a new way of theorizing about intra-ethnic competition.

The analysis centres on a number of particular questions. How does intra-ethnic leadership rivalry affect the dominant position in a conflict? What influences whether or not it fosters radicalization? To whom do the elites direct their competition; whose support is crucial? How is this influenced by the transitional situation, the ethnification of politics and the outbreak of violence? The dependent variable is the position of Serb leaders in Croatia and Bosnia: is the leader or the dominant party willing to accept inter-ethnic accommodation and compromise? Or do they insist on maximalist demands and violent strategies? The independent variable, and the main focus, is intra-ethnic elite competition: rivalry between Serb parties and leaders over power and policies.

When analysing rivalry among Serb elites, three audiences should be included. These audiences are significant in all phases of the conflict, although their relative importance varied greatly. Their significance stems from the resources they supplied the rivalling elites with: resources that were needed to emerge victorious from the competition, such as economic and coercive resources. Some of these resources can also be regarded as goals, in particular the economic resources, but their primary function is as means in the competition. The first audience is found within the party/movement or linked organizations, and resources include party membership, party structures, financial resources, media access and control of the military. Secondly, what will be termed the kin-state should be considered. Belgrade exerted considerable influence over Serb politics and it is even often argued that the influence was so great that local Serb leaders should not be regarded as independent actors. Intra-ethnic competition differs from conventional political competition since claims are made on behalf of the ethnic group and the kin-state leader is, consequently, afforded at least symbolic importance and can, furthermore, supply valuable resources. Finally, the general population is an important audience to the competition, and popular support can prove a powerful resource for competing elites. In existing theorizing, outbidding is about 'mass responsiveness to playing the ethnic card',[4] but the general

4.   T. Sisk. 1996. *Power Sharing and International Mediation in Ethnic Conflicts*, Washington, DC: United States Institute of Peace, 17.

population is not the only audience of importance for rival elites. The relative importance of these three audiences varies in different phases of the conflict and this affects *inter alia* the significance of the 'other side': does the politically relevant audience have to be convinced that the nation is under threat? Was Serb radicalization primarily a response to the wider Yugoslav context?

As a significant addition to existing literature on the Yugoslav disintegration, the empirical analysis presented here points to the very high level of Serb disunity throughout the conflict and war. This disunity, at times, included the inability of Milošević to control local Serb leaders. It is concluded that the dominance of hard-line Serb forces, which proved so important in the development of the conflict and the outbreak of war, was not based on the overwhelming power of ethnicity, it was not based on elites successfully playing the ethnic card. Resources other than popular support proved crucial and intra-Serb rivalry was largely decided by control of coercive resources. The theory of outbidding holds that radicalization is the preferred response to intra-ethnic challenges but the analysis proposed here finds that radicalization or defeat were not the only options available to challenged leaders: intra-ethnic competition can also have no effect on the dominant elite position or can even lead to relative moderation. Furthermore, the effect of the position of 'opposing' ethnic leaders is found to vary considerably in different phases of the conflict and intra-Serb competition was never only an epiphenomenon of inter-ethnic relations. Finally, it is argued that the dominance of the ethnic cleavage was the result of a political struggle, not an almost automatic outcome resulting from a largely voter-driven process. It was not inevitable, but depended, in particular, on the distribution of resources between ethnic and non-ethnic parties. The empirical analysis, therefore, demonstrates the importance of intra-Serb competition for the development of the Yugoslav conflict and its findings question or add to existing theorizing in the field, in particular the widely held assumption of outbidding based on elites playing the ethnic card.

Existing theorizing on intra-ethnic elite competition is briefly reviewed and discussed in Chapter 1 and illustrated with examples from a number of different cases, such as Israel/Palestine, Northern Ireland, Nagorno Karabakh and Rwanda. Based on this discussion, a framework for the subsequent analysis is developed. The framework centres on the different audiences to which rival elites must direct their appeal: party/movement forces, kin-state leaders and the general population. The empirical analysis begins in Chapter 2 with a brief overview of the conflict in Croatia and Bosnia, a discussion of the literature on the Yugoslav disintegration and an analysis of background events and factors. The main empirical analysis in Chapters 3 to 6 is structured according to the different phases of the conflict, prewar and wartime, and each phase is analysed in terms of the different audiences to which the competing parties and leaders addressed their appeals.

Chapter 3 analyses how the Serb Democratic Party (Srpska demokratska stranka, SDS) became dominant in the Serb community in the prewar period, despite having only won a minority of the Serb vote in the Croatian elections. It furthermore analyses the process of outbidding and the victory of hardliners within the party. The chapter finds that the victory of the SDS's hard-line faction was not based on greater popular support, but rather on the control of coercive resources and support from Belgrade. Chapter 4 focuses on the SDS's sister party in Bosnia, which was a much more cohesive party; this is partly explained by a stronger organization but it also depended on a continuous radicalization of the party and on Belgrade's lack of support for challenging factions. There is no evidence to suggest that the party's radicalization was voter-led: the SDS had significant control of the Serb population and alternatives had been marginalized.

Chapters 5 and 6 analyse the wartime period in which a temporary closing of ranks was followed by intensified competition. This period saw the emergence of competition between Serb parties often based on issues other than the war itself, in particular war profiteering. Increasing autonomy from Belgrade also characterized the period and Milošević was not always able to dictate developments in the Serb statelets. The analysis finds that radicalization was not the preferred response to rivalry from outside the party/movement, and relative moderation even resulted in the Bosnian case in 1995. The competition was overwhelmingly dominated by coercive resources, and the growing rift between civilian and political leaders proved of particular importance. Chapters 7 and 8 conclude on the findings of the previous chapters, briefly track post-war developments in both cases to identify change and continuity, and discuss implications for conflict analysis. By analysing intra-group politics in terms of politically relevant audiences and resources it is possible to further refine well-known concepts such as 'spoilers' and conflict 'ripeness'. The empirical findings are used to suggest a new framework for analysing intra-ethnic leadership rivalry that goes beyond an automatic assumption of outbidding based on appeals to mass extremism.

CHAPTER ONE

Ethnic Elites and Internal Competition

The importance of elites in the Yugoslav conflict and war is widely acknowledged, and political leaders such as Slobodan Milošević, Franjo Tuđman and Alija Izetbegović were often portrayed in the media as synonymous with the people they vowed to represent. The underlying media assumption of homogeneous, monolithic communities was a convenient myth rather than reality, but the great significance of elites nevertheless remains and it is generally accepted in the academic literature on the Yugoslav disintegration.[1] In the theoretical literature the crucial role of elites in conflict resolution is likewise emphasized and there is also increasing evidence of elite initiated conflicts.[2] But even though they are crucial actors in situations of conflict, these leaders are rarely unconstrained: they will more often than not find themselves constrained by competing elites or by the fear that such rivals will emerge. Serb leaders were, in both Croatia and Bosnia, constrained by competition from oppositional elites, who frequently perceived radicalization as a fast track to power, and this consequently limited the positions that the leaders could take without jeopardizing their hold on power. In order to study the development of the Yugoslav conflict, and inter-ethnic conflicts in general, one therefore needs to analyse these dynamics of intra-ethnic competition and the ways in which nationalism is contested by both more moderate and more extreme actors.

The framework for the empirical analysis of intra-Serb rivalry in Croatia and Bosnia adopted here has a fairly open and general character, and the theoretical discussion is used to identify dimensions of analysis and hypothesized variables of importance. Due to lack of theorizing on

1. See, for example, N. Andjelić. 2003. *Bosnia-Herzegovina: The End of a Legacy*, London: Frank Cass, 27.
2. B. Reilly. 2001. *Democracy in Divided Societies: Electoral Engineering for Conflict Management*, Cambridge: Cambridge University Press, 177.

intra-communal rivalry in ethnic conflicts, the framework is developed using inputs from a variety of different theories such as theories of party competition, democratic transition and conflict regulation. Firstly, however, this chapter addresses some preliminary issues: what is meant by elites, how is intra-ethnic elite competition addressed in existing theories, and which overall dimensions of analysis should be included in the framework?

By now I have already entered into a minefield of contentious concepts such as 'ethnic' and 'elites' and before proceeding any further, I should make my usage clear.

- *Ethnic*: The term 'ethnic' does not signify anything inherent or permanent. What is decisive are the labels used, the way in which the conflict is legitimized. For example, if the dominant discourse is one of a conflict between Croats and Serbs, then I will characterize it as an ethnic conflict regardless of whether its actual causes are found elsewhere and/or it lacks majority backing. Especially in early phases of a conflict, a great degree of fluidity in ethnic identities is to be expected, but as conflicts intensify there is a tendency for ethnicity to become reified: its proponents seek to make it static and rigid, thereby lending it a homogenizing quality that it did not possess to being with. What is 'ethnic' and, therefore, what is 'intra-ethnic' should not be regarded as static: it is likely to change with the course of the conflict and may very well reflect the interests of sub-groups within delineated ethnic groups.
- *Ethnification*: When politics is ethnicized, the dominant cleavage in political competition is a national or ethnic cleavage and this takes precedence over all other cleavages. For example, a process of ethnification had taken place in the first Bosnian multiparty elections in November 1990 and the dominant cleavage was an ethnic one, whereas the Croatian elections six months earlier were primarily fought on the issue of Yugoslavia's future.
- *Intra-ethnic elite competition*: This is defined as elite competition over dominance within an ethnic group. It encompasses competition both within and between political parties/movements, as well as competition with non-ethnic parties over the definition of politics.
- *Dominant elite position in ethnic conflicts*: By dominant elite position is meant the position adopted by the leader of a community or the strongest party; that is, the winner of the intra-ethnic elite competition. This position should be seen as the standpoint taken on the ethnic conflict: are they willing to accept inter-ethnic accommodation which

entails some form of compromise? Or do they insist on pursuing maximalist goals using all possible means? In both cases a process of radicalization took place. Initially the dominant Serb leaders adopted a relatively moderate position and were willing to accept compromises, whereas the wartime, radical leaders insisted on joining the territory under their control with Serbia and were willing to use military means to achieve that goal.

- *Elites*: The actors of importance in intra-ethnic competition are characterized as elites, or leaders. These are actors who have significant influence over policies directly affecting the development of a conflict.[3] Non-incumbent elites are encompassed insofar as they constitute a threat to the current leaders or possibly a potential threat in the case of a significant change in position. The elites most important to ethnic conflicts are found in the political and possibly the military realm. National and ethnic conflicts are primarily cast in terms of political goals – which state is the territory to be part of? how do we protect our identity? – and the conflict will primarily be fought in the political or military arena. Both cases in this analysis are offspring of a communist system which was characterized by the dominance of politics over all other spheres of social life; however, the army in the former Yugoslavia was accustomed to relative independence.[4] Civilian leaders may lack full control over military leaders who can, consequently, act as effective veto holders when it comes to issues of peace and war. The dominance of politics should be regarded as a variable, especially following the collapse of the state and the outbreak of war. As we will see in the empirical analysis to follow, the rival elites were highly dependent on coercive resources and their links with military and paramilitary leaders were, therefore, crucial for the outcome of intra-Serb competition. An additional group of actors that can be termed sub-elites should also be considered since their support is often crucial for a leader's hold on power. Such actors include party officials and higher-ranking military officials, actors who are not leaders but who form part of an audience to which the competing elites must appeal. As Timothy Sisk argues, these actors can be of great importance in conflict development.[5]

---

3. This definition, with its focus on political power, does not mean that the broader conception of elites, which also focuses on societal position, is without relevance. Serb leaders in Croatia and Bosnia were 'new elites' who lacked the societal position of the 'old elite' which may have fostered insecurity and affected their political behaviour. Thanks to Eric Gordy for this insight.

4. J. Gow. 2003. *The Serbian Project and its Adversaries: A Strategy of War Crimes*, London: Hurst, 53.

5. Sisk, *Power Sharing and International Mediation*, 84.

Intra-ethnic Rivalry and Ethnic Conflict

Although intra-ethnic rivalry constitutes an underdeveloped aspect of conflict studies, it is not completely absent from the literature Elements are found in theories of conflict dynamics and conflict resolution, and the importance of internal politics is frequently mentioned in more empirically-focused studies. A basic assumption is often adhered to: the assumption of ethnic outbidding. The argument is that radicalization will result from internal disputes based on elites playing the 'ethnic card'.

The position adopted by ethnic leaders is crucial for the success of conflict regulation, but conflict regulation theories usually overlook the impact of intra-ethnic competition, beyond some general assumptions. This is especially the case in one of the most influential theories, Arend Lijphart's consociational democracy. The consociational approach argues that given elite willingness to cooperate in a power-sharing government, mass antagonisms and polarization can be overcome and stability can be fostered.[6] Consociational theorists therefore assume that elites are driven by motivations that differ from those of their more radically inclined mass publics.[7] However, despite the importance afforded to elite motivations, consociational theory lacks a theory of these motivations. And not only that: it tends to assume that leaders are entirely voluntaristic actors, unconstrained by competing elites or by the general population. There is a working assumption of monolithic representation and deferential masses, and the theory therefore overestimates the latitude enjoyed by leaders in situations of ethnic conflict.[8] In Donald Horowitz's words, 'compromisers can readily be replaced by extremists on their flanks'.[9]

Other theorists acknowledge the importance of intra-ethnic elite competition and regard such competition rather than the ethnification of politics as the main barrier to moderation: if the elites were monolithic within their own ethnic groups, then an ethnic party system need not be debilitating for the prospect of conflict regulation. As Paul Mitchell argues, 'ethnically exclusive but *stable* party segments could be the building

6. See, for example, A. Lijphart. 1977. *Democracy in Plural Societies*, New Haven, CT: Yale University Press.
7. G. Tsebelis. 1990. *Nested Games: Rational Choice in Comparative Politics*, Berkeley: University of California Press, 162.
8. D. Horowitz. 1985. *Ethnic Groups in Conflict*, Berkeley: University of California Press, 574. B. Barry. 1975. 'Review Article: Political Accommodation and Consociational Democracy', *British Journal of Political Science* 5(4), 500.
9. D. Horowitz. 1997. 'Self-determination: Politics, Philosophy, and Law', in I. Shapiro and W. Kymlicka (eds), *Ethnicity and Group Rights*, New York: New York University Press, 439.

blocks for a negotiated resolution of conflict'.[10] Sisk similarly asserts, 'cohesive and confident ethnic groups – with clearly legitimate and broadly supported leadership – can deliver at the bargaining table'.[11] But monolithic representation is not the norm in situations of ethnic conflict: leaders will usually face internal competition or at least be aware that such competition may emerge.[12] Horowitz therefore argues that 'a principal limitation on interethnic co-operation is the configuration of intraethnic competition, both present and anticipated', and leaders therefore have to be concerned with both political competition and mass sentiments.[13]

The most commonly held view is that intra-ethnic elite competition will lead to radicalization and will, therefore, render conflict regulation profoundly difficult.[14] The proponents of this view contend that in an ethnic party system, the most effective political strategy will be to adopt extreme positions that play on mass antagonisms.[15] Leaders willing to compromise will face outbidding by more extreme rivals and, therefore, not have the necessary leeway: they will either have to radicalize or face defeat. Stephen Stedman analyses how 'spoilers' can use violence to undermine peace processes,[16] but the theory of outbidding holds that such behaviour can also operate in a non-violent way: spoilers can appeal to extreme mass sentiments and thereby undermine more accommodating leaders.

The emphasis is, thus, on the destabilizing aspects of intra-ethnic competition, and Mitchell argues that cooperation across the ethnic divide is severely constrained by the degree of intra-communal party competition; the more competition, the less cooperation.[17] This argument is also often found in empirical literature. For example, James Fearon and

10. P. Mitchell. 1995. 'Competition in an Ethnic Dual Party System', *Ethnic and Racial Studies* 18(4), 776.
11. Sisk, *Power Sharing and International Mediation,* 16.
12. See, for example, M. Esman. 2000. 'Ethnic Pluralism: Strategies for Conflict Management', Paper presented at the conference 'Facing Ethnic Conflicts'. Horowitz, *Ethnic Groups in Conflict,* 574–9.
13. Horowitz, *Ethnic Groups in Conflict,* 574. D. Horowitz. 2000. 'Some Realism about Peacemaking', Paper presented at the conference 'Facing Ethnic Conflicts', 6.
14. See, for example, A. Rabushka and K. Shepsle. 1972. *Politics in Plural Societies; A Theory of Democratic Instability,* Columbus, OH: Merrill. A. Pappalardo. 1981. 'The Conditions for Consociational Democracy: A Logical and Empirical Critique', *European Journal of Political Research* 9(4), 369–70. B. O'Leary. 1989. 'The Limits to Coercive Consociationalism in Northern Ireland', *Political Studies* 18(4), 575, 579. Horowitz, *Ethnic Groups in Conflict,* 359. Mitchell, 'Competition in an Ethnic Dual Party System,' 779.
15. Horowitz, *Ethnic Groups in Conflict,* 331, 346. Reilly, *Democracy in Divided Societies,* 9–10. Sisk, *Power Sharing and International Mediation,* 17. Mitchell, 'Competition in an Ethnic Dual Party System,' 777.
16. S.J. Stedman. 1997. 'Spoiler Problems in Peace Processes', *International Security,* 22(2).
17. Mitchell, 'Competition in an Ethnic Dual Party System', 779.

David Laitin, commenting on Gerard Prunier's *The Rwanda Crisis,* assert, 'it is thus hard to imagine a coherent account of the genocide and the fragility of all peace accords that does not analyse how the divide between moderate and extremist ethnic leaders drove both into violent actions against the ethnic other'.[18] Similarly in the case of Israel/Palestine, it is often argued that the radicalism of Hamas constrained Yasser Arafat's ability to commit to the peace process. As Zartman argues in relation to the Madrid Process, 'pressure from Hamas made results necessary, yet made compromise impossible'.[19] Elections, in particular, are argued to constrain leaders and it is almost conventional wisdom that no progress in peace processes will occur if elections are looming, since elites will fear being outflanked by their rivals. As Minsk Group co-chairman, Yury Merzlyakov, asserted in the case of Nagorno Karabakh, 'We know by experience that any election slows down the peace process … Sometimes, it even brings it to a halt for quite some time'.[20] However, other consequences of intra-ethnic competition are sometimes acknowledged. Sisk argues that strong intra-ethnic splits can actually facilitate inter-ethnic accommodation since it fosters incentives for cross-ethnic alliances.[21] Horowitz similarly asserts that intra-ethnic competition can both lead to radicalization and to cross-ethnic alliances.[22] Intra-ethnic divisions are, furthermore, crucial in his prescription of the Alternative Vote system for conflict regulation.[23] Intra-ethnic competition is two sided and given the prevalence of such competition in ethnic conflicts it is important to analyse its dynamics. As Esman argues, the implications of intra-ethnic divisions 'have not been examined sufficiently or systematically in the literature on ethnic politics'.[24]

Based on the dominant theoretical assumption of outbidding, one would expect that intra-Serb rivalry in Croatia and Bosnia led to a radicalization of the Serb position, and that this radicalization – and hence hard-line dominance – was founded on appeals to mass antagonisms. But

18. J.D. Fearon and D.D. Laitin. 2000. 'Violence and the Social Construction of Ethnic Identity', *International Organization* 54(4): 866.
19. I.W. Zartman. 1997. 'Explaining Oslo', *International Negotiation* 2, 197.
20. A. Babayan and J-C. Peuch. 2006. 'Nagorno-Karabakh: Russia Calls For Mutually-Acceptable Solution', *RFE/RL*, 6 April. From: http://www.rferl.org/featuresarticle /2006/04/6825B16B-8FC1-41F6-88CE-89484C98818F.html.
21. Sisk, *Power Sharing and International Mediation,* 16.
22. Horowitz, *Ethnic Groups in Conflict,* 359–60. D. Horowitz. 1990. 'Ethnic Conflict Management for Policy-Makers', in J.V. Montville (ed.) *Conflict and Peacemaking in Multiethnic Societies,* Toronto: Lexington, 122.
23. See, for example, D. Horowitz. 1991. *A Democratic South Africa? Constitutional Engineering in a Divided Society,* Berkeley: University of California Press.
24. Esman, *Ethnic Politics,* 20.

the assumption of outbidding rests on a rather simplified view of political competition and depends on the overwhelming power of ethnicity: intra-ethnic rivalry is decided by appeals to extreme popular sentiments and the only direction of such competition is therefore radicalization. According to Chaim Kaufmann, ethnic leaders are unlikely to be receptive to compromise under conditions of violence and hyper-nationalist mobilization, and even if they are, they cannot act without being discredited and replaced by hard-line rivals.[25] As an example of the danger of compromise under such conditions he mentions the massacre of the whole Rwandan government in 1994. This argument, however, raises the question of what will happen if ethnification is not dominant and/or if the conflict is not violent, such as in the prewar period in Croatia and Bosnia. The approach, moreover, regards the mass population as the only audience to intra-ethnic elite competition and popular support as the only resource of importance.

Part of the strategy for ethnic or national leaders is a focus on authenticity – a struggle over what defines a 'real' Serb, a 'real' Croat, and so on – and this, by implication, determines who has the right to speak for the group.[26] This struggle involves issues of representativeness – that is, who has the support of the community – but it also involves a struggle over political positions: which interpretation is the 'true' representation of the interests of the ethnic group? Hence, not only effectiveness in popular appeals matters. The general population may not even be the most important audience when it comes to securing and maintaining power since resources other than popular support can be more effective and, furthermore, readily available. The Serbian regime was, in both Bosnia and Croatia, a very significant additional audience to intra-Serb competition and Belgrade provided rival elites with, especially, economic and military resources. Serb elites, furthermore, had access to resources emanating from within their own party/movement and the party/movement therefore constituted another important audience. The existence of several bases of support, several audiences of importance, is also found in other cases. The elites in Nagorno Karabakh could, for example, rely on support from Armenia and from the Armenian diaspora and were, furthermore, able to procure weapons from the Red Army.[27]

25. C. Kaufmann. 'Possible and Impossible Solutions to Ethnic Wars', *International Security* 20(4), 156.
26. V.P. Gagnon Jr. 1995. 'Ethnic Conflict as an Intra-group Phenomenon: A Preliminary Framework', *Revija za sociologiju* 26(1/2), 88.
27. See, for example, T. De Waal. 2003. *Black Garden: Armenia and Azerbaijan through Peace and War*, New York: New York University Press.

In the conflict literature there is an increasing emphasis on resources when explaining the outbreak of violent conflict. Fearon and Laitin, for example, stress the importance of opportunities for insurgency.[28] Their analysis is, however, mostly focused on the distribution of resources *between* different groups, in particular the state and insurgents, whereas the analysis presented here mainly focuses on the distribution of resources *within* ethnic groups, and the relative power of moderates and extremists. Resources used in such rivalry can also be regarded as goals in themselves, as is argued in the literature that emphasizes the importance of 'greed' in ethnic conflicts.[29] However, the focus of this analysis is on resources used as *means*; it is not primarily concerned with elite motivation but rather with the dynamics of their competition and its outcome, and this is strongly influenced by politically relevant audiences and the resources they supply.

Framework for Analysis: Contested Nationalism

The different audiences to which leaders owe their power will form the basis of the framework for the following empirical analysis. These audiences provided competing Serb elites with both political and non-political resources, but the effectiveness and availability of these resources varied in different phases of the conflict and were, in particular, influenced by the outbreak of violence. In addition to the three audiences – party/movement forces, kin-state leaders and the general population – intra-Serb competition was, therefore, also affected by the conflict situation itself as well as by the position of leaders from the other ethnic group(s).

The first part of the framework considers the dynamics of competition within and between parties or movements, focusing on the internal workings of such competition, the impact of institutional factors, and the importance of state, party and movement resources.

Competition between and within Parties/Movements

Intra-Serb competition was rife in both Croatia and Bosnia and involved competition within and between parties, as well as with military leaders and independents. In the prewar period this also encompassed competition

---

28. J.D. Fearon and D.D. Laitin. 2003. 'Ethnicity, Insurgency, and Civil War', *American Political Science Review* 97(1).
29. See, for example, P. Collier. 2000. 'Doing Well out of War', in M. Berdal and D.M. Malone (eds), *Greed & Grievance: Economic Agendas in Civil Wars*, Boulder: Lynne Rienner.

between ethnic and non-ethnic parties, which was crucial for the ethnification of politics and for its subsequent radicalization. The intensity of competition was even greater during the war when there was an array of competing parties, factions, independent candidates and (para)military leaders. Competition between parties will often have a significant influence on competition within parties, and in a very fluid political environment it can be difficult to make a clear distinction. The two forms of competition should, nevertheless, be treated as separate since their audiences differ: competition between parties will, at least nominally, be about appeals to the general population whereas intra-party rivalry will be directed at party officials and members. Attitudes among these audiences are, however, not the only variable of importance for the direction and outcome of intra-ethnic competition.

Competition between Parties/Movements

Depending on the political system, one of the primary means of gaining power is the maximization of popular support. In an ethnic party system this competition for votes takes on a distinct character: due to the near absence of floating voters between ethnic parties, political competition is said to be about mobilizing the faithful. The best way to do so, Horowitz argues, is by using inflammatory and polarizing rhetoric.[30] This is the basis of the theory of outbidding. However, these extreme strategies did not dominate party competition in prewar Croatia and Bosnia. Crucially, the newly formed ethnic parties were faced with significant competition from non-ethnic parties and in order for the Serb parties to emerge victorious, the ethnic cleavage had to become dominant. Ethnification of political competition, therefore, constitutes an important variable in the analysis of intra-ethnic rivalry.

The theory of outbidding, furthermore, regards popular attitudes as the driving force behind intra-ethnic competition. But party competition never completely mirrors popular attitudes as its specific dynamics are influenced by a number of other factors. What electoral system is being used?[31] On what issues is the incumbent party being challenged? Moreover, the configuration of competition also affects the direction and outcome of intra-ethnic rivalry: how many parties are there, what is their relative size, what is the ideological distance between them?[32] Even more

30. Horowitz, *Ethnic Groups in Conflict,* 331.
31. Sisk, *Power Sharing and International Mediation,* 16. Horowitz, *A Democratic South Africa,* 196.
32. G. Sartori. 1976. *Parties and Party Systems,* Cambridge: Cambridge University Press, 135–6, 349–50.

importantly, the significance of popular attitudes should be regarded as variable, and one of the decisive factors influencing its importance is the regime type. The regime underwent a considerable change in both Croatia and Bosnia with the intensification of conflict and the outbreak of war: from a transitional system increasingly marred by undemocratic tactics, to an authoritarian system in the two Serb statelets during the war. Party competition persisted throughout, but the incumbent party will in a context of flawed democracy be able to use the state apparatus to manipulate elections or even repress challengers. Control of state resources can decisively tilt the competition in one party's favour, above all in a situation of authoritarianism and warfare, but even in nominally democratic systems. The distribution of resources may be highly skewed towards one party thereby giving it an advantage in intra-ethnic competition and greater leeway in inter-ethnic relations.[33] Resources of importance in party competition include effective party organization, campaign money and access to the media, but in a non-democratic setting these may be surpassed by control over the police and other coercive resources. Depending on the regime type and the distribution of resources, intra-ethnic competition will, therefore, not necessarily reflect popular attitudes and due to the potential importance of the above-mentioned resources, competing elites will also have to respond to attitudes found within the party/movement and/or linked organizations.

Thus, factors to consider in an analysis of intra-ethnic party competition include the degree of ethnification of the party system, the institutional framework and the distribution of resources, including links with military forces. These factors will influence the direction of competition and its outcome: how will an incumbent party react to challenges? Who will emerge victorious?

Competition from within the Party/Movement

With Eric Nordlinger as a notable exception,[34] theories of conflict regulation that pay some attention to intra-ethnic competition usually limit themselves to a focus on competition between parties. However, in certain situations, the issue of party or movement cohesion can surpass it in importance and the main threat to a leader often comes from within their own ranks: from the party, the movement as such, or the state apparatus. Processes of outbidding can occur within as well as between parties, and

---

33. M. Laver. 1975. 'Strategic Campaign Behaviour for Electors and Parties: The Northern Ireland Assembly Election of 1973', *European Journal of Political Research* 3.
34. E. Nordlinger. 1972. *Conflict Regulation in Divided Societies*, Cambridge, MA: Center for International Affairs, Harvard University, 64–68.

in the two Yugoslav cases discussed here the former often proved to be the more significant challenge – fractionalization prevailed and leadership challenges were frequent. Other examples include Northern Ireland where James Molyneaux was forced to resign as leader of the Ulster Unionist Party in 1995 following criticism of his role in peace talks.[35]

Due to threats from hard-line elements in a party or movement, Nordlinger argues that structured elite predominance is a necessary condition for conflict regulation: leaders must be able to control their party and have the political security to risk engaging in inter-ethnic compromise.[36] Such control will be strongly influenced by organizational variables – how strong are the central party structures? what kind of authority does the leader have over the party? In a transitional situation the party apparatus is generally weak and the leader correspondingly strong,[37] and one could therefore expect the threat of reduced party cohesion to be a problem of minor importance to a leader. However, if leaders are challenged from within, they will lack the organizational apparatus that would strengthen incumbent leaders in a more developed party system. Moreover, newly created parties are generally more vulnerable to intra-party conflicts since initial consensus on the party's position can quickly be undermined.[38]

In a situation of weak party structures and increasingly tense conflict, a particularly important resource in intra-party struggles is control over military or paramilitary forces. In Rodney Barker's words: 'Tank-commanders, after all, not only have guns: they have the state's guns, and their defection places those whom they previously served in double jeopardy'.[39] Barring the possibility of persuading the military of the sense of the leader's position, its loyalty is crucial. Such loyalty can have different bases, and may reflect calculated self-interest, but the key is that the control of resources, including coercive resources, is of great significance for the outcome of intra-party competition.

Finally, the issues on which factions challenge the leadership influence its ability to respond. As Giovanni Sartori argues, one should, therefore, not only consider the size and stability of a faction and the organization of the party as such, but also the ideological or political conflicts underlying any division.[40] In addition, the faction's control of resources will be of

---

35. F. Cochrane. 1997. *Unionist Politics*, Cork: Cork University Press, 331–7.
36. Nordlinger, *Conflict Regulation*, 56, 73.
37. I. Van Biezen. 2003. *Political Parties in New Democracies*, Basingstoke: Palgrave MacMillan, 205–6.
38. Ibid., 216.
39. R. Barker. 1990. *Political Legitimacy and the State*, Oxford: Clarendon, 111.
40. Sartori, *Parties and Party Systems*, 76–80.

great importance for the challenge that it is able to mount. These variables will influence how a leader responds to intra-party challenges: whether or not it will be necessary to radicalize the party's position in order to retain control or if other means are available. The question of party cohesion is, consequently, not a simple question of control or no control, nor does it simply depend on attitudes among party members.

Thus, intra-ethnic competition is affected by a number of variables found within the realm of this competition itself; it is not necessarily led by popular attitudes as argued in the theory of ethnic outbidding.[41] What kind of regime is it? What is the nature of competition faced by the incumbent party? Is the leader challenged by internal dissent? What resources do rivals possess? Different forms of resources are available to the competing parties and leaders: democratic resources such as support from the general population or from party members; other political resources such as party organization and media access; economic resources such as campaign finances or assets that can be used to establish patron–client linkages[42] or buy support in other ways; and coercive resources which include military, paramilitary and police resources.

Kin-state Involvement

In the literature on the Yugoslav disintegration, the Serbian regime is usually accorded overwhelming influence over Serb leaders in Croatia and Bosnia who are, consequently, relegated to the role of puppets. Sisk emphasizes the importance of such transnational, or rather trans-state, linkages since through these linkages 'many ethnic groups derive critical moral and material support'.[43] When elites make claims to speak for an ethnic group, this group is not necessarily delineated by state borders, and another state whose majority shares ethnicity with one of the groups may choose to become involved or may even have initiated the conflict. This shared ethnicity gives a potentially significant role to a kin-state leader who may be recognized as the legitimate leader of the entire ethnic group. In his theory of nationalism, Brubaker sets up a triadic structure of relational fields: a nationalizing state, a minority and a kin-state, which he terms ethnic homeland.[44] The kin-state asserts 'the right, even obligation,

41. Elite autonomy from popular attitudes will be further discussed below.
42. H. Kitschelt, Z. Mansfeldova, R. Markowski, G. Tóka. 1999. *Post-Communist Party Systems*, New York: Cambridge University Press, 48, 57.
43. Sisk, *Power Sharing and International Mediation*, 19.
44. R. Brubaker. 1996. *Nationalism Reframed: Nationhood and the National Question in the New Europe*. Cambridge: Cambridge University Press.

to defend' the interests of its co-ethnics, and Brubaker highlights its importance in the emergence of extreme nationalism and ethnic conflicts.[45] Kin-states can have a very significant influence over local developments, as seen in the case of Cyprus where President Makarios was overthrown in a coup strongly backed by the Greek junta in 1974. However, this level of involvement is not seen in all cases and it can, in extreme cases, even be reversed: in Armenia 'the periphery took over the centre' in 1998 when the former president of Nagorno Karabakh, Robert Kocharian, became the new President of Armenia.[46]

Serbia only technically became a kin-state following the international recognition of Croatia and Bosnia, but due to the great degree of decentralization in the Yugoslav Federation and the explicit goal of Belgrade to protect its co-ethnics, it appears reasonable to consider Serbia's involvement within that framework, even in 1990 and 1991. Belgrade functioned as a very tangible and active influence on Serb politics in Croatia and Bosnia and provided both rhetorical and material support. The Serbian president was, consequently, an audience to which rival elites had to appeal. Despite the gradual cooling of relations between Milošević and the leaders of the Serb statelets, which occurred during the war, many local leaders continued to recognize the authority of the Serbian president. Relations with Belgrade, however, became a salient issue in intra-Serb competition, which Milošević thus participated in by proxy, insofar as local elites with differing views on relations with Belgrade fought his political battles. Brubaker emphasizes that the three fields are not fixed or given, but he nevertheless conceives of them as separate fields. This, however, overlooks the possibility that the leaders of the 'ethnic homeland' can be directly part of the intra-ethnic competition and not just be an external influence. The separation between the local minority and the ethnic kin-state should be seen as a matter of degree: local leaders are more or less autonomous from the kin-state and the spectrum would be from mere puppets to autonomous actors who are in explicit conflict with the kin-state.

Elite–Mass Relations

Despite occasionally asserting Milošević's overriding legitimacy, as the 'president of all Serbs', the competing elites in Croatia and Bosnia frequently

45. Ibid., 57.
46. R. Panossian. 2002. 'The Irony of Nagorno-Karabakh: Formal Institutions versus Informal Politics', in J. Hughes and G. Sasse (eds), *Ethnicity and Territory in the Former Soviet Union,* London: Frank Cass, 152.

made claims of speaking for the local Serb population, of being their true representatives. But to what extent are elites constrained or led by the general population, by the people that they claim to represent and protect?

If the elite is completely united, the general population will have great difficulty influencing elite positions.[47] Elite competition, on the other hand, raises the possibility of mass influence since popular support will in some situations be a decisive resource. Sisk argues that outbidding refers to mass responsiveness to playing the ethnic card,[48] but this responsiveness and its significance in intra-ethnic competition will depend not only on attitudes in the mass population but also on who is playing the card and in which situation. The importance of popular attitudes will vary in different conflicts and its importance is arguably greatest if the conflict has not turned violent and is fought with political means. In Croatia and Bosnia one would consequently expect popular attitudes to be of greatest significance in the prewar period.

The choice is not necessarily between the extremes of leaders 'following their followers' and 'leading them by the nose'. This dichotomy can be avoided by emphasizing the existence of linkages that make voters more inclined to support certain parties and leaders. Popular support thereby becomes somewhat detached from the specific political positions of competing elites. In a transitional context, Herbert Kitschelt and his colleagues point to the possible importance of charismatic leadership or clientelistic exchanges, that is linkages of a recent origin which are not based on programmatic appeals.[49] Nationalism is another basis on which such linkages can be built and this is frequently argued to have been the basis of Serb leaders' popular support. Such linkages will give leaders a certain leeway in their political positioning and it is, for example, often argued that hardliners are better able to compromise: they have established their nationalist credentials and will therefore be better able to withstand outbidding and bring their followers along. In the case of Northern Ireland, the hard-line reputation of Ulster Unionist leader, David Trimble, is frequently seen as having made it easier for him to compromise. However, this does not mean that the leaders are completely unconstrained. As David Beetham argues, 'a given power relationship is not legitimate because people believe in its legitimacy, but because it is *justified in terms of* their beliefs'.[50] These linkages are conditional and the

---

47. R.D. Putnam. 1976. *The Comparative Study of Political Elites*, Englewood Cliffs, NJ: Prentice Hall, 131.
48. Sisk, *Power Sharing and International Mediation*, 17.
49. See, for example, Kitschelt et al., *Post-Communist Party Systems*, 6.
50. D. Beetham. 1991. *The Legitimation of Power*, London: MacMillan, 11.

resulting autonomy is only relative; it will be eroded if the leaders depart too far from the beliefs and values on which their legitimacy is based. Even strong, charismatic leaders with established nationalist credentials can lose power if they are seen as moving too far away from their original position. Or, as Horowitz argues, 'no doubt politicians will later find that it is easier to kindle a fire than to quench one'.[51]

Such linkages with the general population can, therefore, provide elites with a certain measure of autonomy from popular attitudes, but they are not left unconstrained. There are, however, a number of other factors that can further weaken the link between popular attitudes and elite competition, even in a situation of electoral choice. As it has been already mentioned, a highly fragmented opposition will find it difficult to beat an incumbent party regardless of popular attitudes. The choice for the voters is, furthermore, limited to the parties that choose to contest elections and these will also be motivated by goals other than vote maximization, thereby not fully reflecting voter preferences.[52] Finally, more than one cleavage can be politically salient and elites can, to some extent, ignore voter distribution on one political dimension by competing on another.[53]

Even in a fairly free electoral situation, limitations on the impact of popular attitudes on intra-ethnic competition are consequently expected. One of the most important factors influencing the significance of the general population is the distribution of resources: the level of resources available to different parties will affect how dependent they are on securing popular support as well as their possibility for manipulating the expression of popular attitudes. Such tendencies will naturally be even more pronounced in a non-democratic regime, where leaders have additional means at their disposal for countering opposition and rendering popular attitudes unimportant. Popular attitudes are, consequently, expected to have a greater impact on elite rivalry in a democratic setting, such as in the Basque Country, than in an authoritarian setting, such as in Sudan. The importance of popular attitudes will, therefore, vary in different contexts and in different phases of conflict, and is not necessarily significant for the strategies adopted in internal competition or for the outcome of this competition. Its importance is influenced by regime type, by the configuration of competition and by the nature of elite–mass linkages.

51. Horowitz, *Ethnic Groups in Conflict*, 332.
52. For party goals and strategies in different arenas: see, for example, G. Sjöblom. 1968. *Party Strategies in a Multiparty System*, Lund: Studentlitteratur.
53. G. Evans and M. Duffy. 1997. 'Beyond the Sectarian Divide: The Social Bases and Political Consequences of Nationalist and Unionist Party Competition in Northern Ireland', *British Journal of Political Science* 27(1).

The varying importance of popular attitudes is significant since the theoretical assumption of outbidding and radicalization rests on the ability of elites to appeal to mass antagonism in their struggle for power. But the general population is not the only politically relevant audience and popular support is not the only resource of which elites can make use; playing the ethnic card will not guarantee victory, even in case of antagonized mass sentiments. To put it in simple terms: given possession of significant resources, a leader can take a position that runs counter to popular opinion.

Inter-ethnic Relations

The preceding focus on intra-ethnic dynamics – competition between and within parties, kin-state involvement and elite–mass relations – does not imply that the position of ethnic leaders is not also influenced by relations with other ethnic groups.

Internal rivalry was a constant feature of Serb politics in Croatia and Bosnia in the 1990s but its degree and severity varied considerably. Horowitz argues that one of the most important factors accounting for the degree of such competition is the 'collective sense of how many parties an ethnic group can afford without weakening itself in ethnic conflict'.[54] According to this argument, the position of the group and the perceived need for unity are crucial and intra-ethnic competition is, to a large extent, determined by *inter*-ethnic relations, or it at least provides a bottom line. A related argument is often heard from national and ethnic leaders who claim that their radicalization is simply a response to the radicalization of their opponents. As the Serb leaders in Bosnia argued, they had tried everything to find a peaceful solution, but the Bosniak and Croat leaders were unwilling to compromise and their cooperation threatened the Serb people.[55] Changes in the position of leaders are, thereby, argued to be a response to the conflict situation, driven by the proclaimed motive of defending the nation.

Arguments for viewing ethnic conflict as the rational pursuit of organized group interests are widespread in the theoretical literature, where, for example, the interconnectedness of disadvantaged minorities and nationalist mobilization is stressed.[56] In line with this argument,

---

54. Horowitz, *Ethnic Groups in Conflict*, 349
55. See, for example, N. Butorović. 1992. 'Više nema jedinstvene BiH', *Borba*, 6 March, 3. M. Butorović. 2002. *Through Bosnian Eyes: The Political Memories of a Bosnian Serb*, Sarajevo: TKD Šahinpašić, 63, 65.
56. See, for example, T.R. Gurr. 1993. *Minorities at Risk: A Global View of Ethnopolitical Conflict*, Washington, DC: United States Institute of Peace.

Esman holds that the power of ethnic leaders rests on the existence of actual threats posed by another ethnic group and that the collective interests of the community limit intra-ethnic rivalry.[57] Likewise, theories that emphasize situations of stalemate as the main incentive for elites to moderate also point to the importance of inter-ethnic relations.[58] The relative position of ethnic groups would, therefore, be expected to influence the strategies adopted by leaders and, in this respect, there are important differences between the two cases analysed here. In the Bosnian case, there are three significant ethnic groups, while there are only two in the case of Croatia. A tripartite relationship opens up for shifting alliances, which is generally held to have a moderating effect on elite positions, while the bipartisan constellation is held to be the least stable.[59] The relative size of the groups also differs. The Serb community in Bosnia constituted 31 per cent of the 1991 population and even though Bosniaks were the largest group with 44 per cent, the Serbs were not faced with an ethnic majority group. In Croatia, on the other hand, the Serbs constituted 12 per cent of the 1991 population and were faced with a dominant Croat majority of 78 per cent.[60]

If national interests are the primary motivation for elite positions, then inter-ethnic relations will be decisive for intra-ethnic competition – how is 'our' nation threatened? what can be achieved in negotiations? The perceived position of the opposing group and expectations of future moves affect the positions that leaders are willing and able to take, and a useful argument found in both theoretical and empirical literature is that radicalization on one side breads radicalization on the other and that we can, therefore, observe spirals of radicalization.[61] But although this is indeed often the case, one should not overlook the instances when radicalization is not reciprocated or when radicalization occurs without prior radicalization of the other side, or is primarily caused by other factors. As will be shown in the empirical analysis, there are examples of this in both cases and the dynamics are more complex than a spiral of radicalization would suggest. The elites are faced with constraints and

57. Esman, *Ethnic Politics*, 28, 248–9.
58. See, for example, I. W. Zartman. 1995. 'Dynamics and Constraints in Negotiations in Internal Conflicts', in I.W. Zartman (ed.) *Elusive Peace: Negotiating an End to Civil War*, Washington, DC: Brookings Institution.
59. Lijphart, *Democracy in Plural Societies*, 55.
60. According to the 1991 Yugoslav census.
61. See, for example, S. Woodward. 1995. *Balkan Tragedy: Chaos and Dissolution after the Cold War*, Washington, DC: Brookings Institution, 354. R. Hislope. 1997. 'Intra-ethnic Conflict in Croatia and Serbia: Flanking and the Consequences for Democracy', *East European Quarterly* 30(4), 472.

opportunities emanating from within their own groups, and they have to focus their attention on two fronts and cannot refrain from dealing with internal competition. John Darby and Roger MacGinty argue that the loss of followers is a greater threat to political leaders than the collapse of a peace process: 'it is in the nature of political leadership'.[62] Or rather, support from politically relevant audiences will have to take priority. The situation is thereby one of what George Tsebelis terms 'nested games': elites are both actors in the inter-ethnic and intra-ethnic arenas and may, therefore, pursue seemingly irrational behaviour in one due to constraints in the other.[63] Consequently, intra-ethnic competition will not merely be an epiphenomenon of relations between ethnic groups.

The importance of the position of 'opposing' leaders is arguably greatest if popular attitudes are of significance for the intra-ethnic competition: the elites will then have to persuade the general population that their position is justified in view of the threat, or lack thereof, posed by another group. Other audiences may be influenced by different incentives – material benefits, for example – and hence be in less need of such persuasion. But the relative importance of the different audiences is, in turn, affected by the phase of the conflict and hence by inter-ethnic relations: popular attitudes are expected to be of greater importance in a non-violent conflict than in a violent one.

This framework moves beyond a simple dichotomy between greed and grievance.[64] It focuses on the interaction between elite interests and popular grievances, it examines the opportunity structure facing elites and argues that the exact mix of greed and grievance differs depending on context. The result is a complex interplay between intra-ethnic competition and inter-ethnic relations. The argument presented here is, thus, that intra-Serb rivalry had a significant impact on the development of the conflict in Croatia and Bosnia, but this rivalry was itself influenced by inter-ethnic relations, by the phase of the conflict, by the military and demographic balance, and by the position of Croat and Bosniak leaders.

Conclusion

The power of leaders rests on intra-communal dynamics and in their internal competition and political positioning they must consider the reaction of different audiences. In Croatia and Bosnia, rival Serb elites

---

62. J. Darby and R. MacGinty. 2000. 'Conclusion: The Management of Peace', in J. Darby and R. MacGinty (eds), *The Management of Peace Processes,* Houndmills: MacMillan, 257.
63. Tsebelis, *Nested Games,* 164–72.
64. See, for example, Collier, 'Doing Well out of War.'

had to consider the following audiences that supplied them with resources needed in the competition: forces within their party or movement; the general population; and the kin-state. Attitudes found among these politically relevant audiences underlie the relative capacity of moderates and hardliners.

Conflict context	Decisive audiences	Outcome of rivalry
• Institutional framework • Degree of violence ➡ • Degree of ethnification	• Party/movement, incl. military forces ➡ • Kin-state leaders • General population	• Radicalization? • Based on popular attitudes?

Relations between groups

Figure 1.1 Variables and Audiences Influencing Intra-ethnic Rivalry

As an important corrective to existing theorizing, I hypothesize that intra-ethnic elite competition will not necessarily be characterized by ethnic outbidding based on appeals to extreme popular attitudes. This is due to the existence of other politically relevant audiences, for not only the general population matters for the success of spoilers. The significance of the different audiences and the resources they supply is likely influenced by the three context variables: institutional framework, ethnification and violence. Popular attitudes are expected to be of greatest significance in a non-violent, democratic context, but this is not to say that radicalization cannot occur in a different setting. It is just as likely to be based on support from a different audience, such as the 'men with guns' or the 'men with money'.

Serb Elites in Croatia and Bosnia

Although the two cases are similar in many respects, the dynamics of Serb elite rivalry nevertheless differed between them and they also differ in terms of those variables which are hypothesized to be of importance: ethnification did not proceed at an equal speed; there were differences in party structures; kin-state involvement had different degrees and forms; and the relative strength of the ethnic groups differed. This makes the cases well suited to a comparative analysis. The empirical analysis is based on a number of different sources reflecting the complexity of intra-ethnic elite competition. These include interviews with key actors, political programmes, public statements, analyses and reports from the local media, surveys, election results, and transcripts from trials at the International Criminal Tribunal for the former Yugoslavia (ICTY).[65]

In order to analyse the differing impact of different audiences on Serb elite rivalry, the empirical chapters are structured according to the dimensions identified above:

1) *Intra- and inter-party competition.* This section analyses the form and direction of the competition: what were the dominant dynamics? What state/party/movement resources dominated?

2) *Kin-state involvement* focuses on the changing forms of Serbia's involvement and its impact on the local dynamics of intra-ethnic competition.

3) *Relations between the elites and the general population.* This section examines the importance of popular attitudes for intra-Serb competition in Croatia and Bosnia.

4) *Inter-ethnic relations.* The conflict situation and the position of 'opposing' ethnic leaders are expected to affect attitudes found among the three audiences, the relative importance of these audiences and, more directly, the strategies chosen by the leaders. This section analyses how inter-ethnic relations, thereby, affected the direction and outcome of leadership rivalry. The influence of international factors is also covered in this section, since the changing policies of the international community impacted on the military balance and the amount of room for manoeuvre available to the Serb leaders. International factors also had a significant impact on Belgrade's changing position, and its influence is, therefore, also analysed in the section on kin-state relations.

Since the dynamics of competition are expected to differ in different phases of the conflict, the analysis is, moreover, divided into prewar and wartime phases. The time frame of the main analysis is 1990 to 1995. In 1990, the first Serb parties were formally established and the first multiparty elections were held, and the year therefore seems an appropriate starting point for the analysis of political competition, even if preceding developments are also considered. As it marks the end of the war, 1995 is an obvious chronological endpoint, although postwar developments are also briefly examined.

65. The interviewees were mostly political leaders, but a few interviews were with journalists, academics and international officials. The key selection criterion for political leaders was that they had been involved in, or witnessed, intra-Serb competition and therefore had personal knowledge of events taking place.

CHAPTER TWO

Conflict and War in Croatia and Bosnia

Ever since the creation of the Kingdom of Serbs, Croats and Slovenes in 1918, Serb elites have played a crucial role in Yugoslav political developments. This is, of course, no coincidence given that the Serbs constituted the largest ethnic group in both the first and the second Yugoslavia.[1] As an independent state prior to 1918, Serbia had, moreover, played a decisive role in the unification of 'South Slav lands' and some members of the Serbian elite in the first Yugoslavia had a preference for viewing Serbia as Yugoslavia's Piedmont, with the accompanying added legitimacy of the Serbian position. The importance of the position of the Serb elites, however, does not only stem from Serb demographic strength or from Serbia's role in the creation of the Yugoslav state and subsequent dominance of the first Yugoslavia, but also from the existence of a considerable Serb population outside the borders of Serbia proper. In both Bosnia and Croatia, there was a sizeable Serb minority: 31 per cent of the 1991 population in Bosnia and 12 per cent in Croatia.[2] The Serbs in Croatia and Bosnia not only affected political life in these republics but also in Yugoslavia more broadly, and they ultimately played a critical role in the disintegration of the second Yugoslavia.

Although the Serbs in the two republics were, in many ways, different from the Serbs in Serbia, they also included a large segment that harboured wishes for stronger links with the Republic of Serbia.[3] Such sentiments were augmented by the atrocities committed against Serbs in Croatia and Bosnia by the pro-Nazi Independent State of Croatia (Nezavisna država Hrvatska, NDH) during the Second World War. NDH's leader, Ante Pavelić, institutionalized a genocidal regime in which

1. 'The first Yugoslavia' is used to describe the Kingdom of Yugoslavia, while 'the second Yugoslavia' refers to Tito's Yugoslavia which was created after the Second World War
2. According to the 1991 Yugoslav census.
3. L. Cohen. 1995. *Broken Bonds: The Disintegration of Yugoslavia*, Boulder, CO: Westview, 127.

the Serbs in the Krajina region especially suffered[4] and the Second World War memories created a self-perception of being a people under threat, of being the most vulnerable of all Serbs.[5] Tito's Yugoslavia was created as a communist state based on the Partisans' struggle against the Nazis. The political and military ranks of this second Yugoslavia were consequently dominated by Partisans and, since the Serbs from Croatia and Bosnia had been over-represented in the Partisan army, also by Serbs.[6] In times of crisis the over-representation of Serbs provided fertile ground for resentment and hence provided Croat and Bosniak leaders with a measure of ammunition for nationalist agitation. As Lenard Cohen points out, there were, therefore, three major background factors that made the 'Serb question' in Croatia and Bosnia potentially explosive: historical yearnings among Serbs for closer ties with Serbia, the Second World War genocide and the relatively privileged position of the Serbs.[7]

The importance of Serb elites for Yugoslav political development does not, however, mean that all conflicts in Yugoslavia took an ethnic dimension, nor that ethnicity was constantly conflictual or even central. Both inter-ethnic cooperation and conflict characterized Yugoslav history and political conflicts were, furthermore, often characterized by *intra*-ethnic divisions since ideological issues were primary.[8] However, the aforementioned background factors did mean that if ethnicity became conflictual in Yugoslavia, then the issue of the Serbs in Croatia and Bosnia would invariably become central. Such centrality is, however, complicated by the existence of internal divisions to which Serbs, in particular, have been prone. As Ivo Banac points out, there are 'vast cultural – not just linguistic – differences between the Serbs of the Habsburg Monarchy and those of the Ottoman Empire'.[9] Likewise, Tim Judah argues that Serb politicians are 'adepts at backbiting and flaunting their divisions, especially when the times call for unity'.[10] The intra-Serb divisions between 1990 and

---

4. Brubaker, *Nationalism Reframed,* 72. Most of the victims of the Ustaša-regime were Serbs but they also included Jews and Romas as well as dissidents of all nationalities.
5. L. Silber and A. Little. 1996. *The Death of Yugoslavia,* London: Penguin, 93.
6. S.K. Pavlowitch. 2003. 'Serbia, Montenegro and Yugoslavia,' in D. Djokić (ed.) *Yugoslavism,* London: Hurst, 66. I. Banac. 1992. 'The Fearful Asymmetry of War: The Causes and Consequences of Yugoslavia's Demise', *Daedalus* 121(2), 154.
7. Cohen, *Broken Bonds,* 127.
8. D. Jović. 2003. 'Yugoslavism and Yugoslav Communism: From Tito to Kardelj', in D. Djokić (ed.) *Yugoslavism,* London: Hurst, 161, 167.
9. I. Banac. 1996. 'Foreword: The Politics of Cultural Diversity in Former Yugoslavia', in S.P. Ramet. *Balkan Babel,* Boulder, CO: Westview, xiii.
10. T. Judah. 2000. *The Serbs: History, Myth and the Destruction of Yugoslavia,* New Haven, CT: Yale University Press, 253.

1995 actually share many similarities with earlier intra-Serb rivalry, such as in the interwar period when 'the Yugoslav political scene continued to be cross-cut by *inter*-"tribal" as well as by *intra*-"tribal" contests between political parties'.[11] Serb politics was then, just as in the 1990s, characterized by internal divisions and shifting positions, and significant Serb forces existed that opposed Belgrade's centralization.[12] Some of the actors from the 1990s explicitly acknowledge these similarities and two of the Serb parties in Croatia argued that they followed the tradition of Svetozar Pribićević's Independent Democratic Party (Samostalna demokratska stranka, SDS), which was founded in 1924 and espoused a position that was independent from the Belgrade Government.[13] Intra-Serb divisions have, at times, created incentives for inter-ethnic cooperation, such as when Pribićević joined forces with Stjepan Radić's Croatian Peasant Party in the Peasant Democratic Coalition,[14] but they have also led to radicalization. In Yugoslav history and in the conflict of the 1990s, the position of the Serb leaders as well as their internal divisions have played a decisive role, and one cannot understand the development of the conflict and the outbreak of war without analysing the position of the Serbs.

The status of the Serbs in Croatia had already been at the centre of the conflict surrounding the 'Croatian Spring' of 1970/71: as demands radicalized, anti-Serb sentiments and calls for Croatian statehood were increasingly heard and the Serbs in Krajina began taking up arms and demanding extensive autonomy.[15] However, at that time the Yugoslav state was not on the brink of collapse and a solution was found – with a not insignificant use of strong-arm tactics by Tito. But history repeated itself with a vengeance in 1990 with many of the same actors, the same demands and the same means. And this time there was no Tito to quell dissatisfaction; Yugoslav institutions were deadlocked and radicalization was egged on by Slobodan Milošević. The Serb nationalist movements in Croatia and Bosnia emerged in the late 1980s in the swell of Milošević's 'anti-bureaucratic revolutions'. The first murmurings began in Croatia, in February 1989, when the Serbs of Knin organized to protest against

---

11. D. Djokić. 2003. '(Dis)integrating Yugoslavia: King Alexander and Interwar Yugoslavism', in D. Djokić (ed.) *Yugoslavism*, London: Hurst, 145.
12. Ibid., 144–5.
13. Author's interview with Milorad Pupovac, co-founder of the SDSS (Zagreb, 11 August 2003). V. Zorić. 1990. 'JSDS je jugoslavenska', *Danas*, 27 March, 6.
14. Djokić, '(Dis)integrating Yugoslavia,' 145.
15. Judah, *The Serbs*, 165. Z. Isaković. 2000. *Identity and Security in the Former Yugoslavia*, Aldershot: Ashgate, 62. S.P. Ramet. 1992. *Nationalism and Federalism in Yugoslavia 1963–1983*, Bloomington: Indiana University Press, 112, 117–8.

Slovenia's and Croatia's support for the Kosovo Albanians.[16] In July of that year, the Serb cultural society, Zora, was re-established and it helped organize a mass rally in Krajina to celebrate the Battle of Kosovo. Following this rally, the president of Zora, Jovan Opačić, was arrested and sentenced to three months in prison. This further strengthened the momentum of the emerging movement and in February 1990 the Serb Democratic Party (Srpska demokratska stranka, SDS) was founded. In Bosnia, the establishment of a Serb movement proceeded more slowly since the Bosnian authorities were cautious not to allow expressions of nationalist sentiments given the ethnic makeup of the republic. Thus, Kosovo mass rallies were not allowed[17] and an institutionalized Serb nationalist movement only emerged with the re-establishment in June 1990 of the Serb Cultural Society, Prosvjeta, and with the formation of the Bosnian version of the SDS the following month.

The period from the first multi-party elections in 1990 until the outbreak of war saw an increasing build-up of tensions and radicalization on all sides. Both versions of the SDS adopted progressively more radical positions spurred on by their own internal rivalry, by pressure from Belgrade and by the interplay with the radicalizing positions of other ethnic leaders. Following a ten-day war in Slovenia, Croatia was the first republic to descend into open warfare in the late summer of 1991. In Bosnia, a precarious partnership between the three nationalist parties kept war at bay for longer, but Serb leaders were taking an increasingly separate and radical course and, following a last attempt to reach a solution with the Cutilheiro peace plan, war broke out in earnest the day after Bosnian independence was internationally recognized. In Croatia the radical Serb leaders established the Republic of Serb Krajina (Republika srpska krajina, RSK) while their counterparts in Bosnia proclaimed the Serb Republic (Republika srpska, RS). During the war, several attempts were made at reaching an agreement but most proved futile, often due to the intransigence of the Serb side. In January 1992 the so-called Vance Agreement was, however, reached in Croatia and although it took direct intervention from Belgrade to secure local Serb acceptance, it succeeded in at least freezing the situation. Proceeding beyond a frozen situation nevertheless proved difficult. The RSK leaders refused to budge from their uncompromising position but they were playing a losing hand, which became clear in August 1995 when most of the Serb-held territories were

16. J. Dragović-Soso. 2002. *Saviours of the Nation: Serbia's Intellectual Opposition and the Revival of Nationalism*, London: Hurst, 234.
17. A major celebration of the Battle of Kosovo was, nevertheless, held on Mount Romanija on 16 August 1989. Andjelić, *Bosnia-Herzegovina*, 111.

retaken by the Croatian army. Similar intransigence was found among the Serb leaders in Bosnia and this led to a break with Milošević: first over the rejection of the Vance-Owen Peace Plan in May 1993 and then more forcefully following the rejection of the Contact Group Plan in August 1994. It was not until the late summer of 1995 when the RS leaders were cornered by internal divisions, Belgrade pressure, NATO bombings and changing military balance, that intransigence finally gave way to greater willingness to accept a compromise solution. Finally, in November 1995, Milošević on behalf of the RS leaders accepted the Dayton Agreement.

In the literature on the Yugoslav disintegration, the Serbian regime is commonly assigned overwhelming influence over the Serb leaders in Croatia and Bosnia, whose status as independent actors is consequently questioned. Especially in the immediate prewar period and in the first years of war, Belgrade's influence was very tangible and helped strengthen radical forces through the use of media propaganda as well as through the arming and funding of extremists. However, relations between Milošević and the Serb leaders in Croatia and Bosnia underwent a considerable change from 1990 until 1995: Belgrade distanced itself, while the local leaders were able to curtail Milošević's influence and became increasingly independent. The effect of these fluctuations will be analysed in Chapters 3 to 6, but it is worth dwelling for a while on the developments in Serbia proper that affected Milošević's attitude towards the Serbs outside the republic.

Milošević and Political Competition in Serbia

In his speech at the 1989 Kosovo celebrations, Milošević reinstated the Serb nationalist call for unity when he argued that the 1389 defeat and later Serb failures had occurred owing to a lack of unity within the ranks of the Serb elite.[18] Following from that sentiment, Milošević later that year adopted the cause of the Serbs in Croatia and Bosnia and cast himself in the role of their protector.[19] Over the years, however, the close relations between Belgrade and the Serb leaders in Croatia and Bosnia deteriorated. This change was affected by developments in Serbia, especially by challenges to Milošević's powerbase and increasing dissatisfaction brought on by international isolation and sanctions.

---

18. L. Cohen. 2002. *Serpent in the Bosom: The Rise and Fall of Slobodan Milošević*, Boulder, CO: Westview, 145.
19. See, for example, L. Sell. 2002. *Milosevic and the Destruction of Yugoslavia*, Durham, NC: Duke University Press, 108–110.

Cutting the Strings

In the deepening Yugoslav crisis, Milošević's hold on power initially seemed secure. This dominance was aided, in no small way, by changes to the Serbian Constitution which were enacted prior to the first multiparty elections in December 1990 and which would allow Milošević's Socialist Party of Serbia (Socijalistička partija Srbije, SPS) to continue with a one-party system under the guise of a formally democratic structure.[20] The electoral system translated the SPS's plurality of votes into an absolute majority in Parliament, and parliamentary resistance was, therefore, not of great concern. Extra-parliamentary opposition did, however, prove a concern when the opposition arranged a mass demonstration in Belgrade on 9 March 1991 against Milošević's authoritarian rule. These demonstrations were led by Vuk Drašković, leader of the Serb Renewal Movement (Srpski pokret obnove, SPO), who accused Milošević of war-mongering and called for negotiations in order to realise the interests of the Serbs.[21] The Serbian state-controlled media fought back by carrying articles quoting Serbs from Croatia who warned that they would be left at the mercy of Croatian nationalists if the Serbian government continued being undermined.[22] One of the upshots of the demonstrations was the adoption of a dual strategy: Milošević officially espoused a more moderate line and accepted the principle of a confederation but behind the scenes he promoted a crisis atmosphere in order to deflect attention away from the challenge to his position.[23] The increasingly tense situation in Croatia and the eventual outbreak of war reinforced the call for unity and consequently strengthened Milošević's hold on power.

Despite obvious evidence to the contrary, the Serbian government vehemently denied that Serbia was at war. But the consequences of war could not be denied and they were strongly felt in Serbia. The lack of popular enthusiasm for the war was illustrated in 1991 when the Yugoslav People's Army (Jugoslovenska narodna armija, JNA) had great difficulty mobilizing soldiers, and draft dodging and desertion took place on a significant scale.[24] The opposition was still weak but it gradually began to

---

20. Cohen, *Serpent in the Bosom*, 162. See also E. Gordy. 1999. *The Culture of Power in Serbia*. University Park: Pennsylvania State University Press, 37.
21. V.P. Gagnon Jr. 2004. *The Myth of Ethnic War: Serbia and Croatia in the 1990s*, Ithaca, NY: Cornell University Press, 102.
22. R. Thomas. 1999. *Serbia under Milošević*, London: Hurst, 83.
23. Gagnon, *The Myth of Ethnic War*, 103–4. Sell, *Milosevic and the Destruction of Yugoslavia*, 137–8.
24. Cohen, *Serpent in the Bosom*, 197.

condemn the war. Drašković had abandoned his staunchly nationalist position and in October 1991 he criticized the Serb leaders outside Serbia: 'the heart of the nation ... finds itself in disagreement with the nation's periphery'.[25] A clearer anti-war position was adopted by the Democratic Party (Demokratska stranka, DS) which stated, 'we want to stop this shameless and senseless war immediately'.[26] Nevertheless, the outbreak of war had greatly aided Milošević's strategy of destroying alternatives and the opposition lacked influence.[27] The Belgrade government contended that Serbia was defended in Croatian Krajina but, despite such assertions, Milošević – probably realizing that the war did not gain him many popularity points – did not act as a typical war-leader – for example, he never visited Serbian forces at the front.[28]

One of the political actors who was more than willing to defend Serbia outside the republic was Vojislav Šešelj, leader of the Serb Radical Party (Srpska radikalna stranka, SRS). Officially the Belgrade government distanced itself from Šešelj's radicalism, and his Serb Radicals, therefore, performed the function as a more extreme opposition to Milošević. In reality, however, Šešelj was useful for Milošević. Until the war in Croatia started, Šešelj was a marginal political figure but following expressions of support for Milošević he became the 'officially acceptable extremist' in the Serb-controlled parts of Croatia and he was given unprecedented prime time in the Serbian state media. Milošević could use someone to do his dirty jobs[29] and his cooperation with the radical Šešelj provided protection against any risk of outbidding.

Although Milošević was not challenged by significant opposition on the war issue, it nevertheless became a liability. The failure of the JNA to win decisively, the threat of international sanctions against Serbia and the looming war in Bosnia made Milošević willing to accept the Vance Plan in late 1991. This brought about an unexpected conflict with the Croatian Serb leader, Milan Babić, but after successfully orchestrating his ousting, the Belgrade government could focus its attention on Bosnia. Meanwhile, the opposition parties used the end of fighting in Croatia to launch a renewed offensive against the Milošević regime, but when war broke out in Bosnia in April 1992 the call for unity dampened their fervency for a while.

25. F. Švarm. 1994. 'Kidnappers and Hostages', *Vreme NDA*, 13 June. From: http://www.scc.rutgers.edu/serbian_digest/.
26. Thomas, *Serbia under Milošević*, 107
27. Gordy, *The Culture of Power*, 24. Gagnon, *The Myth of Ethnic War*, 107–8.
28. Sell, *Milosevic and the Destruction of Yugoslavia*, 150.
29. F. Švarm. 1995. 'Sesejl Goes to Krajina', *Vreme NDA*, 27 March. From: http://www.scc .rutgers.edu/serbian_digest/

It would, however, not be long before Milošević was to encounter the first significant opposition against the war, and this came from people whom Milošević had expected to be his loyal supporters. In April 1992, the Federal Republic of Yugoslavia was established and, as its president, Milošević appointed the former dissident and famous nationalist author Dobrica Ćosić, while Milan Panić, a rich American businessman of Serb origin, was chosen as prime minister. Milošević hoped that by appointing these two figures he would be able to broaden his appeal and present a more moderate image at home and abroad.[30] But the Ćosić-Panić team was not content with being Milošević's lapdogs and they increasingly asserted their independence. Panić even launched a peace offensive and became a rallying point for Serbia's otherwise divided democratic opposition, and he decided to challenge Milošević in the December 1992 Serbian presidential elections. To make matters worse for the Serbian president, he was also faced with rifts within his own party and in June 1992 a reformist faction broke away from the SPS.[31] This opposition did not, however, make Milošević abandon his projects in Croatia and Bosnia. On the contrary, he began taking a harder line and boycotted reconciliation talks with Croatia that Panić had promoted and, in his fight against Panić, he aligned himself with the radicals in the SRS. During the election campaign, however, Milošević adopted a more moderate rhetoric and stressed the need for ethnic tolerance.[32] This vague positioning and use of repressive measures proved successful: Milošević defeated Panić in an election marred by great irregularities and, by May 1993, he had also managed to rid himself of Ćosić.[33] The opposition from Panić and Ćosić, therefore, did not alter Milošević's relations with the Serbs in Knin and Pale: if anything, it strengthened his resolve.

The holding of elections in late 1992 had greatly increased the strength of the Serb Radicals (SRS) who entered into a formal coalition with Milošević's SPS.[34] Such cooperation could be expected to lock the Serbian president into an uncompromising position, but Milošević was faced with cross-pressure since the situation in Serbia was deteriorating: economic sanctions had been imposed in May 1992 and the economic crisis was approaching catastrophic proportions. Therefore, beginning in spring 1993, Milošević cast himself in the new role as peacemaker and increasingly distanced himself from the leaders in the two Serb statelets.

30. Thomas, *Serbia under Milošević*, 122.
31. Ibid., 122.
32. Gagnon, *The Myth of Ethnic War*, 114.
33. Cohen, *Serpent in the Bosom*, 209–214.
34. Thomas, *Serbia under Milošević*, 136.

But the new peace-promoting image led Milošević on collision course with his Serb Radical supporters who vehemently opposed the Vance-Owen Peace Plan. When the strategy to coerce the Bosnian Serb leaders into acceptance failed, Milošević consequently had to consolidate his power in Serbia knowing that his humiliation could be utilized by the opposition. In alliance with Šešelj, Milošević, therefore, went against the individuals in Serbia who had supported the plan.[35]

This renewed alliance and the reversion to radicalism was, however, short-lived and the Serbian president soon began distancing himself from Šešelj, who was no longer of use. In September 1993, the main committee of the SPS attacked Šešelj's 'primitive chauvinism' and stated: 'We care about Bosnia-Hercegovina, the Republika Srpska and the Serbian people outside Serbia, but that is no reason for a politico from Sarajevo, such as Šešelj, to preach to Serbia'.[36] Thus the leader of the Radicals was not only attacked for his radicalism but his legitimacy to have a say in Serbia was also rejected due to his origins outside Serbia proper. The SPS had thereby made a decisive move away from its previous ideology and the fear of outbidding from the increasingly popular Radicals was not decisive for the strategy chosen by Milošević, although he had initially been forced to reverse his position. In order to make sure that the opposition, from one or the other side of the political spectrum, would not capitalize on the Belgrade–Pale rift, the Serbian government renewed its campaign against the independent media and stepped up its attacks on all oppositional forces.[37]

The cooling of relations between Belgrade and the leaderships of the Serb statelets led to a marked change in the rhetoric used by official Belgrade when describing the Serbs outside Serbia. When relations were still unproblematic, the need for assisting them was stressed and it was emphasized that this was also Serbia's fight. However, Milošević later accused the local Serbs of taking Serbia hostage and of being responsible for the hardship suffered in Serbia due to international sanctions.[38] In her public diary, Mira Marković, Milošević's wife, wrote in May 1994: 'the representatives of those Serbs (mainly outside Serbia) who think that the war is their only option ... should not impute that option to the whole of the Serbian people'.[39]

Once Milošević had abandoned the Greater Serbia project, it was in his interest to have as little focus on the Serbs outside Serbia as possible and

35. Ibid., 156.
36. Ibid., 178–9.
37. Ibid., 223–4. Pale was the 'capital' of RS
38. F. Švarm, 'Kidnappers and hostages.' *Vreme NDA,* 13 June. From: http://www.scc.rutgers.edu/serbian_digest/
39. Ibid.

when Croatian forces retook Western Slavonia and Krajina it was all but ignored by the Serbian government. Nevertheless, the anger and humiliation caused by these defeats seriously concerned Milošević, who allegedly confessed to the Croatian envoy, Hrvoje Šarinić, 'the situation [in Serbia] is very difficult and I will soon be unable to control it'.[40] The Dayton Agreement, therefore, came as a welcome lifeline to Milošević and he made sure to describe it as a great vindication of his position. Within his own party, Milošević ensured, by expelling possible vocal critics, that significant criticism would not surface and that his rule would remain unchallenged.[41] But despite such moves, the failure of Milošević's project of the late 1980s and early 1990s was apparent: he had failed to unify the Serbs, Serbia was isolated internationally and the economic situation remained disastrous.[42]

Thus, the kin-state leader's relations with local Serbs were significantly affected by political competition in Serbia. Changes in Milošević's relations with the leaders in Knin and Pale were brought on by the shifting strength of the opposition, by international involvement or by other factors that could serve to weaken or strengthen Milošević's hold on power. Outbidding from more extreme rivals was, however, not Milošević's greatest concern: his strategy was to destroy alternatives[43] and outflanking was not of immediate concern as long as rivals were not considered such threatening alternatives. Milošević was not unconstrained when it came to abandoning the Serbs in the neighbouring republics: local leaders pinned responsibility on the Serbian president and the fate of the Serb minorities was of least symbolic importance. The Belgrade government could, on the other hand, point to prevalent Serb infighting and stubborn intransigence and claim that it could do nothing in the face of such irresponsibility. Furthermore, it systematically changed the rhetoric used when referring to the leaders of the Serbs outside Serbia and denied that they had any legitimate influence in Serbia proper. Moreover, Belgrade was aware that it was one of the most decisive 'audiences' to which rival elites could appeal and this provided the government with considerable means for influencing or ousting obstinate local leaders. However, the leaders in Knin and Pale played an increasingly independent role and, as an important addition to existing literature on the Yugoslav disintegration and war, the following chapters will show how Milošević was at times unable to control the local Serb leaders, even though his support was initially the sine qua non of political power.

40. Sell, *Milosevic and the Destruction of Yugoslavia*, 243.
41. Thomas, *Serbia under Milošević*, 245–6.
42. Cohen, *Serpent in the Bosom*, 250.
43. Gordy, *The Culture of Power*, 7.

Explaining the Yugoslav Disintegration

To describe the literature on the Yugoslav disintegration as vast would be an understatement. There is a plethora of books across the whole range of social science disciplines that analyse the disintegration or various aspects of it. Some common trends can, nevertheless, be detected and in terms of identifying the root causal factors, there seem to be four main explanations. These can be characterized as: the 'ancient hatred' explanation; the 'national ideologies' explanation; the structural explanation; and the 'political elites' explanation. The first, the ancient hatred thesis, has been almost uniformly rejected by scholars but, nevertheless, enjoyed great prominence in the media and allegedly also among certain policy makers. The explanation focusing on national ideologies is primarily associated with Ivo Banac and his analysis of conflicting Serbian and Croatian visions of Yugoslavia.[44] Contrary to this ideological focus, structural explanations have a much more material basis and primarily focus on the 1974 Constitution and/or underlying systemic decay and economic crisis. Finally, the 'political elites' explanations take their starting point in the late 1980s and attribute the primary reason for the Yugoslav disintegration to the self-interested behaviour of a few political elites, Milošević in particular.[45]

Although this analysis will invariably be influenced by competing explanations of the Yugoslav disintegration, I do not wish to offer an alternative explanation and, therefore, will not engage directly in the above debate. First of all, my analysis starts at a later point than would an analysis aiming to explain the disintegration. The starting point is a situation that is already conflictual and it would, therefore, be erroneous to claim to be explaining the root causes of this conflict. Furthermore, I analyse *one* aspect of the disintegration and the war: Serb elite rivalry in Croatia and Bosnia. While the positions of Serb leaders in Croatia and Bosnia represent an important factor in the Yugoslav disintegration, it is not claimed to be the only factor of importance.

What I am arguing is that intra-Serb elite competition is an under-analysed aspect of the Yugoslav disintegration, and an aspect which needs to be more fully explored in order to fully understand the development of the conflict: the radicalization of positions, the outbreak of war and the

---

44. Banac, 'The Fearful Asymmetry.' I. Banac. 1984. *The National Question in Yugoslavia: Origins, History, Politics,* Ithaca, NY: Cornell University Press.
45. This categorization is strongly influenced by a typology presented in A. Dević. 1997. 'Anti-War Initiatives and the Un-Making of Civic Identities in the Former Yugoslav Republics', *Journal of Historical Sociology* 10(2), 140–42.

continuous rejection of settlements. The analysis consequently fills an important gap in the literature on the Yugoslav disintegration and provides a corrective to some common assumptions. This is, however, not to say that analysis of intra-ethnic elite competition is entirely absent from the existing literature; it has in fact been used to explain political developments in both Croatia and Serbia. For example, Susan Woodward attaches great importance to political competition *within* the national communities as a cause of radicalization.[46] As Fearon and Laitin argue in their review of Woodward's *Balkan Tragedy*, 'the political dynamics between moderates and extremists are an important part of Woodward's story'.[47] Similarly, Eric Gordy, in *The Culture of Power in Serbia*, analyses how Milošević maintained power through the destruction of alternatives.[48]

Although, intra-ethnic competition is decisive in these analyses of political developments, they are not primarily concerned with the dynamics of intra-ethnic rivalry. Moreover, such attention to intra-ethnic competition is decidedly lacking when it comes to Serb politics in Croatia and Bosnia, including analyses of relations between local Serb leaders and the government in Belgrade. There is a pronounced tendency to view the Serbs as monolithic and hence little attention has been paid to internal divisions. Moreover, there is a lack of focus on internal republican developments since most analyses centre on the Belgrade-Zagreb-Sarajevo axis. Increasingly strained relations with Belgrade are frequently cited in the literature, and rivalry among the local Serb leaders is also mentioned, although mostly in passing, but this is not made the object of in-depth analysis. There are, however, two partial, but important, exceptions to this trend: the work of Robert Hislope and of V.P. Gagnon Jr. In his two articles on intra-ethnic competition, Hislope analyses outbidding affecting Milošević and Tuđman, as well as – more briefly – outbidding within the Croatian SDS.[49] Hislope's analysis, however, falls short of identifying variables affecting this outbidding and furthermore does not touch on intra-ethnic competition among the Bosnian Serbs or on relations with Belgrade. In his excellent analysis of 'demobilization' in Croatia and Serbia, Gagnon affords some space to intra-Serb rivalry in Croatia when he argues that violence was a strategy used by the elites to 'silence, marginalize, and demobilize challengers and their supporters in

46. Woodward, *Balkan Tragedy*, 353–4.
47. Fearon and Laitin, 'Violence and the Social Construction,' 867.
48. Gordy, *The Culture of Power*.
49. Hislope, 'Intra-ethnic Conflict.' R. Hislope. 1998. 'The Generosity Moment: Ethnic Politics, Democratic Consolidation and the State in Yugoslavia (Croatia), South Africa and Czechoslovakia', *Democratization* 3(1): 64–89.

order to create political homogeneity'.[50] While Gagnon and I reach similar conclusions concerning the lack of importance of popular attitudes, my analysis differs in important respects. Firstly, our starting points are different: Gagnon is not primarily interested in the dynamics of intra-ethnic competition and does not offer a detailed analysis of the process of demobilization, such as the resources used. Secondly, Gagnon's analysis does not cover the Bosnian Serbs or the link between the local Serb leaders and Belgrade. It, therefore, does not offer a full analysis of Serb disunity in the Yugoslav conflict.

The present analysis, unsurprisingly, presupposes the importance of political elites: their interests, constraints, deliberate choices and miscalculations are regarded as crucial for the development of the conflict. This focus is shared by the majority of the literature on the former Yugoslavia. Neven Andjelić argues that, since the Yugoslav system in the late 1980s and early 1990s was still tightly controlled from above, much of what happened will have to be explained in terms of elite behaviour.[51] During the war, this elite control only became stronger and the influence of popular attitudes in war-affected areas was almost non-existent: a continued elite focus, therefore, seems defensible. Such a focus should, however, not descend into reductionism and an argument that *only* the elites should be analysed. On the contrary, the degree and form of elite predominance should be established empirically, and this research will question the proposition that the dominant elites were the ones who most effectively appealed to mass antagonisms. This clearly departs from the 'ancient hatred' explanation but the findings are also at odds with an explanation much more prevalent in the academic literature: that the conflict was driven by elites 'playing the ethnic card'.

An aspect of the structural explanation which is not generally afforded a prominent position in the literature on Yugoslavia is the transitional context. However, the emergence of ethnic parties, the first multiparty elections, the ethnification of politics and political competition in general were bound to be affected by the transition from communism: it affected party developments, party competition and linkages between the elites and the voters.

Communist Legacy and Political Competition

Kemal Kurspahić argues that, due to Yugoslavia's higher standard of living, more open borders and greater freedom of the press, its citizens

---

50. Gagnon, *The Myth of Ethnic War*, xv.
51. Andjelić, *Bosnia-Herzegovina*, 27.

were less enthusiastic about dramatic changes.[52] He argues, in other words, that the communist system enjoyed greater legitimacy in Yugoslavia than in other East European countries. The legitimacy of the system was, however, far from undamaged and the 1990 elections were not only characterized by an ethnic cleavage, or by a cleavage based on the future of Yugoslavia, but also by a divide between reformed communists and anti-communists. Moreover, the League of Communists had in Bosnia experienced a marked decline in support since the so-called Agrokomerc scandal in 1987. This corruption scandal penetrated the highest echelons of the League of Communists of Bosnia and almost all high-ranking officials were replaced within a year.[53] But the scandal also had longer-term consequences: the new leadership was weak and inexperienced and the legitimacy of the party and the system was irreparably weakened.[54] Although the erosion of support was most marked in Bosnia, republican leaderships elsewhere also faced uncertainty when contemplating a transition to democracy. But the League of Communists in both Croatia and Bosnia were nevertheless convinced that they could win freely contested elections and, in Croatia, they even designed the electoral system so that a plurality of the votes would translate into an absolute majority and thereby, supposedly, ensure communist dominance. Even though they failed to achieve these expected victories, the reformed communists in Bosnia and Croatia provided a non-ethnic alternative to the emerging ethnic parties, and together with other left-leaning parties they made the ethnification of politics far from a foregone conclusion. In Serbia, on the other hand, the League of Communists of Serbia under the leadership of Milošević chose to reform itself with a strong nationalist touch and, rather than countering nationalist forces, it promoted and encouraged them and, therefore, helped foster the ethnification of politics.

More broadly, the transitional situation had a strong impact on political competition. Political parties were not formed until late 1989 or early 1990 and they were primarily formed on an ethno-national basis. Most of the ethnic parties were political movements rather than conventional political parties: they lacked cohesion and had weak programmatic identities, undeveloped party organizations and weak societal linkages. The significance of the ethnic cleavage was strongly influenced by the Yugoslav institutional structure and the already conflictual relations between republics, but it also reflected a lack of well-defined socio-

52. K. Kurspahić. 2003. *Prime Time Crime: Balkan Media in War and Peace,* Washington, DC: United States Institute of Peace, 24.
53. Andjelić, *Bosnia-Herzegovina,* 61.
54. Ibid., 64, 69. Kurspahić, *Prime Time Crime,* 8–9.

economic cleavages, which is a common trait in postcommunist transitions.[55] Moreover, Yugoslavia lacked well-organized anti-communist opposition parties, or opposition alliances, as existed in other East European countries such as Poland, Hungary and Czechoslovakia.[56]

For the elites, nationalism offered an opportunity to gain or stay in power, a way of providing a 'quasi-democratic' authorization for authoritarian rule.[57] The population was used to one-man, one-party rule and unfamiliar with democratic competition, and Ivan Vejvoda argues that the communist monopoly had created a sense of political impotence and futility in the population, which barred political engagement.[58] An authoritarian political culture is often held to prevail in the former Yugoslavia:[59] the expectation that elites are supposed to lead and the population supposed to follow. In an oft-quoted story, the Serb politician Vuk Drašković met a peasant who expressed great enthusiasm for him and vouched that if Drašković became president then he would surely vote for him![60] A strong acceptance of authority can hamper the development of pluralistic politics and encourage a tendency to close ranks behind an emerging leader. Mirjana Kasapović uses the term 'plebiscitary emotionalism' to describe political competition in which support and loyalties are linked to the character of candidates and not to actual political content.[61] Such a political culture will limit the influence popular attitudes have on the position of leaders and hence increase their room for manoeuvre. The postcommunist transition, therefore, must be taken into account when discussing elite autonomy and the ethnification of politics.

Ethnic Conflict?

In the subsequent chapters, the Yugoslav conflict will, as a convenient shorthand, be described as national or ethnic. This usage is by no means

55. Kitschelt et al., *Post-Communist Party Systems,* 391.
56. S. Radošević. 1996. 'The Collapse of Yugoslavia: Between Chance and Necessity', in D. Dyker and I. Vejvoda (eds), *Yugoslavia and After,* London: Longman, 76.
57. V. Tomanović. 1996. 'Nationalism, Transition and Democracy', in S. Bianchini and D. Janjić (eds), *Ethnicity in Postcommunism,* Belgrade: Institute of Social Sciences, 156. See also M. Kaldor. 1993. 'Yugoslavia and the New Nationalism', *New Left Review* 197, 109.
58. I. Vejvoda. 1996. 'Yugoslavia 1945–91: From Decentralization without Democracy to Dissolution', in D. Dyker and I. Vejvoda (eds), *Yugoslavia and After,* London: Longman, 22.
59. See, for example, M. Kasapović. 1992. 'The Structure and Dynamics of the Yugoslav Political Environment and Elections in Croatia', in J. Seroka and V. Pavlović (eds), *The Tragedy of Yugoslavia,* Armonk, NY: Sharpe, 28.
60. Sell, *Milosevic and the Destruction of Yugoslavia,* 127.
61. Kasapović, 'The Structure and Dynamics,' 42.

meant to identify the causes of the conflict; rather, it addresses the legitimation used by the leaders, who claimed to represent 'their' nation and argued that it was threatened and in need of protection. The Croats, Serbs and Muslims were recognized as nations in the Yugoslav Constitution and the most appropriate term to use, therefore, would be 'national' rather than 'ethnic' conflict. However, this presents some linguistic problems when referring to dynamics within and between the national communities: intra-ethnic and inter-ethnic are less open to misunderstanding than intra-national or, especially, inter-national. While it presents some conceptual problems, the term 'ethnic' will, therefore, mostly be given preference.

The use of the term 'ethnic' should not, however, blind us to the fact that these divisions were, at times, still fluid and that the groups were internally divided. In terms of Serb elites, it is, for example, striking how reluctant the urban elite was to define itself in ethnic terms.[62] Other divisions continued to be of importance and one should not forget that there were Serbs fighting in both the Croatian and Bosnian armies. Only a few years before the outbreak of war, ethnic tensions and ethnic divisions were difficult to register in Yugoslav surveys.[63] As late as 1989, researchers concluded that ethno-centrism was not widespread, with 90 per cent of Bosnian respondents describing inter-ethnic relations as 'good' or 'very good'.[64] In surveys covering the whole of Yugoslavia, the ethnic distance between Serbs and Croats was found to be particularly low: only 7 per cent mutual rejection in 1985.[65] Nevertheless, even if relations were generally not conflictual, divisions still remained, especially in rural areas far away from the more multi-ethnic centres of Belgrade, Zagreb and Sarajevo. In the case of Bosnia, Andjelić even speaks of two parallel worlds, while Sumantra Bose asserts that several Bosnias co-existed in the prewar period.[66] Although the characteristics of urban Bosnia might have dominated public rhetoric, rural Bosnia was demographically more significant: Bosnia's five largest towns accounted for barely 25 per cent of the population in 1992 and outside these towns

62. See Chapters 3–4.
63. Gagnon, The Myth of Ethnic War, 34.
64. S. Malešević. 2000. 'Ethnicity and Federalism in Communist Yugoslavia and Its Successor States', in Y. Ghai (ed.) Autonomy and Ethnicity, Cambridge: Cambridge University Press, 163. Z. Golubović. 1996. 'The Causes of Ethno-mobilization in the Former Yugoslavia', in S. Bianchini and D. Janjić (eds), Ethnicity in Postcommunism, Belgrade: Institute of Social Sciences, 161.
65. V. Marković. 1996. 'Three Misconceptions of Nationalism as Revealed through Empirical Experience', in S. Bianchini and D. Janjić (eds), Ethnicity in Postcommunism, Belgrade: Institute of Social Sciences, 167.
66. Andjelić, Bosnia-Herzegovina, 134. S. Bose. 2002. Bosnia after Dayton, London: Hurst, 17.

attitudes and inter-community relations were of a markedly different character.[67] Moreover, from the late 1960s the Yugoslav institutional structure was built on national identity, and Woodward argues that people in 1990 voted in terms of the politically relevant categories of this system, since they did not have time to shape new political identities.[68]

The existence prior to 1989 of national divisions should, therefore, not be overlooked, nor should collective Serb memories from the Second World War, the Yugoslav institutionalization of national identity and the resentment against alleged Serb dominance. These factors facilitated the ethnification of politics and provided ammunition for extremists. However, 'nationality' or 'ethnicity' is, in the following analysis, not ascribed much independent explanatory value. The ethnification of political competition was not a given in the first multiparty elections; it was part of the political struggle. Nor was the radicalization of dominant forces and the marginalization of moderates an inevitable outcome.

67. Bose, *Bosnia after Dayton*, 14.
68. Woodward, *Balkan Tragedy*, 124.

CHAPTER THREE

Prewar Croatia: Ethnification and Radicalization

The introduction of multiparty politics launched a new Serb elite onto the political scene in Croatia, an elite which claimed to represent the homogeneous interests of the Serbs. However, disunity prevailed and became even more dominant as the conflict intensified. In their quest for power, Serb elites, moreover, had to compete with non-ethnic parties and, in this competition, the nature of 'the political' was at stake.[1] The Serb Democratic Party (Srpska demokratska stranka, SDS) managed to achieve dominance in the Serb community, despite disappointing election results, and subsequently radicalized its position.[2] This chapter analyses how the ethnic cleavage became dominant, how the process of ethnification affected political competition and why radicalization ensued. The SDS itself was plagued by intra-party strife that led to a radicalization of the party and, ultimately, to it being taken over by hardliners who pursued a policy more in tune with Belgrade's wishes. The audiences decisive in this takeover are also analysed and I ask if it was a question of extremists more successfully playing the ethnic card.

Theoretically, the emergence of ethnically defined parties is generally held to lead to a radicalization of politics, a radicalization which is primarily voter-driven. Horowitz argues that once an ethnic mass party is created, other parties will be pressured to define themselves in ethnic terms in order to compete effectively and, in the resulting ethnic party system, the most successful parties will be those who use inflammatory

---

1. 'Non-ethnic parties' are defined as parties that do not compete on the ethnic cleavage and direct their appeals to all ethnic groups.
2. For an initial analysis of the changing Serb position from 1990 to 2003, see N. Caspersen. 2003. 'The Thorny Issue of Ethnic Autonomy in Croatia', *Journal on Ethnopolitics and Minority Issues in Europe* 3, 1–27.

and polarizing rhetoric.[3] An ethnic party system is, furthermore, seen as being prone to the politics of centrifugal outbidding since leaders who choose to moderate risk being accused of betraying the nation by more extreme leaders who can successfully appeal to the general population.[4] However, Horowitz takes as his starting point an already successful ethnic party, a party that has managed to become a mass party, and such success cannot be taken as a given. Ethnic parties face competition from non-ethnic parties and this competition needs to be analysed in order to understand the impact of ethnic parties on the radicalization of politics. Moreover, resources other than popular support can be used in this competition and these can be decisive for both ethnification and radicalization.

The prewar phase was transitional and this influenced the nature of political competition: parties were newly established, weak party structures were the norm and political positions and programmes were yet to be consolidated. Societal groupings were restructured, while new parties were searching for their social bases and programmatic profiles, and this transitional context facilitated electoral mobilization along ethno-national rather than socio-economic lines.[5] The transition from communism weakened the non-ethnic parties and strengthened the ethnic ones. Even before violence broke out, the situation was, therefore, far from conventional political competition and, as sporadic violence began, coercive resources gained importance in the arena of political competition. In addition to competition with non-ethnic parties, the main challengers to the Serb leaders came from within their own ranks and intra-party struggles intensified as non-ethnic alternatives were marginalized. Intra-Serb competition reflected different views of the goals and strategies in the inter-ethnic conflict, ideological differences as well as personal power ambitions.[6] This competition led to radicalization, as expected in the theory of outbidding, but what were the factors causing this radicalization? What resources were used by the winning forces in the party? How were they able to marginalize more moderate factions?

After analysing the dynamics of competition, the ethnification of politics and the use of party and movement resources, this chapter will turn its attention to the other audiences of importance for the intra-Serb

3. Horowitz, *Ethnic Groups in Conflict,* 306, 331, 333.
4. Hislope, 'Intra-ethnic Conflict,' 472.
5. I. Šiber and C. Wenzel. 1997. 'Electoral Behaviour in Croatia', in I. Šiber (ed.) *The 1990 and 1992/3 Sabor Elections in Croatia,* Berlin: Sigma, 80–1.
6. For a detailed analysis of the sources of intra-group divisions, see N. Caspersen. 2008. Intragroup Divisions in Ethnic Conflicts: From Popular Grievances to Power Struggles', *Nationalism and Ethnic Politics* 14(2), 239–65

competition: the kin-state and the general population.[7] Given the ethnification of politics and the casting of the conflict in ethnic terms, the kin-state cannot be ignored and, furthermore, it possessed resources needed by rival SDS elites. Belgrade intellectuals had played an important role in the political organization of the Serbs in Croatia, in particular Dobrica Ćosić who helped organize the SDS in both Croatia and Bosnia and handpicked its leaders.[8] However, political and military leaders played a more important role than these intellectuals in the further development of Serb politics for they were better able to supply the resources most needed in the intra-Serb competition, especially coercive resources. The influence of kin-state leaders can be predominantly based on their position as leaders of the *kin*-state or as leaders of the kin-*state*. That is, it can be mostly symbolic and closely linked with the process of ethnification or it can primarily be based on the state resources to which they have access. Both forms of influence proved important in intra-Serb competition in prewar Croatia. Theoretical discussions of intra-ethnic elite competition are usually focused on the issue of outbidding, which is argued to be about mass responsiveness to playing the 'ethnic card'. But was popular support that important in intra-Serb competition? Or, was its importance dwarfed by other resources and hence other audiences to which rival elites addressed their appeals? Finally, inter-ethnic relations are often seen as the primary cause of elite positioning in ethnic conflicts. The chapter will conclude with an analysis of this interplay and its effect on the direction and outcome of intra-Serb competition. How was the process of ethnification affected? Was radicalization a response to the radicalization of the 'other side'?

Ethnification of Politics and the Marginalization of Moderates

The clear winner of the first Croatian multiparty elections in April/May 1990 was the Croatian Democratic Community (Hrvatska demokratska zajednica, HDZ). But despite the victory of a predominantly ethnically defined party, non-ethnic parties still played an important role and the SDS only won a minority of the Serb vote. The ethnification of politics gained speed, however, after the elections and non-ethnic parties, as well as more moderate voices within the SDS, became increasingly marginalized.

7.   The issue of kin-state involvement is also analysed in the following articles: N. Caspersen. 2007. 'Belgrade, Pale, Knin: Kin-state Control over Rebellious Puppets?' *Europe-Asia Studies* 59 (4), 619-39; N. Caspersen. 2008. 'Between Puppets and Independent Actors: Kin-state Involvement in the Conflicts in Bosnia, Croatia and Nagorno Karabakh', *Ethnopolitics* 7(4), 357-72

8.   Dragović-Soso, *Saviours of the Nation*, 237

The 1990 Elections

The SDS was founded in Knin in February 1990 under the leadership of psychiatrist Jovan Rašković. Initially the party took a fairly moderate position and in its programme it advocated democracy, human rights, national equality as well as cultural autonomy for the Serbs, and the redrawing of administrative borders to create Serb-majority regions and municipalities. The SDS supported the continued existence of the Yugoslav Federation and vowed to protect the interest of Serbs in Croatia.[9] However, since the national cleavage was not the only political cleavage of importance, the SDS would, in the competition for the Serb vote, face significant competition from non-ethnic parties. Anticipating such competition, Rašković agreed with Mile Dakić that the latter would form a nominally non-ethnic party, the Yugoslav Independent Democratic Party (Jugoslavenska samostalna demokratska stranka, JSDS), which would appeal to Serbs who would otherwise vote for the reformed communists.[10] This agreement was not publicly known and the official position of the parties differed: the JSDS denied being a Serb party and presented itself as a party open to all nations. It also did not share the SDS's staunch anti-communism.[11] The cooperation between these two parties reflected the incomplete ethnification of politics; the SDS knew that it would have problems capturing the non-ethnic ground. Constituting the ethnic cleavage as the dominant cleavage was, thus, part of the political struggle.

The reformed communists in the League of Communists of Croatia – Party for Democratic Changes (Savez komunista Hrvatske – Stranka demokratskih promjena, SKH-SDP) emphasized their determined resistance to Milošević and their independence from the League of Communists of Yugoslavia, but at the same time advocated the preservation of the federal structure.[12] The party had, contrary to Belgrade's expectations, not split along ethnic lines[13] and it could, therefore, still appeal to the Serbs in Croatia who were opposed to the

9.   Srpska demokratska stranka. 1990. 'Programski ciljevi', *Naše Teme* 34(3/4).
10. Author's interview with Mile Dakić (Belgrade, 29 August 2003).
11. J. Babić. 1990. 'Mile Dakić: Zamjena za savez komunista', *Danas,* 13 March, 15. V. Zorić. 1990. 'JSDS je jugoslavenska', *Danas,* 27 March, 6. Jugoslavenska samostalna demokratska stranka. 1990. 'Politički program – deklaracija', *Naše Teme* 34(3/4).
12. N. Zakošek. 1997. 'Political Parties and the Party System in Croatia', in I. Šiber (ed.), *The 1990 and 1992/3 Sabor Election in Croatia,* Berlin: Sigma, 42. Savez komunista Hrvatske: Stranka demokratskih promjena. 1990. 'Za miran, sretan život u suverenoj i demokratskoj Hrvatskoj,' *Naše Teme* 34(3/4).
13. Author's interview with Dušan Plećaš, Secretary of the SDP's Council (Zagreb, 26 March 2004).

organization: it was more a political movement than a structured political party[26] and, after the de facto defeat of the SKH-SDP, open conflict between the SDS's factions soon emerged. This internal competition strongly affected the position adopted by the party.

Intra-party Outflanking

During 1990 and culminating in early 1991, the leader of the SDS, Jovan Rašković, became increasingly constrained by hardliners in the party who forced him to take an ever more uncompromising position and attacked his willingness to negotiate with the Croatian government. Therefore, from its formation in early 1990, the demands made by the SDS underwent a gradual radicalization. On 25 July the so-called Serb Assembly was held in Srb, Krajina, and constituted the Serb National Council (Srpko nacionalno vijeće, SNV) as its executive body, adopting the 'Declaration on Sovereignty and Autonomy of the Serb People'. The declaration stated, 'the Serb people in Croatia have the right to autonomy. The content of that autonomy will depend on the federal or confederal structure of Yugoslavia'. 'In case of a confederal state structure of Yugoslavia, the Serb people in Croatia have the right to political-territorial autonomy'.[27] In his book *Luda Zemlja,* Rašković stated that territorial autonomy would also be demanded in case Yugoslavia ceased to exist.[28] However, Rašković declared the following day: 'In the event that Croatia secedes, the Serbs in Croatia have a right to decide in a referendum with whom and on whose territory they will live'.[29] It was, therefore, unclear what would be demanded in the event that Yugoslavia dissolved.

The assembly also decided to hold a referendum on the declaration of autonomy. This referendum was declared illegal by the Zagreb government and following rumours that it would be prevented, roadblocks were mounted by cutting down trees, effectively barricading the Knin region, an event which came to be known as the 'log revolution'. The referendum went ahead on 19 August but was marred by irregularities, and the organizers duly reported that close to 100 per cent of the Serb voters supported the proposal for autonomy.[30] Subsequently, on 30 September, autonomy was declared.

26. Author's interview with Veljko Džakula.
27. 'Deklaracija o suverenosti i autonomiji Srpskog naroda u Republici Hrvatskoj' (author's copy).
28. J. Rašković. 1990. *Luda Zemlja,* Belgrade: Akvarijus, 251.
29. Woodward, *Balkan Tragedy,* 120.
30. There were, for example, no voter registers and Serbs outside the SDS strongholds did not take part. I. Goldstein. 1999. *Croatia: A History,* London: Hurst, 219.

Despite this radicalization, Rašković's position in the party was by no means secure. He had failed to build a cohesive core of leaders and two of the founders of the party, Jovan Opačić and Dušan Zelembaba, became dissatisfied early on with what they regarded as their lack of power in the party.[31] They were, furthermore, known as hardliners and their dissatisfaction also included Rašković's political stance. Their rivalry, therefore, reflected personal ambitions and political differences, and also regional differences between Serb-majority areas in Krajina and the rest of Croatia. In May 1990, Rašković had already been forced to suspend relations with the Croatian parliament,[32] but the pressure increased exponentially when President Tuđman's adviser decided in late July 1990 to leak a transcript of secret negotiations between Tuđman and Rašković. This transcript was seriously damaging to Rašković since it portrayed him as weak and confused, and he, furthermore, reiterated his moderate demands, described the Serbs as a crazy people and admitted having difficulty controlling hardliners in the party.[33] Rašković denied the authenticity of the transcript and sought to bolster his position within the party by making more uncompromising statements.[34] But this did not suffice to quell criticism and in September 1990 an extraordinary meeting of the SDS main board was called. At this meeting Opačić and Zelembaba attempted to replace Rašković as party president but they failed to win sufficient support and consequently resigned from their party functions.[35] Although he survived the attack, Rašković was obviously weakened and Milan Babić, who was the Mayor of Knin, pressured Rašković to leave Croatia and go on a support-raising tour in the US.[36] Babić would then take over the de facto leadership of the party.[37]

One of the causes of Opačić's and Zelembaba's discontent had been the number of influential posts given to the party's new de facto leader.[38]

31. S. Radulović. 1991. 'Ko režira deobe: Šta se dogaču Kninu', *Vreme*, 25 February, 26–27.
32. M. Jajčinović. 1990. 'Lineja koja dijeli', *Danas*, 5 June, 18–19.
33. Transcript published in *Danas*, 31 July 1990, 12–15. See also J. Lovrić. 1990. 'Bitka za Hrvatsku', *Danas*, 7 August, 10–12.
34. J. Lovrić. 1990. 'Bitka za Hrvatsku', *Danas*, 7 August, 10–12. J. Lovrić. 1990. 'Srpski puč u Hrvatskoj', *Danas*, 21 August, 7–9.
35. ICTY. 2002. 'Transcripts: Prosecutor vs. Slobodan Milošević (IT-02-54)', Transcripts from Milan Babić's testimony, 18 November–9 December, 13563. Opačić left the party as such, while Zelembaba remained a member. At the same meeting, the vice-president of the main board, Branko Perić, also resigned. *Borba*, 19 September, 4. S. Stamatović. 1990. 'Ostavke nisu pobuna', *Borba*, 20 September.
36. S. Radulović. 1991. 'Ko režira deobe: Šta se dogaču Kninu', *Vreme*, 25 February, 26–27.
37. Author's interview with Filip Švarm, journalist *Vreme* (Belgrade 13 September 2004).
38. S. Radulović. 1991. 'Ko režira deobe: Šta se dogaču Kninu', *Vreme* 25 February, 26–27.

Rašković mistakenly saw Babić as an ally and promoted his career within the party: Babić became president of the Serb National Council (SNV) and Rašković transferred significant authority to him.[39] Babić was initially careful not to make extreme public statements and he even managed to reach some local agreements with the Croatian authorities.[40] However, he made no secret of his demands for more extensive Serb autonomy and, with the purpose of defeating Rašković, he began to build an alternative power base. The territorial autonomy that he demanded was given its first form when SDS-dominated municipalities were joined together in late June 1990 in the Community of (Serb) Municipalities of Northern Dalmatia and Lika.[41] Babić used this community as a powerbase and he extended it by persuading or even forcing other municipalities to join. Moreover, he started building a loyal militia.[42] Letting Babić acquire that much power could, therefore, be seen as a grave mistake by Rašković but it may conceivably have been a political strategy gone wrong. The existence of hardliners gave Rašković an excuse for the radicalization of the party and also gave him bargaining power in negotiations with the Croatian government since concessions were necessary to avoid, as he put it, 'the collision of two flocks of haws'.[43]

Rašković had support in the central structures of the party, especially in the main board which comprised the founders of the party. Babić, on the other hand, relied more on local structures of power centred around Knin: the local SDS committee, the Knin municipal council, the Community of Municipalities and the SNV. His control was enhanced by imposing a hard line on local SDS organizations and forcing out SDS moderates.[44] In late October 1990, it came to the first open conflict between the two leaders: Vojislav Vukćević, who was a close associate of Rašković, vice-president of the SDS and one of the founders of the party, took part in negotiations with the Croatian government. But when these negotiations were made public, the SDS in Knin denied the legitimacy of Vukćević to act as a negotiator. It was stated that no one but the president of the SNV, Milan Babić, had the right to negotiate on behalf of the Serb people.[45] In response, Rašković issued a letter affirming that Vukćević

39. M. Čulić. 1990. 'Rob države u državi', *Danas,* 21 August, 16–17. J. Babić. 1990. 'Čije je oružje', *Danas,* 18 September, 13–15.
40. See, for example, S. Stamatović. 1990. 'Građanski ili etnički suverenitet', *Borba,* 5 July, 14. S. Modrić. 1990. 'Krčenje staza za buduće pregovore', *Borba,* 12 September.
41. 'Odluku o osnivanu i konstitusanju Zajednice općina sjeverne Dalmacije i Like', in M. Dakić. 1994. *The Serbian Krayina: Historical Roots and Its Birth,* Knin: Iskra, Enclosure no. 3.
42. M. Glenny. 1996. *The Fall of Yugoslavia,* London: Penguin, 17.
43. M. Čulić. 1990. 'Intervju: Jovan Rašković', *Danas,* 29 May, 13–15.
44. Gagnon, *The Myth of Ethnic War,* 143, 146.
45. M. Vasić. 1992. 'Babic's Swan Song', *Vreme NDA,* 10 February. From: http://www.scc. rutgers.edu/serbian_digest/.

was the legitimate representative of the SDS and was authorized to negotiate.[46] The conflict further escalated in connection with the December 1990 elections in Serbia, which Rašković wanted the SDS to contest. Babić was against this and in a main-board vote on 22 November he beat Rašković with the smallest possible margin: one vote.[47] Less than a month later, the Croatian parliament enacted a new Constitution, which included cultural autonomy for the Serbs (art. 15) but deprived them of their position as a constituent people. This was a severe setback for Rašković. The day before the Constitution was enacted, Babić had once again demonstrated his strength when the Community of Municipalities proclaimed the Serb Autonomous Region (Srpska autonomna oblast, SAO) of Krajina. The SDS in Knin subsequently launched a campaign against Rašković in an attempt to deliver a final blow to the beleaguered party leader.[48]

The first internal challengers, Opačić and Zelembaba, had meanwhile returned to the SDS and they were expected to strengthen Rašković due to their antipathy towards Babić.[49] Consequently, Rašković decided to challenge his rival directly at a meeting of the SDS main board in mid February 1991. The issues under discussion were the removal of two Babić loyalists from the main board, changing the SDS statute and Babić's proposal for the creation of an SDS party organization in Krajina.[50] On the issue of the statute, Babić advocated making joining Serbia the official goal, whereas Rašković supported the preservation of Yugoslavia as official party policy.[51] In the vote, which was perceived as a vote for or against Babić and his policies, the Mayor of Knin was clearly defeated: 38 out of 42 board members supported Rašković.[52] Vukćević argues that at that point Babić was 'politically dead'.[53] However, the moment of triumph was short-lived, since the main board lacked the power to implement its decision.[54] The Babić-led SNV had for several months not adopted a single proposal bearing Rašković's seal[55] and, exactly one month after the main board defeat, Babić

46. J. Rašković. 1990. 'Mišljenje', Document dated 29 October (author's copy).
47. S. Radulović. 1990. 'Sokolovi u jatu', Vreme, 31 December, 26.
48. Vjesnik, 1 February 1991, 8. S. Radulović. 1991. 'Ko režira deobe: Šta se događu Kninu', Vreme, 25 February, 26–27.
49. S. Radulović. 1990. 'Sokolovi u jatu', Vreme, 31 December, 26.
50. S. Radulović. 1991. 'Ko režira deobe: Šta se događu Kninu', Vreme, 25 February, 26–27. V. Vresnik. 1991. 'Rašković izjavljuje da će se 'Krajina' proširiti na Slavoniju i Baranju!' Vjesnik 19 February, 4.
51. Author's interview with Vojislav Vukćević (Belgrade, 7 August 2003).
52. S. Radulović. 1991. 'Ko režira deobe: Šta se događu Kninu', Vreme, 25 February, 26–27.
53. Author's interview with Vojislav Vukćević.
54. Author's interview with Filip Švarm.
55. Vjesnik, 20 February 1991, 7.

went on to form a separate party organization, the SDS of Krajina. While this could be seen as the formation of a new party, the divide between the two parts of the SDS was fluid and Babić argued that he, as leader of the SDS of Krajina, spoke for the SDS as a whole. Formal institutions were at this point not of great importance and despite Babić's defeat in the 'main' SDS he was barely weakened. Events unfolded quickly and polarization was increasing.

Violence first broke out in the Western Slavonian town of Pakrac in early March 1991 when Serb militias confronted the Croatian police.[56] Even though the rebellion failed, the arrest of 400 Serbs still threatened to bring an end to the more moderate SDS leadership in this part of Croatia. The local leader of the SDS, Veljko Džakula, feared that if the arrests were upheld, the local SDS leaders would be killed by the relatives of the people arrested.[57] In order to avoid complete marginalization by hardliners, the Slavonian leaders therefore decided to go to Zagreb to seek a solution with President Tuđman and, as a result of these talks, the Croatian authorities released those arrested. The crisis was, therefore, temporarily suspended.

SDS Faction Seeks Cooperation with Non-SDS Serbs

The talks between the Slavonian SDS leaders and the Croatian government coincided with the submission of three proposals to the parliament's special commission on inter-ethnic relations. The most comprehensive of these proposals suggested 'maximalist' cultural autonomy and the creation of a Club of Serb Deputies in parliament. At the meeting, the SDS leaders also proposed the creation of a Club of Serb Deputies and indicated that the SDS deputies might return to parliament.[58] It therefore seemed that a rapprochement between the SDS and the nine remaining Serb deputies was possible[59] and this could potentially strengthen the moderate faction of the SDS. Such an alliance, however, never materialized: the SDS moderates were becoming increasingly marginalized and cooperation could, furthermore, have met resistance from the leader of the SKH-SDP, who was wary of his party being perceived as the representative of the Serbs.[60]

56. Z. Daskalović. 1991. 'Rat u Pakracu', *Danas,* 5 March, 28–29.
57. Author's interview with Vojislav Vukćević.
58. Z. Krušelj. 1991. 'Srbi u Banskim Dvorima', *Danas,* 19 March, 22–23.
59. Number based on list of MPs in Ž. Sabol (ed.) 1992. *Sabor Republike Hrvatske 1990–1992,* Zagreb: Hrvatski Sabor. In addition to the nine remaining Serb MPs, there were nine other MPs who did not declare their nationality and three MPs of other nationality. In total, 28 Serb MPs had left parliament, 5 of whom were from the SDS.
60. Author's interview with Simo Rajić.

As late as July 1991, when violence had already broken out in parts of Slavonia, the Serb Democratic Forum (Srpski demokratski forum, SDF) was founded. The then president of the SDF, Milorad Pupovac, argues that the SDF was formed by a group of Serb intellectuals when they realized that the conflict would take 'explicit extreme ethnic dimensions' and that the non-ethnic parties were not doing anything to stop the conflict.[61] Among the founders of the SDF were Rašković and other members of the SDS, and one of those SDS members, Veljko Džakula, argues: 'We wanted to create a large front, where the voice of reason could be heard'.[62] The SDF constituted the first significant 'ethnic' alternative to the SDS and it tried to prevent the radicalization of the dominant Serb forces in Croatia, but when the initiative was finally under way, when former non-ethnic forces had accepted that the conflict was centred on an ethnic cleavage, the conflict had already spiralled out of control and the SDF was no match for the Knin faction of the SDS.

The hardline SDS consolidated its position when, on 18 March 1991, the Municipal Assembly of Knin adopted the decision to separate SAO Krajina from Croatia; two weeks later it decided to join Serbia. Similarly, in Eastern Slavonia, the SNV decided in late March 1991 that Vukćević, Rašković's associate, should no longer represent the region and it was declared that the region had joined Serbia. The leader of the Serb Radicals, Vojislav Šešelj, arrived to support the separation from Croatia and he declared that Vukćević should be shot: 'Shoot him down in front of his house like a dog'.[63] This finally led Vukćević to resign from the SDS leadership, later stating 'I stepped aside in order not to be killed'.[64] With this leadership change in Eastern Slavonia, Babić had won over another SDS faction. In the summer of 1991, the moderate wing of the SDS still had considerable support in the central structures of the party but the hardliners were in firm control in Knin and Eastern Slavonia. The hardliners achieved their victory through their support in local and regional party structures and through their control of economic, political and especially coercive resources. One audience was crucial in the supply of these resources: Slobodan Milošević, the 'President of all Serbs'.

61. Author's interview with Milorad Pupovac.
62. Author's interview with Veljko Džakula.
63. Author's interview with Vojislav Vukćević.
64. F. Švarm. 1996. 'Interview Vojislav Vukcevic: Unlearned lessons', *Vreme NDA*, 10 August. From: http://www.scc.rutgers.edu/serbian_digest/

Kin-state Involvement: Building Up and Arming Extremists

Belgrade's rhetorical response to the HDZ's electoral victory was to argue that the new Croatian authorities had nothing but harmful intentions towards the republic's Serb population. This undoubtedly aided the more extreme forces among rival Serb leaders, but Belgrade's involvement was not limited to this more general fanning of flames, and the Serbian authorities took an active part in the SDS infighting.

Support for the Radical Wing of the SDS

During the course of 1990 and early 1991, Milošević became increasingly frustrated with Rašković, and Babić argues that in early 1991 the Serbian president told him to replace the SDS leader.[65] Rašković had not only showed willingness to negotiate but had at times also opposed Milošević in public.[66] Rašković, furthermore, decided to let the SDS's branch in Serbia run against Milošević's SPS in the Serbian elections in late 1990.[67] Babić, on the other hand, had no problem with expressing his unreserved support for the Serbian president: on the eve of the Serbian elections he sent a letter of support to Milošević and reiterated his support following the anti-Milošević demonstrations on 9 March 1991.[68] These letters demonstrate that the Serb leaders in Croatia were not merely passively following Belgrade's moves; Babić was very actively seeking Milošević's support, knowing that it could prove decisive in his rivalry with Rašković.

Belgrade's involvement in internal SDS rivalry was of two main forms: the arming of the paramilitary police and support for Babić through the state-controlled media. In the Belgrade media, a public profile was created for the formerly relatively anonymous Knin mayor, and an image of him was created as a champion of Serb patriotism, the undisputable leader of Serbs in Croatia and a key figure for realizing the 'all Serbs in one state' plan.[69] The military side of the involvement started earlier with radical elements in the Serb movement being armed and organized by the Serbian security service and the Serbian Ministry of the Interior, by the JNA and by semi-private

65. ICTY. 2002. 'Babić's testimony', 13565.
66. Rašković, *Luda Zemlja*, 328. M. Čulić, 1990. 'Pohod udruženih voždova', *Danas*, 10 July, 13–15. J. Lovrić. 1990. 'Bitka za Hrvatsku', *Danas*, 7 August, 10–12.
67. S. Radulović. 1991. 'Ko režira deobe: Šta se događu Kninu', *Vreme*, 25 February, 26–27.
68. F. Švarm. 1993. 'Love that'll never die', *Vreme NDA*, 22 November. From: http://www.scc.rutgers.edu/serbian_digest/.
69. S. Cerović. 1992. 'Troubles with a bit player', *Vreme NDA*, 13 January. From: http://www.scc.rutgers.edu/serbian_digest/.

channels organized by retired generals like Dušan Pekić.[70] With regard to this aspect of Belgrade's involvement, Milan Martić, the then police inspector of Knin, played a key role, and from the 'log revolution' until the JNA began interfering in March 1991, his police represented the only law in Krajina.[71] These so-called Martićevi were organized by the Serbian security service and came to function as a form of parallel structure in Krajina: they were never subjected to the JNA's control and took orders directly from Belgrade.[72] The military side of Belgrade's involvement may not have been directly targeted to assist Babić but to strengthen radical elements in general and to ensure control over developments. However, through an alliance with Martić, Babić had access to military resources and, therefore, was considerably advantaged in his competition with Rašković, who only possessed resources of a political nature.

Through the supply of resources necessary in the intra-SDS competition, Belgrade played an important role in Babić's victory and in the marginalization of the more moderate faction of the SDS. But it was not only one-sided: Babić realized the importance of Belgrade's support and actively pursued it. Moreover, after consolidating his power within the SDS, Babić also began asserting his independence. Already in March 1991, he challenged Milošević's right to reach agreements on behalf of the Krajina Serbs and reminded the public that Milošević was the president of Serbia but not Krajina.[73] For a while though, the mutual mistrust seemed to evaporate after the JNA intervened on behalf of the Serbs in late March 1991, thereby giving Knin a sign that they would get the needed support from Belgrade.[74] At the time, the stance of the international community also still seemed to favour the Serb position: in March 1991, both U.S. and EC leaders expressed their support for the territorial integrity of Yugoslavia.[75] Over the next year, however, the international position changed considerably, causing a change in Belgrade's strategy[76] and, consequently, a rift with the Serb leaders in Croatia.

70. F. Švarm. 1993. 'Love that'll never die', *Vreme NDA*, 22 November. From: http://www.scc.rutgers.edu/serbian_digest/. M. Vasić, M. Milošević, U. Komlenović, P. Svačić and F. Švarm. 1995. 'The Fall of Western Slavonia', *Vreme NDA*, 8. May. From: http://www.scc.rutgers.edu/serbian_digest/. Sell, *Milosevic and the Destruction of Yugoslavia*, 116.
71. F. Švarm. 1993. 'Milan Martic's Flying Circus,' *Vreme NDA*, 13 December. From: http://www.scc.rutgers.edu/serbian_digest/
72. Ibid. Gow, *The Serbian Project*, 80.
73. *Danas*, 26 March 1991, 24. S. Radulović. 1991. 'Nedosledni Babić', *Vreme* 1 April, 11.
74. Silber and Little, *The Death of Yugoslavia*, 145.
75. S. L. Burg and P. S. Shoup. 1999. *The War in Bosnia-Herzegovina: Ethnic Conflict and International Intervention*, Armonk, NY: Sharpe, 80.
76. Ibid., 84.

The General Population: Radicals Lacking Popular Support

The SDS managed to achieve dominance from a minority position at the time of the elections. Was this change in the party's fortunes driven by changing popular attitudes? Was its subsequent radicalization? The great significance of non-democratic resources, and the resulting importance of kin-state support, would seem to suggest otherwise.

The 1990 Elections: Support for a Non-ethnic Alternative

At the time of the 1990 elections, ethnic divisions were still not dominant and most Serb voters supported the SKH-SDP. According to a poll conducted shortly before the elections, 44 per cent of Serb voters would support the SKH-SDP, 22 per cent the SDS and 14 per cent the JSDS.[77] This even overestimated the support enjoyed by the SDS since, at the elections, only 2 per cent of all voters supported the party, which translates into around 13.5 per cent of the Serb vote.[78] It would seem, therefore, that a part of the Serb electorate decided in the last minute to close ranks behind the SKH-SDP or refrained from voting. This indicates a fairly low level of polarization or ethnification.

Judging from pre-election surveys, supporters of the SDS, the SKH-SDP and the JSDS differed significantly in their political attitudes. Among Serb respondents, JSDS and SKH-SDP supporters were markedly less religious than the supporters of the SDS. They were, moreover, more inclined to advocate the preservation of the existing federal structure, whereas the SDS's supporters advocated a more centralized federation or even a unitary state. In addition, the majority of the JSDS's and the SKH-SDP's Serb supporters did not feel that Serbs were discriminated against, whereas the majority of the SDS's supporters argued this to be the case and consequently regarded inter-ethnic relations in Croatia as the most important election issue.

The SDS's supporters expressed views that could be difficult to accommodate but the surveys and the election results suggest that such attitudes were not widespread. One must, however, consider that the disappointing result for the SDS was partly explained by its poor organization: the party was only properly organized in the Knin area and this naturally hampered its electoral performance elsewhere.[79] Moreover,

---

77. Pre-election survey 'Anketa: Izbori 1990', Fakultet političkih znanosti, Sveučilišta u Zagrebu. This dataset was kindly made available to me by Professor Ivan Šiber.
78. Gagnon, *The Myth of Ethnic War*, 35.
79. Kovačević, *Kavez*, 29–30.

Table 3.1 Serb Supporters of the SDS, the JSDS and the SKH-SDP

	SDS	JSDS	SKH-SDP
Percentage of Serbs among supporters	100 pct	66 pct	28 pct
Percentage who are not religious*	35 pct	69 pct	79 pct
Support for preservation of federal structure*	16 pct	46 pct	36 pct
Percentage who agree that Serbs and Croats are equal*	14 pct	56 pct	63 pct

*Only Serb respondents. The differences between the parties are all significant at the 0.001 level (the two latter at the 0.000 level). Source: Pre-election survey 1990, dataset made available by Ivan Šiber.

the results did not signify that a socio-economic cleavage dominated political competition,[80] and the ethnic cleavage was to become increasingly important after the elections.

Post-electoral Ethnification

After the elections, the SDS loudly questioned the SKH-SDP's right to represent the Serbs in Croatia. The SDS's assertions were mostly based on the SKH-SDP's cooperation with the new Croatian authorities and on it being a non-ethnic party, but the SDS leaders, furthermore, pointed to declining Serb support for the reformed communists. Based on this alleged alteration in support, the SDS demanded new elections in order to demonstrate their popular legitimacy. Such elections were never granted, but reduced support for the reformed communists was not just dreamed up at SDS headquarters as surveys point to a sharp decline in support for the SKH-SDP among Serbs. Thus, in August 1990, only 24 per cent of the surveyed Serbs had a positive view of the party's leader, Ivica Račan, compared with 47 per cent in June and 33 per cent in July. From being the staunchest supporters of the SKH-SDP, the Serbs had become the group with the least positive view of the party's leader.[81] At the same time, 75 per cent of Serb respondents had a positive view of Rašković and 67 per cent indicated their support for the SDS-organized referendum on Serb autonomy.[82]

What caused this rapid decline in support? Attitudes among the SKH-SDP's Serb supporters shortly before the elections indicate an answer. When asked to list values of importance to them in the election campaign, three were clearly predominant: Yugoslav community (76 per cent), peace

80. Šiber and Wenzel, 'Electoral Behaviour in Croatia,' 83.
81. D. Jović. 1990. 'I Tuđman i Rašković rastu', Danas, 28 August, 30–33.
82. Ibid.

and security (61 per cent) and national equality (59 per cent).[83] By August 1990, Serb voters could increasingly argue that the SKH-SDP had failed on all three counts. The preservation of Yugoslavia was looking less likely, peace and security was seriously under threat and national equality was undermined by the new Croatian authorities with whom many Serb SKH-SDP voters felt that their party was working too closely. Judging from the available survey data, it does appear that the Serb electorate abandoned the SKH-SDP. In short, they abandoned the main non-ethnic party which seems to indicate that ethnification was also characteristic of the general population and not just of elite competition. However, there is no clear evidence that support was transferred to the SDS in the same proportions. It should, in any case, be recognized that there was no real alternative to the SDS: the JSDS was marginal and the SKH-SDP made clear its disinclination to be the representative of the Serbs in Croatia. But the SDS was eager to legitimize its position and one way of doing so was through referenda.

In August 1990, the SDS leadership decided to hold a referendum on autonomy, partly to counter claims that the Serb Assembly did not represent the opinions of Serbs in Croatia.[84] The result showed overwhelming support for autonomy and this gave added impetus to the continued radicalization of the party. The referendum exercise was repeated by Babić in the spring of 1991, when Serb voters were asked to vote on the joining of SAO Krajina with Serbia and remaining part of Yugoslavia. Again, the result was overwhelmingly supportive: according to the Krajina authorities, 93 per cent supported the proposal and in the Knin area the turnout was reported to be a staggering 99.7 per cent.[85] With this result, Babić's hard-line faction could point to increased legitimacy for their position. These referenda, however, should not be seen as a perfect test of public opinion: their democratic credentials were doubtful,[86] the 'urban Serbs' did not take part and the voters, therefore, only represented a minority of Croatian Serbs. Rašković explained the absence of the 'urban Serbs' by citing the greater fear that he argued existed in the cities[87] but, if previous patterns are anything to go by, less support could have been expected from Serbs in the cities. Babić's

---

83. Pre-election survey 'Anketa: Izbori 1990', Fakultet političkih znanosti, Sveučilišta u Zagrebu.
84. Author's interview with Vojislav Vukćević.
85. S. Stamatović. 1991. 'Za prisajedinjenje – 93 od sto', Borba, 14 May, 4.
86. There were no voter registers and in August 1990, 48,000 people are reported to have voted in Belgrade. Goldstein, Croatia, 219.
87. J. Lovrić. 1990. 'Jovan Rašković: To se ne može zaustaviti', Danas, 21 August, 8.

support base was in the Knin region and this was also the centre of his 1991 referendum. But even though the referenda cannot be seen as a precise reflection of popular opinion, they do indicate that the SDS was supported by a large part of the Serb population and they played an important role in strengthening the party. In the increasingly tense atmosphere and with the successful elimination of alternatives, the SDS hardliners managed to take the voters along, but this does not mean that the process was driven by popular demands.

Popular Attitudes and the Marginalization of Moderates

The clearest example of the limited significance of popular attitudes is the leadership rivalry within the SDS. Rašković's popularity among Croatian Serbs and among SDS supporters was unmatched but it was not enough for him to hold on to power. His popularity remained intact after the leaking of his talks with Tuđman[88] but it was not sufficient when Babić enjoyed the support of local and regional party structures, paramilitary formations and Belgrade.

When Babić began his assent to the top of the SDS, his ratings approached those of the party leader, but never surpassed them: in September 1990, 84 per cent of the SDS's supporters had a positive view of Rašković, while 76 per cent held that opinion of Babić. Similarly, in November 1990, 71 per cent of the Serbs had a positive view of Babić and 76 per cent had a positive view of Rašković.[89] However, Babić's support among the Serbs plummeted as the internal rivalry became public and as Babić radicalized his position. Thus, in December 1990, only 54 per cent of Serbs had a positive view of Babić compared with Rašković's 86 per cent. This meant that Babić was less popular among Serbs than the federal prime minister Ante Marković and the president of the Croatian Peasant Party Ivan Zvonimir Čičak, both of whom were Croats.[90] Therefore, not only popular support for radicalization but also the dominance of the ethnic cleavage among the general population can be questioned. While Babić could not match Rašković's popularity, as Mayor of Knin he nevertheless had a popular mandate that Rašković lacked. This may have earned him support in the Knin region that he could use in challenging the party's leader. But while such local popularity may have played some role in elite competition, the outbidding that took place within the party was not based

88. D. Jović. 1990. 'I Tuđman i Rašković rastu', *Danas,* 28 August, 30–33.
89. D. Jović. 1990. 'Jastrebovi niže lete', *Danas,* 2 October, 16–19. D. Jović. 1990. 'Slavlju je kraj', *Danas,* 4 December, 7–9.
90. D. Jović. 1991. 'Čemu se nadaju', *Danas,* 1 January, 28–31.

on greater support in the Serb population: Rašković continued to be more popular than Babić among the Serbs in Croatia. Babić's victory and the radicalization of the party was, therefore, based on the availability and effectiveness of other resources: localized party support, non-democratic resources – especially (para)military resources – and kin-state support.

Even in the prewar period, when elections were held and violence was still not the defining characteristic of politics, intra-ethnic competition was consequently not voter-driven, it was not about who could most successfully play the ethnic card. One of the consequences of this was the use of a vague position by the SDS, a position from which the party could appeal to the middle ground while at the same time seeking to increase tensions. Thus, while the demands were moderate and the need for peaceful means was stressed, the rhetoric was often inflammatory, designed to create inter-ethnic tensions. This brings us to the final aspect of the analysis, inter-ethnic relations. Theoretically, one would expect this to be important, but how significant was it for prewar intra-Serb competition in Croatia and the resulting ethnification and radicalization of politics?

Inter-ethnic Relations: Lost Moments of Generosity?

One factor which is often pointed to when explaining the marginalization of moderate Serb forces and the SDS's increasing radicalization is the actions of the HDZ-led Croatian government. This argument is both straightforward and compelling. In their election campaign, the HDZ highlighted the over-representation of Serbs in official positions, and following the election victory many Serbs were fired from their jobs or forced to sign oaths of loyalty.[91] In July 1990, amendments to the Constitution were passed which replaced the five-pointed star on the Croatian flag with the *šahovnica* symbol, which Serbs associated with the pro-Nazi Independent State of Croatia. The 'Croatian literary language', moreover, became the sole official language, and the requirement of a two-thirds majority in decisions on inter-ethnic issues was removed.[92]

Robert Hislope argues that through these actions, the Croatian government helped fuel Serb radicalism and strongly contributed to the ousting of Rašković from the SDS's leadership: it was a case of lost generosity moments.[93] Mark Thompson similarly argues that the actions of the Croatian authorities made moderate Serbs look implausible and

91. Silber and Little, *The Death of Yugoslavia*, 108.
92. Hislope, 'The Generosity Moment', 73–4.
93. Ibid., 75.

provided ammunition for the extremists.[94] This argument is echoed by Susan Woodward, who asserts that the failure of Tuđman to meet the initial demands for cultural autonomy led to a radicalization of demands and ultimately to the change of leadership in the SDS.[95] The question is, however, how decisive these actions were in the competition between Rašković and Babić: was it a case of radicalization breeding radicalization? It would, furthermore, be a mistake to view the HDZ or the Croatian government as wholly unified as there were, in fact, great divisions. How did this fractionalization of the 'opposing side' affect Serb elite competition? Finally, one more issue must be considered when analysing the interplay: how did it contribute to the ethnification of politics? How did it influence the dominance of the ethnic cleavage?

The Ethnification of Politics

The victory of the HDZ was a shock to most Serbs and resulted in increased support for the SDS,[96] but the new Croatian government also aided the party in a more direct way: Rašković was considered the main interlocutor when Serb issues were concerned and, in October 1990, the SDS became formally recognized as the legitimate representative of the Serbs in Croatia. This recognition was obviously influenced by the unwillingness of the SKH-SDP to take on the role as the representative of the Croatian Serbs. However, by negotiating with the SDS and recognizing its legitimacy, the Croatian government also reinforced its own position and its own ethnic definition of politics; like the SDS, it had an interest in the dominance of the ethnic cleavage. The HDZ was still facing competition from the SKH-SDP and, therefore, also sought its marginalization. As a consequence of this convergence of interests, the SDS and the HDZ even cooperated on the local level to force SKH-SDP deputies out of office.[97] The interplay between the HDZ-led Croatian government and the SDS thereby helped reinforce the ethnic cleavage and served to weaken non-ethnic alternatives.

While the interests of ethnic leaders, therefore, overlapped on the issue of the ethnification of politics, there was not unanimous backing for this policy within the HDZ. In negotiations with Rašković, Tuđman argued

---

94. Thompson, *A Paper House*, 269.
95. Woodward, *Balkan Tragedy*, 170.
96. M. Kasapović and N. Zakošek. 1997. 'Democratic Transition in Croatia: Between Democracy, Sovereignty and War', in I. Šiber (ed.) *The 1990 and the 1992/93 Sabor Elections in Croatia*, Berlin: Sigma, 24.
97. Gagnon, *The Myth of Ethnic War*, 145–6.

that he had problems justifying to HDZ deputies why he negotiated with the SDS.[98] Rašković was increasingly unpopular with Croatian voters and persistently rated as the least liked of all politicians in Croatia. Furthermore, even though hawks within the HDZ certainly supported the ethnic conception of politics, they opposed contacts with the SDS leader. Although radicals benefit from the existence of another ethnic party – it legitimizes their existence – cooperation is precluded by their hard-line position: if it were possible to cooperate, then a radical stance would not be needed. Therefore, it may paradoxically have been the greater strength of the more moderate wing of the HDZ that helped the SDS become dominant in the Serb community: its willingness to recognize the SDS as a negotiating partner aided the ethnification of politics.

The Weakening of the SDS Moderate Wing

Negotiations with Tuđman were, however, not always to Rašković's benefit: the SDS leader was persistently criticized by hardliners in the party for his alleged softness. Their critique was strengthened by the leaking of the transcript from the Tuđman-Rašković talks, which the hardliners used to support their claim that Rašković did not represent the interest of Serbs in Croatia, that he was, in fact, playing a double game.[99] Rašković never managed to regain his former position of strength and his position was even further weakened when it became clear that the Croatian government would not meet his demands. One of the biggest failures for Rašković's more accommodating course was the passing of the new Croatian Constitution in December 1990. Although it contained provisions for cultural autonomy, the preamble declared that Croatia was the national state of the Croats and Rašković had thereby failed to achieve his most important demand: that the Serbs retain their constituent status in Croatia. The SDS officially maintained that its position was contingent on the policies pursued by the Croatian government, and that the extent of demands depended on the future status of Yugoslavia. It was, therefore, at least nominally, dependent on the position of the Croatian side.

Tuđman's adviser who decided to leak the transcript argues that they wanted to counter Rašković's public accusation that President Tuđman was taking an extreme position; the proclaimed intention was to demonstrate the willingness of the Croatian government to negotiate.[100]

---

98. *Danas*, 13 July 1990, 12–15
99. Author's interview with Drago Hedl, journalist *Feral Tribune* (Osijek, 11 September 2003).
100. Author's interview with Slaven Letica (Zagreb, 18 September 2003).

However, there were limits to their willingness to compromise and this struck at the heart of Rašković's demands: they would not concede constituent status to the Serbs, since this was felt to undermine Croatian sovereignty.[101] Furthermore, while cultural autonomy and, later, some degree of self-government for Knin and Glina were acceptable, more extensive autonomy arrangements were not. On this basis, therefore, it was very difficult to reach a compromise which would have helped Rašković bolster his position within the SDS. Once it became clear that Rašković was no longer in control of the SDS, incentives to negotiate diminished since Babić was not interested in negotiating a solution within the framework of a Croatian state. At this point, the position of the Croatian government became increasingly irrelevant for intra-Serb rivalry.

HDZ Factions and Serbs Politics

When analysing the inter-ethnic interplay, not only must the actions and rhetoric of Tuđman be considered but also those of the different factions within the HDZ. Like the SDS, the HDZ was far from unified: despite Tuđman's cohesive power, it contained a number of different factions. These divisions fed into the government which was prone to constant ministerial changes.[102] In interviews, Rašković warned against the extreme HDZ factions and argued that they were a reason for his ambivalent position – for his willingness to negotiate, while at the same time using inflammatory rhetoric.[103] Furthermore, Rašković continuously emphasized that his problem was not with Tuđman and he asked the president to publicly distance himself and the HDZ from the hawks.[104] After the 1990 elections , the more moderate wing of the HDZ seemed to be stronger[105] but the radical wing gradually asserted its position. One of the turning points in Eastern Slavonia came when Josip Riehl-Kir, the moderate regional police chief, was murdered by HDZ extremists in July 1991. With this murder, hard line HDZ officials gained the upper hand in

---

101. Ibid.
102. M. Kasapović. 1997. 'Parliamentary Elections in Croatia: Electoral Models and their Effects', in I. Šiber (ed.), The 1990 and the 1992/93 Sabor Elections in Croatia, Berlin: Sigma, 57. Silber and Little, The Death of Yugoslavia, 96.
103. Like the SDS, the HDZ employed a dual strategy: it generally portrayed itself as a moderate party, but also made use of more extreme rhetoric. Gagnon, The Myth of Ethnic War, 137–8.
104. See, for example, Danas, 7 August 1990, 11. M. Čulić. 1990. 'Intervju: Jovan Rašković', Danas, 29 May, 13–15.
105. See, for example, N. Gaće. 1990. 'Na rubu pameti – opet', Borba, 15/16 September, 5.

both the police and civil administration.[106] Similar, if less violent, strengthening of the hardliners was also taking place elsewhere in Croatia.

The existence of the hardliners in the HDZ, their extreme public statements and the possibility that they might become more powerful further weakened the position of more moderate forces in the SDS, thereby adding to the party's radicalization. The existence of hardliners within the SDS and their apparent increasing strength likewise bolstered HDZ hardliners and facilitated the radicalization of their party. Fractionalization on one side risks spurring radicalization on the other since it provides the radicals with ammunition in internal rivalry, and a spiral of radicalization may, therefore, result.

Lost Moments of Generosity?

The position of the Croatian Government, as well as divisions in the ruling party, therefore affected intra-ethnic competition in the SDS: the radicals could use the alleged extremism of the 'other side' to legitimize their own position and discredit attempts to find a negotiated solution. However, the question is to what extent Babić and his followers needed the extra ammunition. They were already in a good position to outbid Rašković and prevent agreements from being made through the use of intimidation, blockades and even physical assaults. The audience to which the hardliners appealed were intra-party forces and the kin-state leader. The latter was not interested in a solution within the framework of a Croatian state and the intra-party forces that mainly mattered were radicalized forces in Krajina and various paramilitary forces who were early on espousing an extreme position. The attitude of the Serb general population was not the driving force in the radicalization of elite positions and the impact of lost generosity moments, therefore, should not be sought in their influence on mass antagonisms. That said, a more accommodating course from the Croatian government would likely have reduced the number of followers that the extremists could take along and, furthermore, have strengthened the moderate forces.[107] But it appears unlikely that this would have prevented the radicals in the SDS from becoming dominant: the interplay with the Croatian government and the HDZ, while certainly important, was not the decisive variable for intra-Serb competition. Thus, inter-ethnic relations had a very significant impact on the ethnification of politics and the dominance of the SDS, and

---

106. Silber and Little, *The Death of Yugoslavia*, 140. Author's interview with Drago Hedl.
107. Goldstein, *Croatia*, 217.

it also affected Babić's ability to oust Rašković without it being solely, or even primarily, about 'lost generosity moments'.

Prewar Ethnification and Radicalization

The ethnification of politics in Croatia had as its starting point a Serb party that only received a minority of the Serb vote: the SDS had not succeeded in 'ethnicizing' politics prior to the elections and the main cleavage in Croatian politics was the future status of Yugoslavia. However, due to internal divisions in the SKH-SDP, the actions of the Croatian government, the institutionalization of the SDS and its use of non-democratic tactics, the reformed communists soon lost their advantage. As a result, the SKH-SDP became increasingly marginalized and the SDS achieved near-monolithic status in the Serb community. An ethnically defined alternative to the SDS was not created until violence had already broken out in parts of the country and the alternative lacked the geographically concentrated support on which the SDS had built its power.

The ethnification of politics was part of the political struggle and the speed of ethnification was, therefore, influenced by factors of strength in political competition, which, in this transitional and increasingly tense context, included the use of non-democratic tactics. The dominance of the ethnic party was not due to the overwhelming power of ethnicity; it was not a voter-driven process, although voters did abandon the main non-ethnic party which had increasing difficulty presenting itself as such an alternative. One important factor in the ethnification of politics, which sets it apart from conventional political competition, was the inter-ethnic interplay. The Croatian government's recognition of the SDS as the legitimate Serb representative and local cooperation between the SDS and the HDZ greatly strengthened the ethnic definition of politics. Inter-ethnic interplay also influenced the SDS's radicalization, although 'lost generosity moments' should not be regarded as the primary factor in the victory of the hardliners.

Within the SDS there was a continuous process of outbidding in the sense that Babić, from a more radical position, sought to undermine Rašković's position. Their rivalry was fuelled by their different positions on the inter-ethnic conflict, by ideological and regional cleavages and, finally, by personal power ambitions. Babić lacked popular support but by building an alternative power base he managed to wrest power from Rašković, resulting in a new leadership with a more extreme position. Babić lacked support in the central structures of the SDS but he relied on support in the local and regional party structures and ensured such support by imposing a hard line from above and removing party moderates. Rašković failed to build a cohesive leadership: he alienated Opačić and Zelembaba, who had the public profile, the hard-line reputation and the support in Knin that could have proved decisive in an attempt to defeat Babić. In addition to support from party structures, the resources of importance in the competition were of a non-democratic nature: Babić controlled the coercive resources and could use these to enforce control. The main audience for intra-party outbidding was consequently not the general population: it was local and regional party structures, paramilitary formations and, above all, Belgrade. In Knin, Babić ensured cohesion by keeping people under constant tension and by frequently changing the political framework to suit his needs.[108] For his hold on power, however, he relied on a very militaristic wing of the SDS, and he therefore likely found himself constrained in the positions he was able to adopt.[109]

One consequence of the gradual ethnification of politics, of the inability of the SDS to successfully play the ethnic card, was the strategic value of a vague position, a position that would not drive away the Serbs still unconvinced by the ethnic definition of politics but would, at the same time, heighten tensions and serve to satisfy hardliners. However, such a vague position also left Rašković open to outbidding. Cultural autonomy in Rašković's demands had no territorial dimension but as the conflict intensified, and Rašković became pressured from forces within the party and from Belgrade, territorial autonomy entered the agenda as a demand in case the federal structure of Yugoslavia was altered. In December 1990, Rašković proposed changes to the draft Croatian Constitution that would affirm Croatia as part of a federal Yugoslavia and included provisions for cultural autonomy. However, it also suggested that the Constitution provided the possibility for territorial autonomy in Serb-majority areas.[110] In addition, in the summer and autumn of 1990, Rašković advocated the unification of Croatian and Bosnian Krajina as Serb-majority areas.[111] The demand for autonomy was therefore marked by a considerable ambiguity when it came to the territorial dimension.

---

108. M. Vasić. 1992. 'Babic's Swan Song', *Vreme NDA,* 10 February. From: http://www.scc. rutgers.edu/serbian_digest/. S. Cerović. 1991. 'Ko je prvi počeo', *Vreme,* 22 April, 28–29.
109. Daskalović. 1991. 'Kula od karata', *Danas,* 26 March, 23-24.
110. V. Vukćević. 1990. 'Primedbe na nacrt Ustava Republike Hrvatske', 11 December (author's copy).
111. *Danas,* 31 July 1990, 12–15. M. Jajčinović. 1990. 'Ispit za Jugoslaviju', *Danas,* 2 October, 12–13.

Even though Babić, before openly clashing with Rašković, also vacillated between antagonistic and moderate rhetoric, he could take advantage of Rašković's vagueness on the issue of autonomy; he strengthened the territorial dimension, thereby creating an alternative power base in Knin, and the ambiguity of Rašković's demands made it difficult for him to counter these moves.

Intra-Serb competition in prewar Croatia was thus marked by a gradual ethnification of politics, by intra-party outbidding and by the increasing dominance of coercive resources, especially those supplied by Belgrade.

CHAPTER FOUR

Prewar Bosnia: Cohesive, Radicalizing Nationalists

The Bosnian and the Croatian cases share many similarities in the pre-war period: the dominant Serb party had the same name; their policies were almost identical; and the leader of the SDS in Croatia, Jovan Rašković, helped establish the SDS in Bosnia as well as helping choose its leader, fellow psychiatrist Radovan Karadžić. Their strategy in radicalizing the position of the party, furthermore, followed the same pattern. Initially the position of the party was fairly moderate, if rather vague; the first step in their radicalization was the establishment of an association of SDS-dominated municipalities; then a Serb Assembly was set up and Serb Autonomous Regions were created; finally, a Serb Republic was proclaimed. Despite these obvious similarities, the two parties fared differently in their competition with non-ethnic parties. The Serb nationalists in Bosnia were, from the outset, in a stronger position than their counterparts in Croatia: they could feed off the increasing tensions in the Yugoslav Federation and they were quicker to establish a well-organized party. This position of strength became clear in the first multiparty elections: while the Croatian SDS secured only a minority of the Serb vote, seven months later the Bosnian SDS was supported by more than 85 per cent of Serbs. Ethnification proceeded at different speeds in the two cases and the Bosnian SDS was much more successful in the electoral competition with the non-ethnic parties. This chapter analyses the reasons for this difference in dynamics.[1]

Dynamics within the SDS also differed and the causes and consequences of these differences are also analysed. The Bosnian version of the SDS was not based around a charismatic leader but was

---

1. This analysis of intra-Serb party competition in Bosnia (from 1990 to 2004) builds on and expands N. Caspersen. 2006. 'Contingent Nationalist Dominance: Intra-Serb Challenges to the Serb Democratic Party', *Nationalities Papers* 34(1).

nevertheless a very cohesive party that was not plagued by the leadership struggles that characterized its sister party in Croatia. Such cohesiveness would theoretically lead one to expect the SDS in Bosnia to be less influenced by radicalizing dynamics, but even though the party's organization provides some explanation for its cohesiveness, another reason is to be found in the ever-increasing radicalization of its position.

In addition, there was a significant difference in the relative demographic strength of the two communities, and this affected the strategies of the Serb leaders as well as those of the other ethnic leaders: in Bosnia, the Bosniak and Croat leaders knew that they could only ignore the Serbs at their peril, whereas the relatively small size of the Serb community in Croatia seems to have led some Croatian leaders to believe that they would not constitute a significant obstacle to a Croatian nation-state. The resulting differences in inter-ethnic relations are marked: the SDS in Bosnia formed an unofficial coalition with the Bosniak SDA and the Croatian HDZ, while the SDS in Croatia was faced with a parliament with an absolute HDZ majority and a government which proved highly reluctant to accommodate Serb demands. Finally, the outbreak of war in Croatia, in the summer of 1991, had a significant impact on Bosnian Serb politics and led to a hardening of positions.

Serb Nationalists Become Near-monolithic

Most of the Serb voters in Croatia had voted for the reformed communists in the SKH-SDP and support for this party only declined after the elections. But the reformed communists in Bosnia, the League of Communists – Party for Democratic Change (Savez komunista – Stranka demokratske promjene, SK-SDP), found themselves in a weaker position. As described in Chapter 2, the League of Communists of Bosnia had been significantly weakened by the corruption scandal surrounding the food company Agrokomerc and this was one of the reasons for the SDS's clear victory. The SK-SDP represented a system in collapse, it had been slow in endorsing multiparty politics, and, even more importantly, it lacked experienced leaders.[2] It was therefore not sufficient for the party to be the only party with an organized network throughout the republic.[3] In competition with the

---

2. The former director of Agrokomerc, Fikret Abdić, received the highest number of votes in the 1990 presidential elections, when he ran for the SDA. This would indicate that it was not so much the corruption scandal that weakened the reformed communists, but rather the way it was handled by the League of Communists.
3. Andjelić, *Bosnia-Herzegovina*, 159, 174.

SDS, it also mattered that the SK-SDP lacked Serbs among its top candidates.[4] This made it more difficult for the party to counter the nationalist claim that a non-ethnic party could not protect Serb interests.

The SK-SDP was, however, not the only non-ethnic competitor to the SDS. Other non-ethnic parties that should be mentioned included the Democratic Alliance of Socialists (Demokratski socijalistički savez, DSS) and the League of Reform Forces of Yugoslavia (Savez reformskih snaga Jugoslavije, SRSJ). The DSS suffered the same problems as the SK-SDP: its roots were in the Socialist Alliance of Working People and it was too closely associated with the old regime. But the Reformists in the SRSJ, formed by the then federal prime minister, Ante Marković, were dangerous for the SDS: they could not be directly identified with the previous regime, Marković's economic programme was successful and he was very popular in Bosnia.[5] Most of the party's leaders in Bosnia were, furthermore, ethnic Serbs. But despite these factors of strength, the Reformists had problems organizing themselves and the party lacked a leader in Bosnia who was strong enough to match Marković's popularity.[6] Prominent political actors had declined invitations to lead the party and no leader was elected at the party's founding congress, which was held only two months before the elections.[7] It took almost another fortnight before the then Rector of Sarajevo University, Nenad Kecmanović, was finally named party president. The Reformists, moreover, covered an array of political opinions and crucially failed to take a clear position on the issue of Yugoslavia's future.[8] Nevertheless, the nationalist parties recognized the potential danger of the Reformists and chose to fiercely attack the party in a bid to undermine its popular appeal.[9]

The non-ethnic parties, on the other hand, primarily directed their competition against each other and, consequently, augmented their already pronounced weakness as they failed to provide a unified, viable alternative to the nationalist parties who had formed an unofficial but highly effective partnership. Some of the leaders were aware of this problem and on 25 October 1990 the leaders of the SK-SDP and the Reformists, Nijaz Duraković and Nenad Kecmanović, signed a secret deal. But when this became known to the Reformists, the most anti-communist elements of the party rebelled and the deal was called off. The political differences between the two parties were small, but personal

4. M. Prstojević (ed.). 1990. *BiH Izbori '90*, Sarajevo: Oslobođenje public, 77–79.
5. Andjelić, *Bosnia-Herzegovina,* 160.
6. Ibid., 162.
7. E. Demirović. 1990. 'Reforma – uslov pobede', *Borba,* 6 September, 1.
8. Prstojević, *BiH Izbori,* 85. Andjelić, *Bosnia-Herzegovina,* 161–2.
9. E. Demirović. 1990. 'Reforma – uslov pobede', *Borba,* 6 September, 1.

grievances and fear of being drawn into the communist collapse proved decisive.[10] The existence of an additional salient cleavage, an anti-communist cleavage, therefore, further weakened the non-ethnic alternatives. The non-ethnic parties were finally weakened by an electoral system that inflated the majority won by the nationalist parties.

The SDS's Strength vis-à-vis Its Non-ethnic Rivals

The SDS's victory was, however, not only based on the weakness of the non-ethnic rivals, and one of the factors that strengthened the party was the strong organization that had been established prior to the elections. The SDS had a wide range of local branches and, by September 1990, the party claimed to have as many as 350,000 members.[11] This building up of the party was significantly assisted by the SDS in Croatia and, more covertly, by the Belgrade government. The SDS, furthermore, followed the strategy used by its sister party in Croatia and established a Serb National Council, albeit before the elections: on 13 October 1990 in front of 30,000 people in Banja Luka. The council in Banja Luka was followed by Serb councils in Tuzla and Trebinje.[12] In its campaign against the non-ethnic parties, the SDS continuously sought to undermine their credibility and Karadžić warned Serb voters that it would be dangerous to vote for the SK-SDP since they would not represent Serb interests.[13] Outside the official campaign the tone was even harsher. In Banja Luka, material was distributed announcing: 'We will not betray you – the League of Communists and the leftists will betray you! The Ustasha knife awaits you again'.[14]

The failure of the non-ethnic parties owed much to their internal squabbles and the weakness of the League of Communists following the Agrokomerc scandal but the main obstacle for the non-ethnic parties was that the elections were fought on an ethnic cleavage. The non-ethnic parties did not succeed in focusing the campaign on other issues: in the Croatian elections the most salient cleavage had been the future of Yugoslavia but in Bosnia all major parties professed their support for Yugoslavia's preservation and, with the HDZ as the only significant exception, they all advocated a federal structure.[15] The nationalist parties, moreover,

10. Andjelić, *Bosnia-Herzegovina* , 180–1. Pejanović, *Through Bosnian Eyes,* 30.
11. *Borba,* 1-2 September 1990, 12.
12. Andjelić, *Bosnia-Herzegovina* , 178.
13. M. Vućelić. 1990. 'Srbi se najsporije bude', *Borba,* 23 July, 5.
14. Pejanović, *Through Bosnian Eyes,* 37.
15. Electoral programmes from Prstojević, *BiH Izbori.* The position of the Reformists was somewhat vague but their programme could only be realized in a federal context. Andjelić, *Bosnia-Herzegovina,* 161–2.

consciously sought to ethnify politics and they succeeded in doing so through the combination of cooperation and the use of inflammatory rhetoric. They prevented the issue of Yugoslavia's future from becoming dominant by focusing on the need for ethnic representation. The nationalist parties were, furthermore, strongly supported in their endeavour by the progressively tenser atmosphere in the Yugoslav Federation. Politics had, consequently, become ethnicized prior to the elections but this was reinforced and augmented by the weakening of the non-ethnic parties.

The Lack of Significant Serb Challengers

The main rivals to the SDS in the prewar period were the non-ethnic parties, but the party was also faced with competition from another Serb party: the Serb Renewal Movement (Srpski pokret obnove, SPO) led in Serbia by Vuk Drašković. This party was, however, never a serious rival to the SDS and apparently did not intend to be: Drašković rejected calls for increasing the activities of the party before the elections as this would serve to divide the Serb vote.[16] Unsurprisingly then, the SPO only won one seat in parliament and never really entered political life in Bosnia.[17] It was, anyway, difficult to notice any difference between the two parties before the elections,[18] although the SPO's programme was more unashamedly nationalistic.[19] The differences only became visible when the SPO in Belgrade took a moderate turn and began criticizing the war in Croatia and accused the nationalist parties in Bosnia of not trying hard enough to prevent war from also breaking out there.[20] Such critique, however, did not find resonance with the SPO deputy in Bosnia, who had all along acted like a member of the SDS and finally chose to join the party.[21] Only immediately before the outbreak of war did the SDS therefore face a more moderate Serb party, but this party was without influence and even lacked control over its own deputy.

The SDS's near-monolithic status in the Serb community was strengthened by the almost complete marginalization of non-ethnic parties

16. Thomas, *Serbia under Milošević*, 56.
17. Andjelić, *Bosnia-Herzegovina* , 167.
18. Author's interview with Slobodan Nagradić, Professor of Political Science (Sarajevo, 19 November 2003).
19. Electoral programme in Prstojević, *BiH Izbori,* 118–20. See also *Vjesnik,* 26 October 1990, 3.
20. M. Milošević. 1991. 'See You in the Next War', *Vreme NDA,* 2 December. From: http://www.scc.rutgers.edu/serbian_digest/.
21. Author's interview with Slobodan Nagradić. See also N. Čurak. 1992. 'Članovi SPO u BiH nemaju ni čakije', *Slobodna Bosna,* 10 January, 7.

following the elections. The nationalist parties made sure of excluding all other parties from influence and the opposition was too weak to have any impact. The Serb representatives from the non-ethnic parties were, furthermore, increasingly pressured by the SDS to join their ranks, and many non-SDS Serb deputies voted with the SDS on the issue of Bosnian sovereignty.[22] In late February 1992, when the constitution of the Serb Republic was proclaimed, a significant number of Serb representatives from non-ethnic parties were present at the session and communication was discontinued with those who refused.[23] The marginalization of non-ethnic rivals and the absence of other Serb parties meant that challenges to the SDS leadership would have to come from within the party.

A Radicalizing SDS Remains Cohesive

Whereas the SDS in Croatia was formed around the charismatic leadership of Jovan Rašković, the SDS in Bosnia lacked a similar personality to attract popular support. The party was initiated by a group of Serb academics from Sarajevo and Radovan Karadžić was an eleventh-hour choice as leader after other better-known Serbs had declined. One of the people whom the Serb academics had unsuccessfully tried to persuade was Nenad Kecmanović, who instead became leader of the Reformists.[24] Karadžić's role as leader was only supposed to be temporary: he should set the tempo in the first few months and then cede his place to a more influential and politically experienced leader.[25] Even shortly before the SDS's founding session, Karadžić publicly declared that he was exhausted and would not stand for the party presidency.[26] Karadžić and the rest of the SDS leadership were, at the time, not well-known[27] and Andjelić argues that Karadžić initially lacked control over the party: the actual decision-making body of the SDS was the party's political council, which consisted of Serb academics and some party officials.[28] In the pre-election period the real power, therefore, seems to have been behind the scenes, not with the official party leadership that was still establishing its public profile.

---

22. M. Tomić. 1991. 'Istorijsko 'Ne' Bosni', *Slobodna Bosna*, 7 November, 3.
23. Pejanović, *Through Bosnian Eyes*, 50.
24. N. Kecmanović. 1992. 'Čas anatomija Nenada Kecmanovića', *Dani*, 17 December, 44–47.
25. N. Stefanović. 1993. 'A Political Portrait of Radovan Karadzic', *Vreme NDA*, 3 May. From: http://www.scc.rutgers.edu/serbian_digest/.
26. Pejanović, *Through Bosnian Eyes*, 17.
27. N. Kecmanović. 1992. 'Čas anatomija Nenada Kecmanovića', *Dani*, 17 December, 44–47.
28. Andjelić, *Bosnia-Herzegovina*, 166. Prstojević, *BiH Izbori*, 115. The considerable influence of the SDS's advisory council made up of Serb intellectuals is, however, denied by one of its former members. Author's interview with Predrag Lazarević (Banja Luka, 12 November 2003).

Karadžić was consequently not a strong leader to begin with; he served the party rather than the other way round. But Karadžić's image was gradually built up and the official leadership became more influential in the decision-making process after the elections. The intellectuals behind the party became increasingly divided when positions of power had to be allocated and greater political differences also surfaced as inter-ethnic conflict intensified.[29] In this development, the structure of the party became increasingly authoritarian and Karadžić began exerting greater control.[30] Of some importance for Karadžić's hold on power was also the fact that he was the president not only of the SDS but also of the Serb National Council; a rival leader with an institutional base was, therefore, less likely to emerge. Despite Karadžić's rising star, the situation was very different to that in Croatia where the SDS was founded by and around Rašković and functioned more as a political movement led by a charismatic leader. One might have expected Karadžić's weaker leadership to give rise to greater fractionalization than Rašković's charismatic authority, but actually the opposite was the case: for the first few years, the Bosnian SDS remained a fairly cohesive party with only few factional disputes.

At its foundation, the SDS did, however, announce the formation of a more radical youth wing called Mlada Bosna (Young Bosnia), led by the writer Vladimir Srebrov.[31] Mlada Bosna was an officially sanctioned faction but its militarism quickly became too much for the SDS leadership, which at the time tried to portray itself as a moderate party. Thus, Srebrov was expelled shortly after the party's foundation subsequent to inviting the JNA to take power in Bosnia and promising assistance from his militants. Karadžić declared that the 'para-militaristic, almost militant outbursts of M.A. Vladimir Srebrov are incompatible with the spirit of the Serb people' and he consequently disbanded Mlada Bosna.[32] The leadership had no problems quelling this attempt at radicalizing the party at a moment when the party's public position was more moderate.[33] The creation of the faction may in fact have been a deliberate attempt by the SDS leadership to demonstrate its moderate stance, while at the same time using Mlada Bosna's radicalism to stir up ethnic tensions.

After the elections, other divisions emerged in the leadership over which position the party should adopt in the intensifying inter-ethnic conflict but

---

29. Author's interview with Predrag Lazarević.
30. Andjelić, *Bosnia-Herzegovina,* 169.
31. M. Lučić. 1990. 'Nema vodećih i pratećih naroda', *Borba,* 13 July, 3.
32. D. Anastasijević. 1995. 'Vladimir Srebrov', *Vreme,* 30 October, 17.
33. Ž. Vuković. 1990. 'Dobavljanje nekorisnih mentora', *Borba,* 22–23 September, 3.

these divisions never developed into actual fractionalization. In October 1991, after the Bosnian parliament adopted the Declaration on Sovereignty, a meeting of the SDS main board brought out these divisions. Some members wanted SDS deputies to remain in the official bodies whereas others advocated a walkout.[34] The outcome of the discussion was that the deputies stayed in the parliament, but this decision was qualified by the formation of the Serb Assembly on 24 October 1991. In the decision to form the assembly, it was declared that the validity of enactments from the Bosnian parliament would only be recognized if they were not contrary to the interests of the Serb people.[35] Furthermore, it was declared that the Serb nation would stay in what remained of Yugoslavia and that this decision would be sent to a referendum.[36] This cleverly crafted compromise served to avoid further divisions in the party leadership. When the Serb Republic was proclaimed in January 1992, Nikola Koljević, one of the leaders of the SDS, urged the deputies in the Serb Assembly, 'Please vote unanimously'.[37] The leadership was aware that if the party could present itself as unified it would be in a stronger position, and the statement also conveyed that Koljević had backed down on his earlier demands. When the establishment of the Serb Republic was first discussed, Koljević and the speaker of the Serb Assembly, Momčilo Krajišnik, were against enforcing the decision immediately in case the appeal for international recognition of Bosnia was withdrawn.[38] However, Karadžić at this point declared: 'There is no going back to the united B&H [Bosnia-Herzegovina]'.[39] Koljević and Krajišnik, although high-standing members of the party, were alone with their position and ultimately had to back down.

The Krajina Faction

While divisions in the leadership of the party were fairly muted, significant regional factions existed; particularly the strong Bosnian

34. Minutes from the SDS main board meeting presented at the ICTY. See: ICTY. 2002. 'Transcripts: Prosecutor vs. Radoslav Brdjanin and Stojan Zupljanin (IT-99-36)', Transcripts from Robert Donia's testimony, 29–31 January, 1115, 1117.
35. 'Odluka o osnivanju skupštine srpskog naroda u BiH', in R. Kuzmanović. 1994. *Konstitutivni akti Republike Srpske*, Glas Srpski: Banja Luka.
36. 'Odluka o ostajanju srpskog naroda u Bosni i Hercegovini u Zajedničkoj Državi Jugoslaviji', in Kuzmanović, *Konstitutivni akti.*
37. Z. Isaković. 1992. 'Another Serbian State', *Vreme NDA,*13 January. From: http://www.scc.rutgers.edu/serbian_digest/.
38. M. Čamo. 1992. 'Pucanje srpskog monolita', *Slobodna Bosna,* 16 January, 5.
39. Z. Isaković. 1992. 'Another Serbian State', *Vreme NDA,*13 January. From: http://www.scc.rutgers.edu/serbian_digest/.

Krajina faction, centred on Banja Luka, which posed a potential threat to the leadership. This rivalry reflected a regional cleavage as well as different views of the appropriate strategy in the inter-ethnic conflict. SDS moderates who had won the elections in Banja Luka had been pressured by the leadership to radicalize their position or be replaced[40] but this engineered radicalization almost backfired.

The Krajina faction had already, in early 1991, criticized what they regarded as the too moderate reaction to the Declaration on State Sovereignty presented in parliament by the SDA and the HDZ.[41] Soon after this demonstration of radicalism, they began demanding a more autonomous role for the region. The Bosnian Krajina region was of great importance for the SDS leadership: Banja Luka was central to the party's strategy and Bosnian Krajina, moreover, bordered on the equally radical Krajina region in Croatia. The central SDS leadership was aware of the dangers of regional centres of power and, at the above-mentioned main board meeting, Milorad Ekmečić, the *éminence grise* of the SDS, warned, 'The Serbs have created regions which are not connected, and these regions must not be allowed to establish their governments which would not be connected'.[42] But the Autonomous Region of Krajina (Autonomna regija Krajina, ARK) was, nevertheless, able to charge a separate course and, in the autumn of 1991, they began challenging Karadžić's leadership. Woodward argues that the rebellion followed a finance scandal in which Karadžić was accused of imposing a surcharge on gas sold in the autonomous regions, thereby robbing local leaders of profitable revenue.[43] In addition, strong forces in Bosnian Krajina wanted unification with Croatian Krajina. This was supported by Babić but was rejected by Karadžić and the latter, in October 1991, expressed concern that the Bosnian Krajina leaders were listening more to Babić than to him.[44] The conflict came to a head at the thirteenth session of the ARK Assembly in late February 1992 when an ultimatum was passed which demanded that Banja Luka become the capital of the Serb Republic and that cantons with the highest degree of autonomy should be established.[45] If these demands were not met in the constitution for the Serb Republic, then 'Krajina should be proclaimed a sovereign republic which will establish relations

40. Gagnon, *The Myth of Ethnic War*, 50.
41. R. Preradović. 1991. 'Bez Jugoslavije nema ni BiH', *Oslobođenje*, 11 February, 3.
42. Minutes from SDS main board meeting presented at the ICTY. ICTY, 'Prosecutor vs. Radoslav Brdjanin,' 1114.
43. Woodward, *Balkan Tragedy*, 511, n45.
44. *Slobodna Bosna*, 7 November 1991, 5.
45. E. Ružić and B. Zorici. 1992. 'Krajiški ultimatum Karadžiću', *Slobodna Bosna*, 27 February, 5.

directly with other parts of BH [Bosnia-Herzegovina]'.[46] Although this ultimatum was clearly radical and a direct challenge to the Sarajevo leadership, it indicated that the most radical wing in Bosnian Krajina was no longer dominating: this wing had demanded immediate unification of the two Krajinas.[47]

Shortly after this session in Banja Luka, Bosnian President Alija Izetbegović rejected the Cutilheiro peace plan, which would have divided Bosnia into ethnic territorial units. In his rejection, he referred to the assembly in Banja Luka and the discussion of a constitution for the Serb Republic. This led Karadžić to fiercely attack the autonomous direction of Banja Luka: 'I promise you, Bosnian Krajina must not become an issue… We cannot allow that five people with personal ambitions destroy our chances'.[48] As a response to this, the SDS club of deputies decided to blame five or six individuals who were second-tier members of the Krajina assembly and then to adopt the constitution of the Serb Republic with Sarajevo as its capital. The constitution, however, did not specify that the territory was indivisible and it assigned the regions certain functions. To reinforce their position, the top brass of the SDS attended the next session of the Krajina assembly clearly indicating that further maverick behaviour would not be tolerated.[49] While the Krajina leaders were still not satisfied with the leadership or its centralization, these steps proved sufficient to make them backtrack from their more radical demands.[50] The SDS leadership, thus, decided to act decisively against any attempts at fractionalization that could undermine their authority and, crucially, the Krajina faction did not penetrate the party leadership, as it did in the Croatian SDS. Another factor that weakened the Bosnian Krajina leaders was their internal divisions: they were not united and the Sarajevo leadership could take advantage of this to regain control. Notwithstanding these points of weakness, the Banja Luka faction forced upon the SDS leadership a more radical position than it had intended during the Cutilhiero negotiations. But the reaction of the central party was fairly mild: only second-tier local leaders were removed and the Krajina leaders were even given some concessions. This could indicate

46. Minutes from the assembly session presented at the ICTY. ICTY, 'Prosecutor vs. Radoslav Brdjanin,' 1145.
47. E. Ružić and B. Zorici. 1992. 'Tri varijante za razbijanje Bosne', *Slobodna Bosna*, 23 January, 10.
48. Minutes from a session of the Serb Assembly presented at the ICTY. ICTY, 'Prosecutor vs. Radoslav Brdjanin,' 1148.
49. Ibid., 150–3.
50. M. Marić. 1992. 'Nema raskola – ima razlika', *Borba*, 17 March, 8.

that the more radical position was not truly contrary to the interests of the leadership and they, furthermore, needed a stable, cohesive leadership in place in Banja Luka for what was to come.

The relative weakness of the Krajina faction was caused by its lack of a foothold in the SDS leadership, its internal divisions and its lack of resources. But what were the general reasons for the existence of relatively few factions in a party that was led by Karadžić who at least initially appeared to be a weak leader? First of all, the SDS in Bosnia was better organized than the SDS in Croatia: it had built a stronger party organization and Karadžić was backed by influential forces working behind the scenes. Divisions were not accepted and, when they emerged, were dealt with immediately, if need be by making concessions as long as unwanted departures from official policy ceased. Secondly, the SDS in Bosnia was in a stronger position politically: it won a landslide victory in the elections and consequently did not have to continue fighting non-ethnic parties. The dominant trend of the party was, finally, one of increased radicalization and this helped pre-empt challengers.

Post-electoral Radicalization

Before the elections, the SDS's position was rather vague: it wanted to stir up tensions but at the same time present itself as a party capable of finding a solution by representing the Serbs in Bosnia. At the party's founding session, Karadžić consequently pledged his support for democracy, national equality and human rights.[51] Rajko Kasagić, who was prime minister of Republika Srpska in 1995/96, contends that the SDS in 1990 was a very different party from what it later became: '[It was] a centrally oriented party … a party of private business, freedom of the press and democracy'.[52] In addition to professed support for democracy and national equality, the SDS did, however, also make clear that the party would demand a referendum for the Serbs in case the goal of a continued Yugoslav Federation could not be achieved.[53] Furthermore, moderate rhetoric did not always dominate at SDS rallies. At one such rally in Banja Luka, Karadžić famously encouraged people to 'sell your cow and buy a gun',[54] and the SDS used the experience of Croatia's Serbs to increase tensions. But at no rally did Karadžić ever call for dividing Bosnia or

---

51. M. Lučić. 1990. 'Nema vodećih i pratećih naroda', *Borba*, 13 July, 3. See also the SDS's electoral programme in Prstojević, *BiH Izbori*, 113–5.
52. Author's interview with Rajko Kasagić (Banja Luka, 11 November 2003).
53. Prstojević, *BiH Izbori*, 115. M. Vućelić. 1990. 'Srbi se najsporije bude', *Borba*, 23 July, 5.
54. Pejanović, *Through Bosnian Eyes*, 36.

for war.[55] The party's official policy was the preservation and survival of Yugoslavia, possibly without Croatia and Slovenia, which was not impossible at the time. Furthermore, Karadžić continuously stated that the Bosniaks and Croats were not the SDS's opponents and he stressed the need for partnership.[56] This resulted in a vague or ambivalent position, similar to the one used by the SDS in Croatia, and one effect of this was to avoid the creation of a more moderate ethnic alternative.

An important difference from the SDS in Croatia should, however, be noted: the SDS in Bosnia early on adopted an uncompromising position. The Serb National Council (SNV) had already been formed before the Bosnian elections and the SDS made clear that they would not accept any decisions which went against their declared goal of preserving the Yugoslav Federation. There was no talk of autonomy, and no solution short of a federal Yugoslavia was acceptable, but to achieve this goal the SDS initially emphasized the need for partnership. The vagueness was, therefore, primarily related to the means used to achieving this goal, but the goal itself was also somewhat ambiguous: was it the preservation of Yugoslavia or a Greater Serbia?

After the elections this rather ambivalent position was replaced by an increasingly radical one. In May 1991, Balaban, a minister in the Bosnian government, warned: 'If Bosnia becomes an independent and sovereign state ... the associated [Serb] communes will break away and create their own autonomous province, with all the functions of a state. Within 24 hours at least one military unit will be set up in each Serb commune'.[57] And when the Bosnian parliament passed the Declaration of Sovereignty in October 1991, the SDS shed any semblance of moderation and Karadžić declared: 'The road you have chosen is the same road that took Croatia into Hell, except that the war in Bosnia will take you into a worse Hell, and the Muslim nation may disappear altogether'.[58] The SDS then continued to realize its fallback option – that is, the joining of large parts of Bosnia to Serbia – and in this they followed a strategy very similar to the one used by the SDS in Croatia. Between September and November 1991, six Serb Autonomous Regions (Srpska autonomna oblast, SAO) were proclaimed. In the SAOs, the SDS monopolized the top posts – the economic, political and, above all, military posts – and the new authorities initiated a policy of

55. Ibid. Gagnon, *The Myth of Ethnic War*, 49.
56. D. Banjac. 1990. 'Stranka koja ukida straha', *Borba*, 16 July, 3. R. Ninčić.1990. 'Udruženi poraz komunista i reformista', *Danas*, 26 November, 12–14.
57. Quoted in X. Bougarel. 1996. 'Bosnia and Hercegovina: State and Communitarianism', in D. Dyker and I. Vejvoda (eds), *Yugoslavia and After*. London: Longman, 100.
58. Ibid.

discrimination and terror against non-Serbs.[59] In late October 1991, the Serb Assembly was created and on 9 and 10 November 1991, a referendum among Serb voters, unsurprisingly, showed an overwhelming majority for remaining part of Yugoslavia. On 21 November, the Serb Assembly proclaimed as part of Yugoslavia all municipalities, local communities and populated places in which over 50 per cent of the Serbs had voted for this option. Shortly afterwards the formation of separate Serb institutions moved from being voluntary to being mandatory for SDS local boards; they had to set up so-called Crisis Headquarters (Krizni štab) that would take power in the municipality when given the order by Karadžić.[60] In early January 1992, the Serb Assembly approved a declaration on proclamation of the Serb Republic of Bosnia-Herzegovina (Srpska republika Bosna i Hercegovina), which would cover 'all the territories of the autonomous [regions] *and* all other regions where the Serbian people represent a minority due to the Second World War genocide'.[61] The republic was proclaimed in Pale on 7 April 1992, and on this occasion, the SDS recalled its two representatives from the Bosnian presidency and appealed to Serb ministers, civil servants and policemen to break with the Bosnian state.[62]

The avoidance of successful outbidding in the Bosnian SDS owed something to this persistent radicalization of the party, as well as the stronger party structure and the relative weakness of the Bosnian Krajina faction compared with the Knin faction in the Croatian case. One of the causes of the relative weakness of the challengers was their lack of kin-state support. As in the Croatian case, Belgrade helped strengthen radical forces but its role was not contested and it did not become involved in intra-party rivalry.

Kin-state: 'We Authorise Milošević to Act on Our Behalf'

In prewar Bosnia, Belgrade's influence was largely covert and Milošević may even initially have been hoping for an ally other than the SDS. Late 1989 and early 1990 saw the League of Communists of Bosnia becoming increasingly divided into pro- and anti-Milošević camps[63] and such divisions could have given Milošević reason to believe that the Bosnian Communists would, in the end, come out in support of his stance. Some

59. Ibid.
60. Document from 19 December 1991, presented at the ICTY. ICTY, 'Prosecutor vs. Radoslav Brdjanin', 1127–9. See also Gow, *The Serbian Project*, 129–30.
61. Z. Isaković. 1992. 'Another Serbian State', *Vreme NDA*, 13 January. From: http://www.scc.rutgers.edu/serbian_digest/.
62. Bougarel, 'Bosnia and Hercegovina', 103.
63. Andjelić, *Bosnia-Herzegovina*, 117. Gagnon, *The Myth of Ethnic War*, 75, 84.

commentators argue that this can explain the late establishment of a Serb party in Bosnia: Milošević was waiting for a possible change within the local communist ranks.[64] Reliance on the SK-SDP instead of on an explicitly Serb party made sense given the meagre election results achieved by the SDS in Croatia. A problem with this explanation is, however, the already considerable ethnification of politics in Bosnia. Milošević was not just hoping for support from the Serbs in the SK-SDP and support from a united party was increasingly unlikely. The timing of the SDS's establishment in Bosnia can, furthermore, be explained by the increasing success for its sister party in Croatia, which may have increased hopes in the electoral fortunes of an explicitly Serb party. But how great was Belgrade's influence over the SDS in prewar Bosnia?

Milošević and the SDS

The SDS's public relationship with Milošević varied considerably between the pre-election and the post-election period. Shortly after the formation of the SDS, Karadžić, when asked about his cooperation with political parties in Belgrade, said that he did not want an alliance with Milošević's SPS, which he considered the bastion of the communist movement.[65] The public profile of the SDS was that of an anti-communist, national party which was willing and able to cooperate across the ethnic divide. Public association with the Serbian president, therefore, was not in the party's interest. Moreover, since the Serbian secret police had a weaker network in Bosnia than in Croatia, more of the organization of the SDS was left to the locals and Belgrade arguably had less influence over the party.[66]

But the paramount role of Milošević was recognized by Karadžić after the elections when, in February 1991, he made statements such as, 'If Yugoslavia is to be dissolved, we authorise Slobodan Milosevic to act on our behalf'.[67] To further demonstrate his loyalty, Karadžić publicly supported Milošević during the 9 March 1991 demonstrations in Belgrade.[68] Even though Karadžić initially downplayed his links with Belgrade, Milošević's legitimacy in representing the Serbs outside Serbia was, thus, not denied by the SDS leader. Such displays of loyalty were, however, not always reciprocated by Milošević, who sought to camouflage his links with the SDS.[69] As late as February 1992, he maintained that he

64. Andjelić, *Bosnia-Herzegovina,* 151.
65. Pejanović, *Through Bosnian Eyes,* 23.
66. Judah, *The Serbs,* 192.
67. Andjelić, *Bosnia-Herzegovina,* 207. Sell, *Milosevic and the Destruction of Yugoslavia,* 129.
68. Gordy, *The Culture of Power,* 34.
69. Sell, *Milosevic and the Destruction of Yugoslavia,* 160.

did not know Karadžić well and that 'Serbia has nothing to do with Bosnia. It's not our problem'.[70] Following the international recognition of Slovenia and Croatia, and mounting U.S. pressure for Bosnia's recognition, Milošević appears to have become more committed to a 'new less extensive Yugoslavia'.[71] In this altered strategy, the Serbs in the neighbouring republics would be not be incorporated into the state but would obtain de facto independent status within Croatia and Bosnia. For this strategy to succeed, Milošević needed the cooperation of the international community[72] as well as less obvious links with local Serb leaders.

Despite Milošević's public distancing from the SDS leadership, oppositional factions within the party could not look to Belgrade for support. Milošević seemed satisfied with Karadžić's leadership and with the party's course, and there was, therefore, no reason to take advantage of possible internal divisions. The most radical wing in Banja Luka was, furthermore, close to Babić and following Milošević's falling out with the Knin leader in early 1992, he was unlikely to support Bosnian Krajina's challenge to Karadžić. There was, consequently, no support forthcoming for intra-party challengers and the kin-state was, therefore, of less significance for the outcome of intra-Serb rivalry in Bosnia than it had been in Croatia. This does not, however, mean that Belgrade did not influence the radicalization of the SDS: Belgrade provided the party with the resources needed to pursue the war option.[73]

In terms of the general population, there were also significant differences between the two cases. Whereas the Serb voters in Croatia had given their electoral support to the reformed communists, and the SDS had to rely consequently on other resources to become dominant, the situation was markedly different in Bosnia where Serb voters closed ranks behind the SDS.

The General Population: Unclear Mandate for Popular Nationalists

The massive level of support for the nationalist parties in the Bosnian elections came as a great surprise, since none of the pre-election polls had pointed to such a landslide and had actually indicated victory for the SK-

70. Ibid., 162.
71. Burg and Shoup, *The War in Bosnia-Herzegovina*, 103
72. Ibid.
73. Pejanović, *Through Bosnian Eyes*, 55.

SDP. Thus, even in a poll in early November, only days before the elections, the SDS looked set to win just 14 per cent of the vote and a majority of the Serbs seemed likely to vote for either the SK-SDP or for the Reformists.[74] It therefore appeared to be a repeat of the Serb voting patterns in the Croatian elections.

There are some problems surrounding the surveys,[75] but one thing they do point to is a rapid development in attitudes and a clear upward trend in support for the nationalist parties. Less than a year before the elections, the nationalist leaders were not a significant political force and popular support for them was not registered. Thus, in December 1989, a poll on the most popular individuals was conducted in urban areas and nationalist leaders failed to be mentioned by anyone surveyed.[76] The lack of popular support for nationalist parties is even better illustrated in a well-known poll from April/May 1990 in which a great majority supported a ban on ethnic political parties.[77] This poll was limited to urban areas but the lack of support for nationalist parties is still striking considering that the situation in Yugoslavia had already become tense at this point. As regards Serb voters, the surveys point to growing support for the SDS: the party increased its share of the vote from 4.5 per cent in late August to 10.2 per cent in early November.[78] For Serb respondents, what was most important for their view of a political party was its programme: whether it had a Yugoslav orientation or not. Interestingly, the Serb respondents reported having very little knowledge of the SDS's programme. The resulting confusion over the SDS's programme must have been augmented by events pointing to possibly greater radicalism: the creation of the Serb National Council in October 1990 and the expressed militancy of at least parts of the party. This uncertainty is reflected in the large proportion of Serb respondents who, in October 1990, said that they were still undecided as to their electoral choice.[79] Crucially for the electoral results, these many undecided voters chose to cast their vote for Serb nationalism. Since the SDS and the non-ethnic alternatives did not differ in their declared programmatic goal, this suggests that ethnification among the population had indeed taken place before the elections.

74. Overview of polls in S. Arnautović. 1996. *Izbori u Bosni i Hercegovini '90: Analiza izbornog procesa*, Sarajevo: Promocult, 57–58.
75. Ibid., 52–3. Andjelić, *Bosnia-Herzegovina*, 181.
76. Andjelić, *Bosnia-Herzegovina*, 129.
77. Ibid., 141.
78. Arnautović, *Izbori u Bosni i Hercegovini*, 57–58. The 10.2 per cent translates into 14.3 per cent if only decided voters are included.
79. Ibid., 54–6.

One of the reasons for the greater degree of ethnification found in Bosnia is obviously the timing of the elections: the Bosnian elections were held six months later than the Croatian ones and the situation in Yugoslavia had become progressively more tense. Ethnification was, moreover, strengthened by the weakness of the non-ethnic parties and by cooperation between the nationalist parties. Consequently, at the time of the 1990 elections, the reformed communists had lost their popular base: the SK-SDP had been replaced by the nationalist parties as the party of the masses.[80] This was the outcome of political competition and was influenced by the distribution of resources between the SDS and the non-ethnic parties; it was not about the overwhelming power of ethnicity, and the SDS resorted to adopting a vague position. Even though more radical sentiments were sometimes expressed by SDS officials, the profile of the party was moderate.

Post-electoral Radicalization

The ethnification of politics and the popular support for the nationalist parties do not automatically entail that Serb voters endorsed the subsequent radicalization and it certainly does not mean that radicalization was driven by voter attitudes.

In a survey conducted to mark the first anniversary of the new authorities, great reservations were expressed by respondents: 77 per cent were in favour of new elections and 43 per cent said that the new government's performance was below their expectations, while only 8 per cent thought it exceeded their expectations. These sentiments were also expressed by members and supporters of the nationalist parties.[81] The population was disappointed with the chaotic rule of the nationalist parties and with declining living standards, and popular protest became more and more widespread.[82] Shortly before the war, protests also emerged over the nationalist policies of the parties: peace movements were organized in the cities and mass peace rallies took place in early 1992. Although the mass protests failed to alter the position of the nationalist parties, along with the above-mentioned survey they do suggest that radicalization did not enjoy popular support, or was at least not led by popular demands.

80. Andjelić, *Bosnia-Herzegovina*, 160.
81. Survey by Oslobođenje and the Department of Journalism. V. Krsmanovic. 1992. 'Memories of a Common Past', *Vreme NDA*, 13 July. From: http://www.scc. rutgers.edu/serbian_digest/.
82. Andjelić, *Bosnia-Herzegovina*, 203.

The Serb leaders in Bosnia had, however, taken note of the successful holding of Serb referenda in Croatia. This was an effective way of bolstering their position by demonstrating popular support for their radicalization, and the result of the referendum was unsurprisingly overwhelming support for staying in Yugoslavia. The preference of the majority of Serbs for staying in Yugoslavia had already been made clear in surveys and the outcome was, therefore, to be expected. But the expressed support for joining parts of Bosnia with what remained of Yugoslavia could be argued to signify a radicalization and the SDS could use this to argue that their position was indeed the majority opinion of the Serb community.

Nevertheless, there were significant irregularities in the referendum and one cannot conclude from the result that the war option, which the SDS increasingly championed, also enjoyed majority support in the Serb community. The Bosnian president, Alija Izetbegović, strongly questioned the referendum result when he stated, 'Of course, the result was a triumph – the response was over one hundred percent – I can't help thinking it was Bolshevik-style voting'.[83] The SDS might have been able to take the voters along to a more uncompromising position but they lacked opportunities to express alternative views. The SDS's ability to control the Serb population was aptly demonstrated by the almost complete boycott of the Bosnian independence referendum in February 1992; the SDS had the resources to manipulate the expression of popular attitudes. Even so, Karadžić used the alleged extremism of the Serb population to justify a radicalization of the SDS's position. Just before the outbreak of war, he stated that the SDS would have to take a tougher stand because the nation wanted extreme leaders and if the SDS did not radicalize they would be outflanked by rival parties and leaders.[84] Rhetorical regard for popular opinion was widespread, but there is no evidence that popular attitudes played a decisive role in the radicalization of the SDS's position.

When the SDS was still competing with non-ethnic parties, and espoused a relatively moderate or vague position, the party did, however, have great success in attracting popular support. One of the important factors influencing this ability was the inter-ethnic interplay, which strengthened the ethnification of politics and thereby helped marginalize the already weakened non-ethnic parties.

---

83. Silber and Little, *The Death of Yugoslavia*, 216.
84. N. Butorović. 1992. 'Više nema jedinstvene BiH', *Borba*, 6 March, 3.

Inter-ethnic Relations: Tripartite Structure

In terms of inter-ethnic relations in Bosnia and Croatia, there are two important differences: the Bosnian tripartite structure introduces the importance of shifting alliances, and the relative demographic strength of the Serb community is, furthermore, decidedly different in the two cases. Beyond these differences many similarities are, nevertheless, found in the two cases and the interplay was, as in Croatia, decisive for the ethnification of politics.

Ethnification and Radicalization

Realizing that none of the ethnic parties would be in a position to rule on their own and, furthermore, aware of the need to undermine support for non-ethnic parties, the three main ethnic parties in Bosnia chose to cooperate. Although they frequently used inflammatory rhetoric to increase tensions, they simultaneously emphasized that their opponents were not the other ethnic parties but rather the representatives of the old system.[85] At the founding assembly of the SDS, the leader of the Bosniak SDA, Alija Izetbegović, received standing ovations and he welcomed the new Serb party with the words, 'we have been waiting for you for some time – for this Bosnia needs you'.[86] Karadžić reciprocated this praise, expressed 'great liking' for Izetbegović and stated, 'Our Muslims are much closer to us … than many Christian people in Europe'.[87] The alliance between the SDS, the SDA and the HDZ was never made formal but the parties openly encouraged their supporters to give lower preference votes to the other ethnic parties.[88]

Cooperation between the ethnic parties aided the ethnification of politics; it strengthened the parties' attempt to define political competition in ethnic terms. This may seem counter-intuitive since this cooperation could be taken to indicate that anti-communism was more important than ethnicity. However, the cleavage between the reformed communists and the anti-communist ethnic parties was merely used to justify their cooperation and the need for ethnic representation was stressed. Thus, the SDS warned

---

85. D. Banjac. 1990. 'Stranka koja ukida straha', *Borba,* 16 July, 3.
86. Bougarel, 'Bosnia and Hercegovina,' 98.
87. N. Stefanović. 1994. 'Dr Radovan Karadzic, President of the Serb Republic in BiH', *Vreme NDA,* 13 June. From: http://www.scc.rutgers.edu/serbian_digest/. In its election programme, the SDS professed its support for equal treatment of the different nations living in Bosnia. Election programme in Prstojević, *BiH Izbori,* 113–5.
88. A. Zulfikarpašić. 1998. *The Bosniak,* London: Hurst, 155.

of the consequences of a non-ethnic vote and the HDZ, in their electoral programme, assured Croat voters that if their neighbours, friends and colleagues were ready to accept them as Croats, then they would also be ready to accept that they had their own party.[89] Since they did not agree on the issue of the future status of Yugoslavia, with the HDZ supporting a confederation, their cooperation, furthermore, prevented this issue from being the most salient issue in the campaign. As in Croatia, the initially relatively moderate position of the ethnic parties, paradoxically, facilitated ethnification: they recognized each other as legitimate representatives and reinforced each other's message of an ethnic definition of politics.

The ethnic definition did not at first preclude cooperation and relations with the HDZ and the SDA, in the pre-election period, scarcely gave the SDS reasons or ammunition for radicalization. The SDS and the SDA, especially, were adamant that they were not opponents and both parties supported the continued existence of the Yugoslav Federation. Nevertheless, the SDS did radicalize during the election campaign, most visibly with the establishment of the Serb National Council, which indicated that the SDS would not necessarily respect Bosnian institutions. The SDS argued, however, that this should not be interpreted as radicalization, that it was a defensive measure in case the rights of the Serbs were not protected.[90] Although this radicalization did not directly mirror relations with the HDZ and the SDA, it did reflect an underlying fear among the Serbs that the Bosniaks and Croats would form an alliance and thereby be able to outvote the Serbs.

Problematic Cooperation Despite Restraint

After the landslide victory in the Bosnian elections, Karadžić continuously emphasized the need for partnership[91] and the three parties proceeded to divide positions of power between them. Although they were to find that cooperation was problematic once substantial questions had to be addressed, it was almost a year before open battles were fought between the parties.[92] Conscious of the increasingly tense situation, especially after war broke out in Croatia, the SDA and the HDZ avoided taking extreme positions on the federation/confederation debate.[93] But the

89. M. Vućelić. 1990. 'Srbi se najsporije bude', *Borba,* 23 July, 5. HDZ BiH programme in Prstojević, *BiH Izbori,* 44–45.
90. *Danas,* 13 November 1990, 11.
91. R. Ninčić. 1990. 'Udruženi poraz komunista i reformista', *Danas,* 26 November, 12–14.
92. Pejanović, *Through Bosnian Eyes,* 40–41.
93. Cohen, *Broken Bonds,* 209.

SDS also showed restraint: despite the continued radicalization of its statements, the SDS leadership held on to the precarious nationalist partnership. Thus, when the partnership with the HDZ and SDA was re-established after a row in early 1991, Karadžić stated that the SDS was a democratic party and had long ago abandoned extreme Serb positions: forces for a unitary Yugoslavia or Greater Serbia.[94] The possibility of changing alliances resulted in a vague position still being of use to the SDS, despite its near monolithic status within the Serb community.

But, ultimately, the SDS chose to adopt a position of staunch intransigence and argued that cooperation was impossible. The blame for this, they argued, was entirely the SDA's and the HDZ's since they refused to accept the SDS's position.[95] The alliance between the Croats and the Bosniaks was something the SDS had warned against from the outset, as Krajišnik stated in early 1991: 'The Serb nation does not want to live in an independent state where they will be afraid of being outvoted'.[96] The SDS could argue that the HDZ and the SDA were violating the national parity principle and they used this to justify choosing the war option.[97] The hardening of the Serb position was further reinforced by movements on the international scene, especially by the U.S. push for Bosnia's recognition, which began in February 1992.[98] While this was the reason used to justify the SDS's radicalization, the position of the party should not be seen as merely reactive: other forces gave the leadership strong incentives to radicalize and the party most often took the lead in radicalization. However, the tripartite constellation was of importance, for the initial period of cooperation but also for the radicalization of the SDS's position. In terms of the latter, the SDS had markedly different relations with the HDZ and the SDA and this was to influence subsequent developments.

The Scepticism of Croats and the Wooing of Bosniaks

The SDS was, from the beginning, much more sceptical of the Croat HDZ than the Bosniak SDA. This was partly based on the HDZ's preference for a confederal solution but should also be seen in the light of the mounting tensions in Croatia. However, there were Croat forces in Bosnia that the SDS could possibly ally itself with. The HDZ was itself divided, between

94. E. Habal. 1991. 'Bosna je suverene u okviru Jugoslavije', *Oslobođenje*, 20 February, 3.
95. Pejanovic, *Through Bosnian Eyes*, 63, 65.
96. D. Stanišić. 1991. 'Ustavno ili neustavno, pitanje je sad', *Oslobođenje*, 4 February, 4.
97. Glenny, *The Fall of Yugoslavia*, 141. Karadžić argued that the SDA and the HDZ were no longer partners, that they were now 'classical opponents'. N. Butorović. 1992. 'Više nema jedinstvene BiH', *Borba*, 6 March, 3.
98. Burg and Shoup, *The War in Bosnia-Herzegovina*, 100.

factions supporting an independent Bosnia and factions dreaming of a Greater Croatia. Greater Croatia was anathema to the Serbs in Croatia but it opened up for potential alliances with the Serbs in Bosnia, with whom it could be possible to reach an agreement on dividing Bosnia. At the time of the November 1990 elections, the pro-Bosnia faction was still in the stronger position, under the leadership of Stjepan Kljuić, but with support from Zagreb the Herzegovin lobby gradually took over and radicalization ensued.[99] This change made a peaceful solution less likely, but for the SDS it opened the door to new alliances, especially following the Karadjordjevo talks between Tuđman and Milošević.

However, in the prewar period the SDS primarily put its faith in the Bosniaks and it was this interplay that had the greater impact on the SDS's position. Izetbegović and Karadžić had, from the founding of their parties, publicly emphasized the necessity and value of their cooperation. The Serbs in Bosnia and Belgrade actively tried to woo the Bosniaks, hoping that they could thereby prevent the disintegration of Yugoslavia. The first sign of a definitive break between the SDA and the SDS came in February 1991 when the SDA began advocating a confederal solution.[100] But although this clearly contradicted the SDS's goal and raised the prospect of a Croat-Bosniak alliance, the partnership did not collapse. A final attempt at reviving the cooperation was initiated by the Muslim Bosniak Organization (Muslimansko-bošnjačka organizacija, MBO) with the so-called Belgrade Initiative in the summer of 1991; an agreement which would guarantee Yugoslavia's continuation.[101] At this point, the Serb leaders felt increasingly isolated and the MBO's leader, Adil Zulfikarpašić, argues that they were pleasantly surprised by the proposal.[102] The agreement, however, failed when Izetbegović refused to sign. After this last attempt it was not long before the HDZ and the SDA declared a sovereign Bosnia and the SDS left parliament and began preparing for the war option.[103] Already at the time of the negotiations over the Belgrade Initiative it was clear that relations between the SDA and the SDS were frosty at best. Thus, Koljević, in Izetbegović's presence, allegedly exclaimed, 'He is lying to us!'[104]

Part of the explanation for this lack of trust is to be found in internal divisions in the SDA. Hard-line forces within the party effected a gradual

99. Judah, *The Serbs*, 165.
100. Andjelić, *Bosnia-Herzegovina*, 207.
101. A Yugoslav Federation dominated by Serbia was by no means an ideal solution for the Bosniaks but it was a last-ditch attempt to avoid war.
102. Zulfikarpašić, *The Bosniak*, 152.
103. Ibid., 178, 180, 181.
104. Ibid., 172.

radicalization and, in negotiations with the Serbs, Izetbegović found himself constrained and he retracted statements on possible settlements following negative reactions within his own ranks.[105] When Zulfikarpašić defended the Belgrade Initiative on Bosnian television, a fax was received from the SDA executive committee stating, 'We are against the very idea of negotiating with the Serbs'. Izetbegović said he had no idea who sent it,[106] which attests to factional disputes in the party or at least to Izetbegović's ambivalent position. The divisions in the Bosniak community permitted the SDS to maintain their hope for Bosniak support but it also contributed to Izetbegović's increasingly uncompromising position and the SDS leadership's lack of trust in him. Both the SDS and the HDZ had tried to win the Bosniaks over and the failure of the SDS to secure their support resulted in a great sense of betrayal.[107]

The tripartite coalition in some ways dampened radicalization since it was not clear from the outset who would end up in the minority position. It encouraged moderation as a means of ensuring cooperation. However, radicalization eventually ensued and it is an interesting point that increased radicalization of all three nationalist parties co-existed with continued partnership and attempts at reaching agreements. This radicalization was significantly influenced by the context of increasing tensions and the outbreak of violence in Slovenia and Croatia. While inter-ethnic relations and overall context, therefore, affected the position of the Serb leadership, it would be mistaken to regard the radicalization of the SDS as merely mirroring these developments: radicalization was strongly pushed by intra-party divisions and by the kin-state, and the SDS often took the first step in radicalizing its position.

Dynamics of Competition and Division

At the time of the Bosnian elections , the ethnification of politics in the republic was considerable and with this issue being dominant, the non-ethnic parties found it very hard to compete with the SDS. The nationalist cooperation was part of a conscious strategy to define politics in ethnic

105. Ibid., 172.
106. Ibid., 183.
107. N. Stefanović. 1994. 'Dr Radovan Karadzic, President of the Serb Republic in BiH', *Vreme NDA,* 13 June. From: http://www.scc.rutgers.edu/serbian_digest/. Serb politicians from that time frequently argue that the position of the Serbs was reactive and that it was in particular a reaction to the SDA's and the HDZ's c-operation. E.g. Author's interviews with Predrag Lazarević, Dragutin Ilić (Banja Luka, 23 October 2003) and Vladimir Lukić (Banja Luka, 2 December 2003).

terms and the initially relatively moderate position of the nationalist parties, paradoxically, aided ethnification and, hence, ultimately the radicalization of politics. The ability of the SDS to attract Serb voters was, furthermore, augmented by the weakness of the non-ethnic parties and their internal squabbles. Moreover, the SDS managed in a short time, from its foundation to the elections, to establish a well-functioning party structure. The existence of non-ethnic rivals meant that a vague position was instrumental for the SDS in its attempt to capture the middle ground. Playing the extreme ethnic card was not successful, but due to the earlier ethnification of politics a vague position soon lost its use: the SDS was almost monolithic within the Serb community, non-ethnic alternatives were marginalized and a significant, more moderate Serb party seemed unlikely to emerge. Rivals to the SDS and its leadership, therefore, had to come from within.

Radovan Karadžić was initially not a strong charismatic leader: the SDS built him up, not the other way round. Power was, at least before the elections, exerted from behind the scenes rather than in the official party leadership. Despite having such a relatively weak leadership from the outset, the party was fairly cohesive and not plagued by fractionalization. The only serious problem of intra-party challenge in the prewar period was caused by the increasingly autonomous Krajina leadership. Like other threatening intra-party divisions, this was, however, solved resolutely through a compromise involving concessions to the hard-line elements. It therefore followed the trend of the continuous radicalization of the party. This radicalization, as well as Karadžić's strong backing from behind the scenes, seems to have preserved an undivided party. Finally, Belgrade's support for the leadership and lack of involvement in intra-party struggles helped Karadžić fend off challengers; they did not posses the resources needed to win in the intra-Serb rivalry.

Despite popular endorsement of the SDS at the time of elections, the party could not necessarily count on popular support for its continued radicalization. Dissatisfaction with the nationalist parties was mounting but the party made clever use of a referendum to point to the support enjoyed by its more radical position. While the party in its radicalized form was certainly not without popular backing, there is no evidence that supports a voter-led radicalization: Serb voters had no chance to support any alternatives to the SDS and with its control of resources in Serb-dominated areas the party had the power to heavily influence popular opinion and its expression. The Bosniak-Croat alliance can, to some extent, be seen as a turning point that temporarily led to greater Serb unity. However, one should not overlook the significance of enforced unity: non-ethnic deputies were subject to very significant pressures to join the SDS's ranks and moderates were often removed from their posts. This had more to do with the dynamics of intra-ethnic rivalry than with inter-ethnic relations.

Prewar Intra-Serb Rivalry

The analysis of intra-Serb competition in prewar Croatia and Bosnia highlighted some interesting dynamics. In particular, popular attitudes were found to be of limited significance in the process of radicalization and the ethnification of politics was part of the political struggle; it was not based on the overwhelming power of ethnicity.[108] The analysis found that intra-Serb rivalry was primarily dominated by non-democratic resources, which were to a large extent supplied by Belgrade, and the dominance of hardliners was, consequently, based on their control of resources outside democratic competition. What was important for rival elites was to have a geographical basis of support, a core area where an alternative power base could be built. Furthermore, the use of distinctly non-democratic tactics to get rid of more moderate rivals greatly aided the victory of the radical faction. The availability and effectiveness of coercive resources strengthened the hardliners and made possible the dominance of centrifugal dynamics. Contrary to what is argued in theories of outbidding, popular attitudes were not the driving force in intra-party struggles; they were not based on popular demands for a harder line. One decisive factor in the victory of the hardliners in the Croatian case was Belgrade's involvement: the Serbian regime provided the resources needed in the competition.

Competition with non-ethnic parties and the process of ethnification progressed differently in the two cases. In the competition with non-ethnic parties, the SDS in Bosnia proved much stronger than the SDS in Croatia: the authority of the League of Communists was eroded to a greater extent, the non-ethnic parties weakened each other by competing internally, the SDS in Bosnia was stronger and better organized than the SDS in Croatia, and the ethnic issue finally had greater political salience in Bosnia than in Croatia. The ethnification of politics was part of the political struggle and should be analysed as political competition: in terms of the dynamics of competition, distribution of resources and the inter-ethnic interplay, which lends it a quality different from more conventional political competition.

---

108. As Gagnon puts it: 'It is the very inability of elites "to play the ethnic card" as a means of mobilizing the population that leads them to use other options'. Gagnon, *The Myth of Ethnic War*, xvi.

The ethnification of politics and the marginalization of non-ethnic rivals was in both cases complete in late 1990 – that is before the outbreak of widespread violence – and was consequently not merely a consequence of violence, as it is sometimes argued.[109] But support for the nationalist parties and their subsequent radicalization was not based on elites successfully playing the ethnic card and mobilizing people from a radical position.

When ethnification was still incomplete and non-ethnic rivals still posed a treat to the ethnic party, a vague position was, therefore, instrumental: a position from which the party could simultaneously promote tensions and compete with non-ethnic forces. The vague position, furthermore, meant that ethnic alternatives to the SDS were unlikely to emerge. The parties presented themselves as 'catch-all' Serb parties, which dissuaded more moderate rivals, and when the non-ethnic rivals were marginalized the SDS was consequently near-monolithic in the Serb community. Once the non-ethnic alternatives were marginalized, the incentive for a vague position disappeared and a more radical position became strategic, especially since radical factions were found within the party. In this sense, ethnification fostered radicalization whereas incomplete ethnification was more compatible with moderate dynamics.

The dominant dynamic of Serb elite competition was in both cases centrifugal: radicalization was the outcome, despite different degrees of division. The SDS in Croatia provide a clear example of intra-party outflanking when more radical factions continuously pressured Rašković to take a more extreme position and ultimately replaced him as party leader. In Bosnia, the SDS leadership was in greater control of the party but this greater cohesion and ability to deal with divisions and factions was accompanied by a constant radicalization of the party. Rivalry was fuelled by differing views of solutions to the inter-ethnic conflict, by ideological and regional cleavages and by personal power ambitions. These issues came together in the SDS's strong regional factions in Knin and Banja Luka. However, the Knin faction reached into the leadership of the SDS, whereas the Banja Luka faction was in conflict with the leadership of the SDS. The primary issue of contention differed: Banja Luka wanted greater autonomy while Knin wanted the party to take a more radical course; thus, while internal competition in Croatia was primarily over the national or ethnic issue, in Bosnia the divisions were also based on other issues. Furthermore, the Banja Luka faction was internally divided and, therefore, weakened vis-à-vis the central

109. See, for example, Gagnon, *The Myth of Ethnic War*. J. Mueller. 2000. 'The Banality of "Ethnic" War', *International Security* 25(1).

leadership. The Banja Luka faction was, consequently, much easier to manage than the Knin faction and the leadership only had to make minor concessions. In terms of the resulting dynamics of competition, these differences, therefore, point to the importance of the structure of the party, the nature of divisions and the cohesiveness of the opposing faction. Both leaderships may have created or deliberately encouraged radical factions in order to be able to stir up tensions while at the same time presenting themselves as the more moderate forces who needed concessions in order to fend off the hawks. This is, however, a dangerous strategy and for Rašković, if such a strategy was ever deliberate, it backfired.

Inter-ethnic relations proved very important for the ethnification of politics but had a less significant impact on the process of radicalization: radicalization of the 'other side' provided ammunition for hardliners, but it was not *the* decisive factor in the outcome of intra-Serb competition. Changes in intra-ethnic elite competition need not be a response to changed rhetoric or actions of opposing ethnic leaders. Inter-ethnic relations primarily matter when popular attitudes are of great significance and the importance was, consequently, reduced by the decreasing significance of this audience. Intra-ethnic competition should consequently not be regarded as just an epiphenomenon of inter-ethnic relations; it is not merely reactive.

Despite the different dynamics of competition, the outcome was, nevertheless, the same in Croatia and Bosnia: increasing radicalization of the dominant Serb position. But the different paths to this radicalization meant that the two SDS leaders, Babić and Karadžić, entered the wars in Croatia and Bosnia with significantly different degrees of political support, fractionalization and threats to their leadership.

Conflict context	Decisive audiences	Outcome
• Transition • Sporadic violence • Gradual ethnification	*Competition within SDS* • Local and regional party structures • Paramilitary forces • Kin-state	Radicalization
	Competition with non-ethnic parties • General population inter-ethnic interplay important • Party structures	Vague positioning until ethnification complete

Figure 4.1 Prewar Intra-Serb Rivalry

CHAPTER FIVE

Wartime Croatia: Disunity Did Not Save the Serbs

With the outbreak of war, we find ourselves in a very different context for political competition: not only has the transition to democracy failed and complete ethnification become a reality, but it is also a situation of war in which other resources, especially military ones, are available and effective in the internal rivalry. Given the importance of coercive resources, links with military and paramilitary forces become of crucial significance for the outcome of intra-Serb competition. These forces exercise their influence either through support for competing political leaders or through direct challenges. Based on such background conditions, intra-ethnic competition is consequently far removed from political competition in a peaceful, consolidated democracy. However, the wartime period also brings with it the emergence of competition between ethnic parties, often also focused on issues other than the conflict itself. Divisions are still fuelled by disagreement over the inter-ethnic conflict, by ideological cleavages and by personal power ambitions, but rivalry now also becomes focused on criticism of war profiteering and differing views of relations with Belgrade. This runs counter to theoretical expectations that unity will increase in a time of crisis and that the outbreak of violence will prevent other issues from becoming salient. Intra-party competition, therefore, ceases to be the only form of intra-Serb competition and other salient issues surface. But while party competition increases in importance, the party structures themselves are even weaker than in the prewar period: other resources are important and the need for democratic legitimacy has been reduced by the outbreak of war.

In the period immediately before the outbreak of war, the dynamics of intra-Serb competition had differed significantly in Croatia and Bosnia, although continuous radicalization was a common feature. But after war broke out – in the summer of 1991 in Croatia and in April 1992 in Bosnia – the dynamics of intra-Serb competition gradually changed and in some ways became more alike. The intensity of competition increased in Bosnia and, in both cases, competition from other parties also became of importance. However, the Serb elites in Croatia remained far more divided than in Bosnia and this affected the positions taken by the leaders and the ultimate defeat of the radicals when Croatian forces retook Krajina in August 1995. Initially, however, the Serb leaders in both cases had great success in achieving their military objectives: by late 1991, Serb forces controlled one third of Croatian territory and by September 1992 Serb forces in Bosnia controlled as much as 70 per cent of the country.

Milošević's pre-eminent role had, in the prewar period, been nearly uncontested among the victorious local leaders but this changed significantly during the war: the local leaders almost invariably fell out with their former benefactor in Belgrade. Rivalry therefore began over who was the true interpreter of Serb interests and goals, and in this competition disgruntled leaders in the two Serb statelets sought alternative alliance partners in Serbia while Milošević found other players more willing to follow his tune. The Serbian president, thereby, utilized the existence of divisions among the local Serbs and, therefore, continued to have a significant impact on the dynamics of intra-Serb competition. However, the local Serb leaders were able to garner alternative support in Serbia, from the democratic opposition, the Serbian Orthodox Church and, in particular, the Serb Radical Party. The existence of resources emanating from within the statelets as well as support from these alternative audiences in the kin-state resulted in a greater level of autonomy from Milošević, who consequently was not always able to dictate developments in the two statelets.

The importance of popular attitudes decreased considerably with the outbreak of war and it was not a significant constraint on rival leaders, even though elections and referenda were held. In David Owen's words, these leaders 'displayed a callousness of mind in which the people's view never seemed to come anywhere near the conference table'.[1] Similarly, the position of 'opposing' ethnic leaders did not significantly impact on the direction of internal rivalry, on changes in a more radical or more moderate direction. The form of inter-ethnic relations that really mattered was the military balance but even when this became detrimental to the Serb leaders, it took changes in intra-Serb competition and kin-state pressure to force a significant change in the dominant elite position.

---

1.   D. Owen. 1995. *Balkan Odyssey,* San Diego, CA: Harcourt, 3.

Radicalization continued to be the dominant response to intra-party challengers but it was not the chosen response to competition from other parties or independent leaders. Such opposition would most often be suppressed and, hence, caused no change in the dominant position, but it also at times led to a relative moderation of the dominant position. Radicalization is, therefore, not the only possible outcome of intra-ethnic competition, not even in a violent, highly polarized situation. This contradicts existing theorizing in the field.

Infighting in the Serb Statelet

Following the outbreak of war in Croatia, there was initially a closing of ranks behind Milan Babić, who had emerged victorious from the prewar intra-Serb competition. Formally, however, Babić was only president of the SAO Krajina as well as president of the Serb National Council. The two other SAOs in Croatia – SAO Western Slavonia and SAO Slavonia, Baranja and Western Srem – were led by Veljko Džakula and Goran Hadžić. The initiative was, nevertheless, with Babić and on 19 December 1991, the parliament of SAO Krajina proclaimed the Republic of Serb Krajina (Republika Srpska Krajina, RSK), with Babić as president. The RSK was, in early 1992, joined by the two other autonomous regions but this did not ensure more than temporary unity; Babić lost power shortly after and subsequently chose to reactivate his SDS of Krajina and constitute it as an actual party. Competition between parties was thereby introduced and the main challenges to the leaders now came from outside their own party or movement: from other parties or from independent candidates. Intra-party divisions persisted but they primarily concerned the ability to take hardliners along to new political positions rather than explicit challenges. The event that set these changing dynamics in motion was a leadership struggle over the Vance Plan in early 1992.

Babić Faces Defeat

The Vance Plan set up four United Nations Protected Areas that coincided roughly with the Serb-held areas that had had a Serb majority or substantial minority before the war. In return for the deployment of UN forces, the JNA would withdraw from Croatia and the paramilitaries would be disarmed. Babić was, however, vehemently opposed to the plan: he refused to accept disarmament and the withdrawal of the JNA, fearing that the mandate of the UN forces would not be extended after six months.[2]

2.   ICTY, 'Babić's testimony,' 13625.

In his opposition, Babić had counted on the support of his loyal followers in Knin, but with the other two autonomous regions joining the RSK the balance of power had changed and support from SAO Krajina was no longer sufficient for Babić to remain in power. The RSK political system was in essence a parliamentary system and the president could, consequently, be removed by parliament. It was, therefore, crucial that the speaker of the RSK parliament, Mile Paspalj, be persuaded by Belgrade to endorse the plan and call a parliamentary session in Glina, away from Babić's stronghold in Knin. This session endorsed the plan, dismissed Babić as president and requested the resignation of the government. Goran Hadžić, who was president of SAO Slavonia, argues that this was merely the result of the joining of the two other SAOs: Babić was only president of the 'small Krajina' and a new parliament had to be constituted and a new president elected.[3] It was, however, not a clear divide between Krajina and the rest of the RSK: the conflict between Babić and Belgrade also brought out divisions between Knin and the regions of Lika, Kordun and Banija, and many deputies from the latter regions chose to go against the RSK president. Divisions were, thus, fuelled by different views of the war, by regional cleavages as well as by personal ambitions. Babić had, however, not given up his fight and convened his loyalists at a parliamentary session in Knin. They decided to call a referendum on the Vance Plan and voted against the dismissal of Babić, whereby double rule was effectively established in the RSK. On 26 February 1992, Hadžić was elected new president of the RSK and after a period of competing centres of power the authority of his government was established.[4]

Although Babić was formally ousted by the RSK parliament, coercive resources and support from military forces were decisive for this outcome. Babić lacked support in the 'enlarged' RSK and he crucially lacked the support of the military. He did not trust the JNA[5] but had counted on support from the local paramilitaries. This was, however, conditional on support from Milan Martić, who controlled the paramilitary police. Babić and Martić had previously clashed due to Babić's desire to control the armed forces, and an additional reason for Babić's rejection of the Vance Plan may have been that the entailed demilitarization would have left Martić's police as the only military force in the RSK.[6] Martić, perhaps

3.   Author's interview with Goran Hadžić.
4.   Dakić, *The Serbian Krayina*, 59. M. Čuruvija. 1992. 'Kordun i Banija napuštaju Babiću', *Vjesnik*, 12 February, 1.
5.   S. Cerović. 1992. 'Troubles with a Bit Player', *Vreme NDA*, 13 January. From: http://www.scc.rutgers.edu/serbian_digest/.
6.   M. Milošević. 1992. 'Babic Caput', *Vreme NDA*, 13 January. From: http://www.scc.rutgers.edu/serbian_digest/. S. Cerović. 1991. 'Balvan čuva Jugoslaviju', *Vreme*, 17 June, 16–17. V. Rajić. 1992. 'Knin – drugi put', *Vjesnik*, 7 January, 5.

realizing this opportunity, sided with Hadžić. As a response to this situation, and in protest over the Vance Plan, Babić formed the paramilitary 'Petar Mrkonjić' brigade in April 1992.[7] He, furthermore, decided to reactivate the SDS of Krajina and constitute it as a separate party with himself as president.[8] Babić's SDS and his paramilitaries were later to become of importance but for now he lacked support for his position and in late March he allegedly narrowly escaped an assassination attempt.[9] Eventually, therefore, he returned to parliament, waiting for an opportune moment for his comeback.

The conflict over the Vance Plan gave Rašković a chance to revive his political career. He reinstated himself as leader of the SDS and announced at a press conference that the party was 'back in Croatian politics' and that the Serb representatives would return to the Croatian Parliament.[10] However, this act was largely symbolic and lacked political significance since Rašković was not able to assert his authority in the RSK. This is illustrated by a letter issued by the local SDS in Benkovac in which Rašković is taunted as the leader of the 'SDS of Croatia' and banned from travelling to Benkovac.[11] Rašković was to remain in a marginal position until his death in the summer of 1992. The moderation entailed by the Vance Plan was, therefore, of a very limited nature but it did, for a while, put an end to centrifugal dynamics.

It soon became clear, however, that the Vance Plan was only intended to freeze the situation and the other provisions of the plan were never implemented. Frustrated with the lack of progress, two members of the RSK government, Veljko Džakula and Dušan Ećimović, initiated negotiations with the Croatian authorities over the return of refugees to Western Slavonia and, together with other SDS leaders from Western Slavonia, they signed the so-called Daruvar Agreement in February 1993. The government in Zagreb quickly distanced itself from the agreement[12] but in Knin the reaction was more severe since it was thought to create an unwanted precedent: if in Western Slavonia why not in Knin? Džakula and Ećimović were relieved of their posts and in September 1993 they

7.   M. Dakić. 2001. *Krajina kroz Vijekove,* Belgrade: Vedes, Hronika p. 15.
8.   Kovačević, *Kavez,* 68–9. Author's interview with Dragan Kovačević, RSK information minister, 1995 (Belgrade, 17 September 2004).
9.   *Borba,* 25 March 1992, 4.
10.   *Vjesnik,* 5 February 1992, 12. See also M. Vasić. 1992. 'Babic's Swan Song', *Vreme NDA,* 10 February. From: http://www.scc.rutgers.edu/serbian_digest/.
11.   Letter printed in Dakić, *Krajina kroz Vijekove,* Appendix 39.
12.   U. Komlenović. 1995. 'Mavericks on the Road', *Vreme NDA,* 3 April. From: http://www.scc.rutgers.edu/serbian_digest/.

were arrested and charged with high treason.[13] The RSK leadership controlled the resources necessary to suppress such challengers and the charges sent a clear signal to others who might be contemplating moderation. By arresting these popular figures, the RSK leadership also made sure that they would not be able to run in the upcoming elections in the Serb-held territories.[14] The Western Slavonian leaders had taken a step too far and misjudged when moderation was tolerated and when it would put them in danger: acceptance of the Vance Plan was necessary in order to obtain power, implementation of the plan was not.[15] Divisions based on different views of the war thus remained significant and continued to have a decisive impact on Serb politics.

Outbidding and Conflict between Civilian and Military Leaders

The new president of the RSK faced considerable problems with more radical forces and, with the added help of hindsight, Goran Hadžić now argues that he could not have supported the Daruvar Agreement since he would have risked being killed.[16] The central force behind the rejection of the agreement and the arrest of the negotiators was Hadžić's main rival, Milan Martić, the minister of the interior and the strongman in Knin.[17] Outbidding was also part of Babić's strategy for returning to power. Thus, following talks at the UN, the SDS of Krajina's executive committee issued a declaration in which it accused the RSK delegation of 'too easily getting into talks ... about giving up part of the Serbian territory – handing it over to our enemies'.[18] Martić's persistent challenges were, however, of greater immediate concern to Hadžić who, although he was president of the whole of the RSK, never managed to establish control in the Knin region: in this area, Martić and his paramilitary police ruled supreme.

13. Author's interview with Veljko Džakula. U. Komlenović. 1995. 'All Dzakula's Arrests', *Vreme NDA*, 15 May. From: http://www.scc.rutgers.edu/serbian_digest/. F. Švarm. 1994. 'Darkness at Noon', *AIM Press*, 20 February. From: http://www.aimpress.ch/.
14. Author's interview with Dušan Ećimović (Belgrade, 29 August 2003).
15. In February 1994, Džakula was kidnapped in broad daylight in Belgrade following a television interview in which he criticized the RSK leaders. The RSK ministry of the interior took responsibility for the kidnapping, stating that Džakula was taken into custody by the municipal court in Glina, where proceedings for 'territorial threat to the RSK and espionage' had been initiated against him. F. Švarm. 1994. 'Darkness at Noon', *AIM Press*, 20 February. From: http://www.aimpress.ch/.
16. Author's interview with Goran Hadžić.
17. G. Jureško. 1993. 'Srpski pregovarači imaju jedno lice za javnost, druge za pregovore', *Vjesnik*, 19 December, 8–9.
18. F. Švarm. 1993. 'Patriots and Godfathers', *Vreme NDA*, 1 March. From: http://www.scc. rutgers.edu/serbian_digest/.

Hadžić eventually had to withdraw to Slavonia and could only come to Knin under heavy guard.[19] In Eastern Slavonia, other paramilitary formations had considerable influence, especially the Serb Volunteer Guard, or the 'Tigers', led by Željko Ražnjatović, better known as 'Arkan'. The presence of the Tigers undermined Martić's monolithic control of the armed forces, but their influence was largely confined to Slavonia and Hadžić's power was similarly constrained.

Hadžić's problems in ruling the RSK were augmented by an economic collapse: there was a shortage of food, electricity and fuel, which spurred the undeniable need for economic negotiations with the Croatian authorities.[20] At the same time, fear of Croatian military attacks became widespread after Croatian forces successfully retook control of the important Maslenica Bridge in early January 1993. Finding itself in an increasingly untenable position, the RSK government actually began negotiating with Zagreb.[21] Thus, despite the continued politics of outbidding, the RSK leaders, lacking any other alternatives, chose a more moderate position. The prime minister of the RSK, Đorđe Bjegović, even stated: 'a loose confederation with Croatia could be envisioned'.[22] Hadžić's government was not strong enough to repress its opponents and this was, therefore, not a viable strategy in the competition. The challenges facing them were, moreover, not limited to outbidding on the issue of the war as they were also accused of war profiteering and incompetence. Further radicalization of their position on the war would, therefore, not make the challenge disappear and it was, furthermore, difficult to imagine a position more radical than the one espoused by Babić and Martić.

In order to gain time, the government had postponed elections scheduled for March 1993, but the situation in the RSK was becoming increasingly chaotic: Hadžić was not in control and the conflict between him and Martić eventually reached breaking point. In October 1993, Hadžić decided that Martić's paramilitary police should be subjected to the RSK army, an army which had been created following the Maslenica offensive and which was formally under the president's authority. To

19. F. Švarm. 1995. 'Orders from Belgrade', *Vreme NDA*, 13 March. From: http://www.scc.rutgers.edu/serbian_digest/.
20. F. Švarm. 1993. 'Patriots and Godfathers', *Vreme NDA*, 1 March. From: http://www.scc.rutgers.edu/serbian_digest/. M. Vasić. 1992. 'Neither Unity nor Law', *Vreme NDA*, 3 August. From: http://www.scc.rutgers.edu/serbian_digest/.
21. F. Švarm. 1993. 'Patriots and Godfathers', *Vreme NDA*, 1 March. From: http://www.scc.rutgers.edu/serbian_digest/.
22. F. Švarm. 1993. 'A Fragile Pontoon Link', *Vreme NDA*, 26 July. From: http://www.scc.rutgers.edu/serbian_digest/.

achieve this, Hadžić ousted Martić in a parliamentary session, but Martić fought back by accusing Hadžić of controlling the oil resources of the RSK[23] and, furthermore, criticizing Hadžić's absence from the RSK – Hadžić mostly stayed in Novi Sad where he was enrolled in the Faculty of Economics. Martić argued that the parliament had not been quorate when it dismissed him and he called another parliamentary session in Plitviće, Krajina. When this session revoked the decision to dismiss Martić, elections were inevitable.[24] As in the case of the Babić-Hadžić conflict, parliamentary sessions called in different parts of the RSK could, due to limited mobility, be used to support contested positions. Issues of war and peace were still significant in rivalry between the elite, but other issues had also become salient and this influenced the dynamics of competition, in particular the strategies available to Hadžić. Moreover, the importance of coercive resources was clearly reflected in the competition, as the control of military forces was crucial.

The holding of elections did, however, not only promise to solve the strife between Hadžić and Martić, it also gave Babić a chance to make a comeback. The elections cemented Hadžić's weakness and his SDS of Serb Lands lost decisively to Babić's SDS of Krajina.[25] In the presidential elections the main competitors were Babić and Martić. Martić ran on a populist platform promising the voters a fight against war profiteers, aid to war invalids and families of killed soldiers, and economic revival.[26] Babić's platform was similar and none of the campaigns envisaged a change in course from the intransigent one followed so far.[27] This campaign reflects a change in the form of competition: the primary source of division was no longer the inter-ethnic conflict.

Babić seemed to have already won in the first round, but the election commission called a second round, which Martić narrowly won after having received substantial support from Belgrade and its media.[28] Before

23. *Croatian International Relations Review.* 2000, 'Chronology 1993, October through December', 6(18/19), 54.
24. Ž. Mataija. 1993. 'Plušte uzajamne optužbe', *Vjesnik*, 13 October, 4. F. Švarm. 1995. 'Political Clashes in the Krajina', *Vreme NDA*, 13 March. F. Švarm. 1993. 'Patriots and Godfathers', *Vreme NDA*, 1 March. From: http://www.scc.rutgers.edu/serbian_digest/.
25. F. Švarm. 1993. 'Milosevic loses Krajina', *Vreme NDA*, 20 December. From: http://www.scc.rutgers.edu/serbian_digest/.
26. F. Švarm, 1993. 'Milan Martic's Flying Circus', *Vreme NDA*, 13 December. From: http://www.scc.rutgers.edu/serbian_digest/.
27. I. Marijačić. 1993. 'Balvanska konstanta', *Vjesnik*, 16 December, 4. F. Švarm. 1994. 'The Return of the District Strongman', *Vreme NDA*, 31 January. From: http://www.scc.rutgers.edu/serbian_digest/.
28. F. Švarm. 1994. 'No Roads for Reality in Krajina', *AIM Press* 20 March. From: http://www.aimpress.ch/.

this final round, Martić had indirectly threatened to use his military might to take over power and, furthermore, he argued that Belgrade would likely abandon the RSK should Babić return to power.[29] By winning, Martić demonstrated that control of the paramilitary and police in Krajina and links with Belgrade were more important than the SDS name and organization when it came to securing the RSK leadership.

Post-electoral Dynamics: Multipartyism and Deadlock

The upshot of the elections was a president, Milan Martić, who had no political party to back him up and who was faced with a parliamentary majority consisting of Babić's SDS and the Serb Radical Party (Srpska radikalna stranka, SRS). Like its mother-party in Serbia, the Serb Radicals in the RSK espoused extreme Serb nationalism and served as an even more radical rival or alliance partner to the SDS. The SRS was founded in the RSK in July 1992[30] and began cooperating with Babić once it became clear that his political death had been prematurely declared.[31] Under the leadership of Rade Leskovac, the SRS became a highly organized party and it made significant inroads into Hadžić's support. Together with the SDS of Krajina's thirty deputies and one of eight independent deputies, the Radicals' sixteen deputies held a majority in parliament and could, therefore, topple any prime minister proposed by Martić.

In addition to the Serb Radicals and the competing versions of the SDS, the elections had given political representation to two more parties.[32] The first of these was the Serb Party of Socialists (Srpska partija socijalista, SPS), which was created shortly before the elections under the leadership of RSK prime minister Đorđe Bjegović and was designed as Belgrade's voice in the Serb statelet. However, its success was limited: the SPS won six out of eighty-four mandates in the parliamentary elections.[33] Likewise, the Social Democratic Party of Krajina proved to have marginal electoral

29. F. Švarm. 1994. 'The Return of the District Strongman', *Vreme NDA*, 31 January. From: http://www.scc.rutgers.edu/serbian_digest/.
30. Author's interview with Rade Leskovac, president of the Radicals in the RSK 1992–1995 (Vukovar, 26 September 2003).
31. F. Švarm, 1993. 'Love that'll Never Die', *Vreme NDA*, 22 November. F. Švarm. 1993. 'Who is Who?' *Vreme NDA*, 25 October. From: http://www.scc.rutgers.edu/serbian_digest/.
32. Dakić, *The Serbian Krayina*, 60. In addition to Babić's SDS of Krajina and Hadžić's SDS of Serb Lands there was also a party named just SDS which espoused a royalist position and only won four mandates in the elections. Author's interview with Dragan Kovačević.
33. F. Švarm. 1993. 'Campaign and Uniforms', *Vreme NDA*, 6 December. From: http://www.scc.rutgers.edu/serbian_digest/.

success and secured only four mandates. It should, however, be noted that this was the only party contesting the elections that did not have 'Serb' in its title, although this was no guarantee for a more moderate stance.[34] Nevertheless, its more ambiguous position made the Social Democratic Party a prime target for attacks, and its then leader, Ranko Bakić, even speaks of murders of some party members.[35] Finally, the 'Generals' party' (Savez komunista – Pokret za Jugoslaviju, SK-PZJ) played some political role, although it did not run in the elections. It represented Belgrade's voice, and through its paramilitary wing – Arkan's Tigers – it had significant influence in Eastern Slavonia.[36] The competition between these parties was primarily based on regional and ideological differences and on differing links with Belgrade, and only secondarily on the issue of the war or on valence issues, such as war profiteering.

No one leader was in clear control following the elections, and intense competition and deadlock ensued. While Martić could rely on his presidential powers, control of the police and support from Belgrade, Babić was also in a strong position: he had the backing of parliament and, since his ousting in 1992, had managed to build up his own paramilitary structure which, through selected assassinations, had helped him retrieve power.[37] Babić, therefore, could not be ignored by Martić and this caused great difficulty in the forming of a government.[38] Babić and his supporters in the SRS opposed Martić's choice as prime minister, Borislav Mikelić, who was very much regarded as Milošević's man.[39] However, Babić eventually conceded: he accepted Mikelić and his own appointment as foreign minister, even though it cost him the support of the Serb Radicals.

Despite this continuous rivalry, negotiations with the Croatian government continued and an agreement on economic cooperation was even reached in December 1994. Outflanking was not decisive and in October 1994, the Radical speaker of parliament, Branko Vojnica, was removed in a parliamentary vote, due to his resistance to continued negotiations.[40] However, it would not be long before intransigence again became dominant.

34. F. Švarm. 1995. 'Springtime Change', *Vreme NDA*, 6 March. From: http://www.scc. rutgers.edu/serbian_digest/.
35. Author's interview with Ranko Bakić (Banja Luka, 23 October 2003).
36. Gow, *The Serbian Project*, 83–4
37. Author's interview with Filip Švarm. Woodward, *Balkan Tragedy*, 221
38. F. Švarm. 1994. 'The Start of the Trade-off', *Vreme NDA*, 28 March. From: http://www.scc.rutgers.edu/serbian_digest/.
39. Mikelić was a member of the League of Communists – Movement for Yugoslavia (SK-PZJ), which was very close to Milošević's wife, Mira Marković.
40. Author's interview with Rajko Ležajić, speaker of the RSK parliament 1994–1995 (Belgrade, 17 September 2004). Dakić, *Krajina kroz Vijekove*, Hronika 27.

Clashes over the Z-4 Plan

In early 1995, the so-called Z-4 Plan was tabled. This plan promised far-reaching autonomy in Serb-majority areas, including a separate currency, parliament, police force, fiscal policy and separate links with Serbia. The agreement thereby came close to creating a state within the state and hence to accommodating Serb demands for self-determination. This was the most generous offer so far and in the above-mentioned spirit of greater willingness to negotiate one could have expected some readiness on the part of the RSK leadership to at least consider it. However, Martić chose to reject the plan outright. He did so for a number of reasons. The official reason was lack of trust in the Croatian authorities, but to this must be added a growing desire to assert his independence from Belgrade as well as lack of paramilitary support. Babić was also faced with resistance from the hardliners and, therefore, was not able to support the agreement,[41] whether he wanted to or not. The two leaders were, despite their strength, not monolithic and they were concerned that they would not be able to bring their 'hawks' along. Furthermore, Martić may have calculated that by distancing himself from Belgrade and by winning the support of the Serb Radicals, he could bolster his position against the ever-stronger Babić. In this atmosphere, only the RSK prime minister, Borislav Mikelić, came out openly in support of the agreement and with that move he lost the support of Martić who decided to get rid of him. For a long time Babić chose to sit on the fence and largely kept quiet, but when Martić, asked the RSK parliament to dismiss Mikelić on 1 March 1995, he failed to get the support of Babić's deputies and Mikelić remained in his post.

While Krajina was caught in infighting, the situation in the region was changing and their position was weakening. In May 1995, the miscalculation became obvious: in Operation Flash, Croatian forces retook Western Slavonia. The fall of Western Slavonia was accompanied by accusations of complicity by Belgrade and Martić argued that the loss of Western Slavonia vindicated his uncompromising position, that it would 'open the eyes of those Serbs who thought we could do a deal with the Croats'.[42] Blame, however, had to be apportioned and turmoil in the Krajina leadership ensued: Mikelić blamed Martić and the military leadership, but Martić managed to retain his post with the help of Babić,[43] who had once again changed sides and now turned against Mikelić.

41. Author's interview with Rajko Ležajić, F. Švarm. 1995. 'Checkmate on Z-4', *Vreme NDA*, 6 February. From: http://www.scc.rutgers.edu/serbian_digest/.
42. F. Švarm. 1995. 'The Dawn of Power Holders', *Vreme NDA*, 22 May. From: http://www.scc.rutgers.edu/serbian_digest/.
43. Owen, *Balkan Odyssey*, 344.

Mikelić argued that Babić, even though he was politically at odds with Martić, feared his hawks and therefore chose to make a deal.[44]

One of the issues that divided Mikelić from the remaining RSK leadership was a proposed union with Republika Srpska in Bosnia. The unification of the two statelets had been declared many times over the years but never realized. In the spring of 1995, however, Martić and Babić set their mind to realizing the union. But one important person in addition to Mikelić was against such a union – Goran Hadžić, who had returned from political obscurity in mid 1994 and had begun charging a more autonomous course for Eastern Slavonia.[45] As part of this strategy, Hadžić formed the coordinating committee for Slavonia, Baranja and Western Srem, which was akin to an autonomous region.[46] And when the RSK parliament unanimously adopted the decision on unification with Republika Srpska in June 1995, the committee issued a letter stating: 'Representatives of Eastern Slavonia will not participate in any way in further implementing this decision … Dismissal procedures are underway for all deputies who are participating or acting counter to those interests'.[47] Regional divisions had, therefore, once again come to the fore.

Only in the eleventh hour did the RSK leadership become willing to negotiate and by then it was too late. On 2 August 1995, Babić accepted the Z-4 Plan as a basis for negotiations, stating that 'a modified version of the Z-4 plan which would treat the eastern and the western part of Krajina equally would provide a good basis for political negotiations'.[48] The Croatian representatives, however, demanded that the Serbs accept Croatian rule immediately, well knowing that their offensive – Operation Storm – would be launched the following day. The RSK army quickly collapsed and no assistance was forthcoming from either Pale or Belgrade. Thus, the only area remaining under Serb control after August 1995 was Eastern Slavonia, and the leadership here needed less encouragement to negotiate. They concluded that unless an agreement was reached, they would face the same destiny as the Serbs in Krajina.[49]

44. F. Švarm. 1995. 'Wrong Choice', *Vreme NDA*, 5 June. From: http://www.scc.rutgers.edu/ serbian_digest/.
45. Woodward, *Balkan Tragedy*, 345.
46. D. Janjić. 1995. 'Union Never Brought to a Close', *AIM Press*, 6 June. From: http://www .aimpress.ch/.
47. F. Švarm. 1995. 'Hadzic Re-activated', *Vreme NDA*, 5 June. From: http://www .scc.rutgers.edu/serbian_digest/.
48. F. Švarm. 1995. 'The View from the Fort', *Vreme NDA*, 7 August. From: http://www .scc.rutgers.edu/serbian_digest/.
49. Author's interview with Vojislav Stanimirović, the president of Eastern Slavonia's executive council (Vukovar, 25 September 2003).

Zagreb Serbs: Go-betweens or Puppets?

The divisions among the Serbs become even more striking if one also looks at the representatives of the so-called 'urban Serbs' – the Serb leaders outside the RSK – who were not only in conflict with the RSK leaders but also competed with each other.[50]

The Croatian Constitution provided for Serb parliamentary representation in proportion to their share of the population, which translated into thirteen seats. However, no Serbs were directly elected in the 1992 elections and the electoral commission, therefore, decided that the thirteen seats should be distributed among parties that had gained parliamentary representation and which had fielded Serb candidates. This would give eight mandates to the SDP[51] and two mandates to the Croatian People's Party (HNS). The SDP had had a catastrophic election, winning only three seats in Parliament,[52] but the party was, nevertheless, far from happy with this unexpected gift which would in effect turn it into a Serb party.[53] The SDP leadership therefore demanded that its Serb deputies either turned down the seats or left the party.[54] Following internal discussions in the party, the outcome was that three of the SDP's Serb deputies stayed in the party and agreed to being SDP representatives and not Serb representatives, while the remaining five deputies left the party.[55] The SDP had, thereby, made clear that it would not perform the function of a representative of the Serbs. As Ivica Račan, the party's leader put it, 'The SDP is not a Serb party and has no mandate from the Serbs'.[56]

This function, therefore, would have to be filled by another party. The Constitutional Court had, in a controversial decision, decided to award the remaining three Serb seats to the Serb National Party (Srpska narodna stranka, SNS), which had failed to pass the electoral threshold. The SNS was led by Milan Đukić, who was elected deputy speaker of the Croatian

---

50. Away from both Zagreb and the RSK, in the remote area of Gorski Kotar still other dynamics were found. Here a moderate faction of the SDS managed to stay in power and reached an agreement with Zagreb whereby peace was upheld in the region. See for example, S. Tatalović. 1996. 'Peaceful Solution of Conflicts in Croatia: Case Study of Gorski Kotar', *Peace and the Sciences* 27.
51. In November 1990, the party had changed its name from SKH-SDP to just SDP.
52. The party only got 5.4 per cent of the vote. D. Plećaš (ed.) *Deset godine Socijaldemokratske partije Hrvatske 1990–2000*, Zagreb: SDP, 270, 273.
53. Author's interview with Dušan Plećaš, SDP.
54. SDP, 1992. 'Stavovi predsjedništva SDPH o srpskim zastupnicima u Saboru Republike Hrvatske' (author's copy).
55. Author's interview with Dušan Plećaš.
56. SDP, 1992. 'Izjava Ivice Račane na konferenciji za novinare 4.9.1992. godine' (author's copy).

parliament in September 1992. Đukić and his party were the creation of the Croatian government and the party was intended to perform the role of 'loyal Serbs', to demonstrate to the world that the RSK leaders did not represent the majority of Croatia's Serbs. Needless to say that Đukić's influence with the RSK leadership was as good as non-existent.[57] Đukić's resonance in the Serb community was limited and another figure emerged as the leader of the urban Serbs: Milorad Pupovac, then president of the Serb Democratic Forum. Pupovac was not accepted by the radical elements of the RSK but he had contacts with more moderate forces in the statelet, some of whom also acted as negotiators with the Croatian government.[58] One of those contacts, Radovan Jović, paid a high price for this link: he was dismissed as a judge in Glina, had his house blown up, had several clashes with Martić and was mobilized by the RSK army in 1995. When he refused, he was sent to prison.[59] The danger involved in contacts with the 'urban Serb' leaders significantly reduced the influence they could have on dynamics in the RSK.

Between Pupovac and Đukić not many warm words were exchanged: Đukić accused Pupovac of being an exponent of Knin and Belgrade, while Pupovac criticized Đukić for keeping quiet about events such as the Gospić massacre[60] and for generally being a mouthpiece of the Croatian government.[61] Even among the urban Serbs, great divisions were therefore found: both supported compromise, but Pupovac also strongly criticized the Croatian government and had to maintain credibility with his contacts in the RSK. To some extent there was a process of outbidding between Pupovac and Đukić, but over the course of the war Đukić moved closer to Pupovac's position. Their competition then became largely focused on valence issue, especially on who was the legitimate representative of the Serbs.[62]

Wartime intra-ethnic rivalry in the RSK was marked by increasing competition and by the dominance of coercive resources. The more moderate voices that did exist were marginalized with sometimes brutal means: they were harassed, threatened and even killed.[63] But even in this

57. Author's interview Milan Đukić (Zagreb, 30 July 2003).
58. Author's interview with Milorad Pupovac.
59. M. Vasić, F. Švarm, T. Tagirov, B. Rašeta. 1995. 'Arrest in Tucepi', *Vreme NDA*, 30 October. From: http://www.scc.rutgers.edu/serbian_digest/.
60. In October 1991, a Croatian military unit committed a systematic mass killing of Serb civilians in the front-line town of Gospić
61. *Vjesnik*, 10 December 1993, 3. Author's interviews with Milan Đukić and Milorad Pupovac.
62. B. Rašeta. 1994. 'Srbi su spremni na pregovore', *Pečat*, 11 October, 14.
63. Gagnon, *The Myth of Ethnic War*, 5.

violent and polarized environment, radicalization was not the only possible outcome of intra-ethnic competition and temporary, relative moderation even ensued. Competition from other parties or independents was not met with a radicalization of the dominant position, but centrifugal dynamics once again became dominant when the status of the RSK was on the table and the leaders feared not being able to bring their own hawks along. Thus, the position that eventually won out was one of persistent radicalization, which ultimately led to the fall of Krajina in August 1995. This happened despite pressure from Belgrade for a change of course. The Krajina leaders displayed a growing appetite for independence, but Milošević was by no means deprived of influence: he, if anyone, knew how to take advantage of changing alliances and could still supply resources needed in local elite competition. But Belgrade's support was no longer the sine qua non of political power in the RSK: alternative resources were available and it was possible to redefine the borders of legitimate political influence.

Kin-state: Serbia Is Defended in Knin, For a While

Military failures, international pressure and a German push for Croatia's recognition gradually led to a change in Belgrade's strategy and goal. The Serbian government now appeared willing to accept the notion of 'special status' for the Croatian Serbs, even if it also insisted on the Serb right to self-determination. The message to the Krajina Serbs contained in this policy was 'You are on your own'[64] and this was to significantly influence relations with the kin-state. A possible difference of opinion was already indicated during the negotiations over the Carrington Plan in the autumn of 1991. Both Belgrade and Knin eventually rejected the plan, but Milošević had been willing to accept earlier versions, whereas the Krajina leadership refused it all along.[65] These were, however, minor skirmishes compared with the rift created by the Vance Plan a few months later.

Babić's rejection of the Vance Plan brought out the wrath of the Serbian president who, in an unusual move, issued a public letter to the RSK president in which he rejected his right to make decisions that would harm the Serb people: 'You have turned a deaf ear to the explicit attitudes ... of the Serbian leadership more than once, giving yourself the right to

64. Burg and Shoup, *The War in Bosnia-Herzegovina*, 89
65. L. Silber. 1991. 'Divisions Emerge among Serb Leaders over EC Proposals', *Financial Times*, 1 November. ICTY, 'Babić's testimony,' 14074.

make decisions, the price of which, unfortunately, has to be paid in blood by the entire Serbian nation'.[66] The main board of the SDS of Krajina did not, however, take this lying down, and they issued a response letter in which they described Milošević's move as 'a call for overthrowing the legally elected president'.[67] Since Babić was clearly not poised to abandon his intransigent position, Belgrade instead chose to make use of internal divisions in the RSK and installed a new loyal leadership, and for a while Belgrade's control in the statelet seemed unproblematic.

But the RSK elections in late 1993 were a shock to Milošević. Belgrade had put its bet on Martić but instead witnessed a decisive comeback by Babić, which indicated that the Serbian president was losing control. No effort was spared to secure Martić's victory in the crucial second round of the presidential election and Martić, in return, made his loyalty to Milošević painstakingly clear when he stated that he would like to be president of Krajina for five days only, after which he would step down in favour of 'all-Serb President Milosevic'.[68] When Martić won the second round, Belgrade thereby secured the continuation of a loyal leadership but the new RSK president, like other leaders before him, eventually also fell out with the Serbian president.

The first step in the cooling of relations between Milošević and Martić was taken by Belgrade when the Yugoslav government signed a joint statement on the normalization of Croatian-Yugoslav relations in January 1994.[69] However, relations became even frostier after Milošević chose to punish the Bosnian Serb leaders following their rejection of the Contact Group Plan. The introduction of sanctions also hurt the RSK, which now found itself geographically isolated and fearing abandonment.[70] Martić avoided taking Milošević's side and he even went to the Bosnian Serb statelet to vote, in the name of the RSK, against the Contact Group Plan. Moreover, in the spring of 1995, Martić sought to free himself of Belgrade's influence by ousting Milošević's man, Borislav Mikelić. It is significant that Mikelić's more moderate position was not successful, despite Belgrade's support. Milošević may actually not have been too

66. M. Milošević. 1992. 'Babic Caput', *Vreme NDA*, 13 January. From: http://www.scc .rutgers.edu/serbian_digest/.
67. Ibid.
68. F. Švarm, 1994. 'The Return of the District Strongman', *Vreme NDA*, 31 January. From: http://www.scc.rutgers.edu/serbian_digest/.
69. F. Švarm,1994. 'The Start of the Trade-off', *Vreme NDA*, 28 March. From: http://www.scc.rutgers.edu/serbian_digest/.
70. U. Komlenović. 1994. 'The Fate of the Krajina', *Vreme NDA*, 17 October. From: http://www.scc.rutgers.edu/serbian_digest/. F. Švarm. 1994. 'Knin: sam na svijetu', *Pečat*, 11 October, 15.

unhappy about this, since it made it easier to abandon the RSK leadership and Martić argues that he actually followed orders from Belgrade when he rejected the Z-4 Plan.[71] But Mikelić's demise does attest to Belgrade's markedly reduced influence in Knin.

After Martić's public defiance of Milošević, the Serbian president had no great qualms abandoning his former protégés and leaving them to their fate. When Western Slavonia was retaken in Operation Flash, Serbian television and the newspaper *Politika* limited their coverage to the protests lodged by Yugoslavia's foreign minister and to the flood of refugees.[72] Milošević did not react publicly and it is indeed remarkable that the only official reaction came from the foreign ministry and not from the 'President of all Serbs'. Similarly, when the Croatian army launched Operation Storm and Knin fell within twenty-four hours, Milošević's reaction was reportedly to exclaim, 'Imagine, those fools withdrew'. The SPS attributed the defeat to the failures of Martić and Karadžić and the Serbian media was ordered to follow this line in their reporting.[73] It was as if Milošević had never supported the unruly leaders in Knin.

In Eastern Slavonia, which was the only area remaining under Serb control after August 1995, the situation was different. The then president of SAO Slavonia, Goran Hadžić, had, throughout the war, been closely in tune with Belgrade. One of the reasons for this closeness, in addition to geographical proximity, was the greater presence in Eastern Slavonia of paramilitaries from Serbia, in particular Arkan's Tigers. Thus, in July 1995, Knin only had support in one municipality in Eastern Slavonia, the rest were with Hadžić and Milošević. After the fall of Knin and in the face of an impending military attack by the Croatian army, Belgrade had little difficulty exerting its influence on the eastern part of the RSK. Even though negotiations were taking place between local leaders and the Croatian government, the Erdut Agreement, which created a transitional UN administration in Eastern Slavonia, was actually the result of negotiations in Dayton between Milošević and Tuđman.[74]

During the war, all the leaders of the RSK either fell out with Belgrade when they sought greater autonomy or, as in the case of Hadžić, were abandoned when they failed to retain control in the statelet. Hadžić argues that Milošević was deliberately looking to support leaders who were likely to defect and that he lost Belgrade's support because he continued being

71. Kovačević, *Kavez*, 81–4.
72. Gordy, *The Culture of Power*, 73.
73. Sell, *Milosevic and the Destruction of Yugoslavia*, 250.
74. R. Holbrooke. 1999. *To End a War*, New York: Modern Library, 267. Author's interview with Goran Hadžić.

unquestionably loyal.[75] The cooling of relations and the stubborn intransigence of the Knin leaders certainly made it easier for Milošević to abandon them without this resulting in a backlash in Serbia. However, Belgrade did not only seek to increase the distance between itself and the maverick RSK leaders, the Serbian authorities also actively sought to affect internal competition in the RSK in order to secure influence in the statelet.

Disunity as a Means of Influence

When Milošević fell out with Babić over the Vance Plan, he successfully utilized cleavages found in the statelet and played on personal power ambitions. The competing RSK leaders actively vied for Belgrade's support sensing that it would make the difference between ascent to the top and political oblivion. Thus, when Hadžić and Paspalj saw their chance to seize power, they sent a letter to Milošević in which they described Babić as an autocrat, adventurer and Bolshevik who was guiding the Serbs to ruin. Likewise, in the run-up to the 1993 elections, several RSK leaders, including Hadžić and Martić, sent a letter to Milošević in which they derided Šešelj, whom Milošević had recently fallen out with, describing him as a man who 'has discarded all interests of the Serbian people'.[76] Over time, however, the importance of Belgrade as an audience decreased due, in particular, to the availability of alternative resources.

As the RSK leaders expected, Belgrade did indeed take a very active role in the 1993 elections. Martić was chosen as Milošević's new man in Knin and he, according to some reports, received as much as 200,000 Deutschmarks for financing his campaign.[77] But Babić's strong showing called for more forceful intervention. The electoral commission, which was under Belgrade's strong influence, quickly declared that there had been irregularities in the presidential election and subsequently annulled the results in several of Babić's strongholds. This did the trick and it was announced that Babić had received 49.89 per cent of the votes in the presidential race, thereby narrowly securing a second round for Martić.[78] Commentators speculated that Babić had built a parallel military

75. Author's interview with Goran Hadžić.
76. F. Švarm. 1993. 'Love That'll Never Die', *Vreme NDA*, 22 November. From: http://www. scc.rutgers.edu/serbian_digest/.
77. F. Švarm. 1993. 'Milan Martic's Flying Circus,' *Vreme NDA*, 13 December. From: http://www.scc.rutgers.edu/serbian_digest/.
78. F. Švarm. 1993. 'Touching the Untouchables', *Vreme NDA*, 27 December. From: http://www.scc.rutgers.edu/serbian_digest/.

infrastructure and, since power in Krajina depended on the control of military resources, he had, therefore, been able to successfully confront Belgrade's candidate.[79] This may have aided Babić in the first round but in the second round Belgrade created a clear perception that it would abandon the RSK if it were not satisfied with the elected candidate.[80] Belgrade's promised support rather than actual involvement seemed crucial but Belgrade's influence thereby came to depend on the credibility of its continued involvement. Belgrade's willingness to support the RSK was increasingly questioned and, combined with the apparent existence of power resources in the RSK that were outside Belgrade's control, Milošević's ability to influence internal politics was reduced. This became clear when Mikelić was ousted by Martić and Babić, despite being Belgrade's preferred man. Martić had given up on Belgrade's support and relied instead on the military, the police, Karadžic's SDS, the Radicals and finally on his growing popularity resulting from increasing popular anger with Milošević.[81]

Countering Belgrade's Moves

Even though Belgrade's influence in the RSK waned, the statelet still depended on kin-state support. The economy was a shambles and the only thing keeping it from complete collapse was help from Serbia.[82] The RSK elites were, therefore, limited in their ability to react against unwanted changes in Belgrade's position. Instead, they had to rely on resources found within the RSK and on making new alliances, with the Bosnian Serbs in Pale and with the Serbian opposition.

The possibility of creating a common front with Republika Srpska (RS) was continuously used as an implicit bargaining strategy by the RSK leaders and hence as a way of increasing their autonomy from Belgrade. In 1993, a referendum was held in the RSK on unification with the RS. This referendum was a show of force on the part of RSK leaders who knew that the referendum, which resulted in a clear endorsement of unification, was powerful political capital which could be utilized at a strategic point. Babić optimistically stated: 'The referendum is probably

79. Ibid.
80. F. Švarm. 1994. 'The Return of the District Strongman', *Vreme NDA,* 31 January. From: http://www.scc.rutgers.edu/serbian_digest/.
81. U. Komlenović. 1994. 'The Fate of the Krajina', *Vreme NDA,* 17 October. From: http://www.scc.rutgers.edu/serbian_digest/.
82. M. Milošević. 1992. 'Babic Caput', *Vreme NDA,* 13 January. From: http://www.scc. rutgers.edu/serbian_digest/.

making Milosevic's hair stand on end... In the end they'll swallow what we cook up here'.[83] Unification was kept in store as a possibility in case relations deteriorated rapidly and, in the meantime, as a blackmailing devise. The leaders in Pale were, however, reluctant alliance partners. The RS was in a much stronger position than the RSK and less dependent on Belgrade's support. Any cooperation, therefore, would be on terms decided by the leaders in Pale. As a replacement for cooperation with Pale, or as a supplement, the RSK leaders sought to ally themselves with the Serbian opposition.

The Serbian opposition party most clearly present in the RSK was the Serb Radical Party (SRS), which had created a strong branch party that had close political and institutional links with the SRS in Serbia.[84] For the remaining opposition parties, alliances with parties and leaders in the RSK was the only way of influencing RSK politics since they had not managed to gain a foothold in the statelet. Notwithstanding the ideological affinity between the SDS and some of the Serbian opposition parties, the effect of these links, however, appears to have been negligible.

In the first conflict between Milošević and the RSK leaders, Babić had unsuccessfully tried to muster the support of the Serbian opposition, but he largely failed in his endeavour, even though he did win the support of the Serbian Orthodox Church.[85] No support was forthcoming from the SPO, whereas the DS was more equivocal on the issue. In parliament, Zoran Đinđić spoke of the need to 'determine the western borders of Serbdom' and stated, 'We do not intend to turn our backs on the Serbs outside Serbia'.[86] Nevertheless, the party accepted the Vance Plan and little support materialized.[87] Support from ultra-nationalist circles would have been more likely but Šešelj was still in tow to Milošević, and the Radicals, therefore, remained quiet. After Šešelj fell out with Milošević he tried to make use of his strength in the RSK to improve his position in Serbia proper. He, therefore, embarked on toppling Milošević's man Hadžić, pressed for elections and presented himself to the RSK leaders as the only politician who would not shun total war. He, furthermore, told

83. N. Stefanović. 1993. 'A Referendum by Candlelight', *Vreme NDA*, 28 June. From: http://www.scc.rutgers.edu/serbian_digest/.

84. The leader of the local party was also vice-president of the party in Serbia. Author's interview with Nikola Poplašen, founder of the SRS in Bosnia (Banja Luka, 3 December 2003).

85. M. Milošević. 1992. 'Serbia in a Broken Mirror', *Vreme NDA*, 27 January. From: http://www.scc.rutgers.edu/serbian_digest/.

86. Thomas, *Serbia under Milošević*, 110.

87. F. Švarm. 1994. 'Kidnappers and Hostages', *Vreme NDA*, 13 June. From: http://www.scc.rutgers.edu/serbian_digest/.

the local leaders that he was their only chance of remaining in power.[88] Thereby, Šešelj's support became important for local leaders in their conflict with Milošević: it became another resource in the ongoing competition between pro- and anti-Milošević forces.

Shortly after the presidential election in the RSK, Šešelj further stepped on Milošević's toes by forming a coalition with Babić.[89] But Šešelj and Babić did not remain friends and the Radical leader instead turned to the newly rebellious Martić. In May 1995, Šešelj visited Krajina in order to demonstrate the SRS's influence in RSK politics and to help and encourage Martić in his intransigent position. Moreover, Šešelj aimed to solidify the offensive of the Serbian nationalist opposition and the Bosnian Serb leaders against Milošević, but Babić was wavering and without his participation the front was weakened.[90] The cooperation between the RSK leaders and the SRS never decisively weakened Milošević but the existence of another Serbian leader whom the local leaders hoped could substitute for Milošević undoubtedly strengthened their intransigence. The rest of the Serbian opposition had a more limited impact, even after they also decided to seek utilizing internal divisions in an attempt to weaken Milošević. Thus, in the elections in 1993, the opposition leaders sent premature expressions of congratulations to Babić whom they had shunned nearly two years earlier.[91] This support for any leader in the RSK who expressed resistance to Milošević continued, but with little impact: the democratic opposition in Serbia was too weak to be of great significance.

There is little doubt that the Belgrade government had an important influence on RSK politics but its influence decreased during the four years of war. From being loyal supporters, the Krajina leadership came out in defiance of Milošević and his change to a more accommodating position. As relations became frostier, a common rhetorical ploy by both sides was to deny the other's legitimacy, thereby altering the space of intra-ethnic dynamics. The fractionalization of the RSK elite, nevertheless, made considerable Belgrade influence possible even when parts of the top echelons distanced themselves from Milošević. Support from Belgrade was a valuable resource in the fierce competition and Milošević generally

88. F. Švarm. 1993. 'Love That'll Never Die', *Vreme NDA*, 22 November. From: http://www.scc.rutgers.edu/serbian_digest/.
89. F. Švarm. 1995. 'Sesejl Goes to Krajina', *Vreme NDA*, 27 March. From: http://www.scc.rutgers.edu/serbian_digest/.
90. Ibid.
91. F. Švarm. 1994. 'The Return of the District Strongman', *Vreme NDA*, 31 January. From: http://www.scc.rutgers.edu/serbian_digest/.

had no problems finding new loyalists. However, Belgrade's resources gradually became of less importance: two of the main contenders for the top of the hierarchy – Martić and Babić – had, to varying degrees, access to their own paramilitary resources and Belgrade's influence became dependent on the credibility of its continued support. Hence, when fear of abandonment grew, Belgrade's influence on internal developments was reduced. The countermoves available to the RSK leaders remained limited but the existence of other potentially relevant audiences, especially the Radicals, encouraged intransigence. Autonomy from Belgrade was, moreover, a potential basis for popular support and it was the only significant issue separating the candidates in the RSK elections.[92]

The General Population: Referendum and Elections but Doubtful Voter Influence

Despite the possible benefits of popular support, the attitudes of the general population became even less significant for intra-Serb rivalry than it had been in the prewar period. Few of the deputies making up the RSK parliament had popular mandates from the 1990 elections; the remaining deputies were appointed by the SDS and they were often people with connections to the Serbian secret police.[93] Nevertheless, the extreme divisions within the leadership actually provided an opportunity for voter influence when elections became the only way out of the political stalemate.

The 1993/94 Elections

The holding of elections does, however, not necessarily mean that popular attitudes were decisive for internal competition and hence the position of leaders. In fact, a number of factors prevented a direct link between the elites and the mass population from materializing. The first problem was the lack of clear political differences. The electoral competition between the parties and candidates was primarily about allegations of corruption and war profiteering and not very much about the war itself; on this issue the parties were united in their radicalism. The only war-related issue that separated the parties was their views on links with Belgrade. Thus, on this issue the voters had a chance to make their opinions heard. Another

92. Author's interview with Filip Švarm.
93. F. Švarm. 1993. 'Campaign and Uniforms', *Vreme NDA*, 6 December. F. Švarm. 1995. 'Orders from Belgrade', *Vreme NDA*, 13 March. From: http://www.scc .rutgers.edu/serbian_digest/.

problem, however, was the existence of factions and frequent splits which made the effect of a party vote highly unpredictable. The value of a party vote was, moreover, reduced by the limited role of parties and their low level of cohesion which left deputies largely unconstrained. To these problems, which are not uncommon in transitional elections, should be added the dubious democratic credentials of the elections. Before the elections, the arrest of popular leaders from Western Slavonia ensured that the RSK leadership would not be faced with these more moderate voices.[94] This of course limited the choice available to voters. The elections themselves were, moreover, far from free and fair: physical attacks on political rivals were reported, the parties did not have equal access to the media and, most importantly, the election commission was under heavy influence from Belgrade and annulled the results in selected electoral districts.[95]

Despite these limitations, the election results did indicate support for Babić's uncompromising stand and his autonomous course: he managed to make a comeback in spite of Belgrade supplying resources to his rivals. However, following the election results, Filip Švarm commented that as long as Babić's victory was based exclusively on the will of the voters, then this need not worry Belgrade too much. What should worry the Serbian regime was the possibility that the victory was based on the control of paramilitary resources.[96] This argument brings out the limited value of popular support in the RSK: other resources could be used to undermine rivals and an unwelcome result was unlikely to be respected by a candidate in control of more important resources, such as the military. Even so, 'the will of the people' was persistently used to legitimize political positions, especially positions in conflict with Belgrade. When Martić fell out with Belgrade, he was hoping to win the support of other audiences and alliance partners, in particular Babić, Karadžić, the SRS and his own hardliners. But he publicly pointed to the general population and stated: 'The people will decide the fate of the Krajina and I certainly won't accept a solution against the will of the people'.[97] The supposed 'will of the people' was thereby invoked as an alternative resource in elite competition, but this was also done more formally through referenda.

---

94. Author's interview with Dušan Ećimović.
95. I. Marijačić. 1993. 'Balvanska konstanta', *Vjesnik,* 16 December, 4.
96. F. Švarm. 1993. 'Touching the Untouchables', *Vreme NDA,* 27 December. From: http://www.scc.rutgers.edu/serbian_digest/. Author's interview with Filip Švarm.
97. U. Komlenović. 1994. 'The Fate of the Krajina', *Vreme NDA,* 17 October. From: http://www.scc.rutgers.edu/serbian_digest/.

The Use of Referenda

Calling a referendum had, before the war, been one of the SDS's preferred strategies when needing to bolster its position. Following the fallout over the Vance Plan, Babić again sought to emulate this strategy by calling a referendum on the plan. This demand was, however, in vain – a referendum was never held and this illustrates the difficulty of playing the 'referendum card' from a weak position. It is a powerful instrument for the already powerful and thereby does not change the dynamics of competition significantly. The only referendum that was held during the war was on unification with Republika Srpska. The official result was 99 per cent in favour with a 97 per cent turnout.[98] At this point, Babić had recovered from his defeat over the Vance Plan and the referendum was seen as important political capital in dealings with Belgrade.[99] However, unification was never realized. It was only a useful threat when the leaders needed greater space for manoeuvre, and the actual impact of expressed voter attitudes was consequently limited.

Thus, despite holding elections and a referendum in the RSK, the impact of popular attitudes on the position of the Serb leaders was very limited. Changes in the dominant position were not driven by popular demands, although popular support was not completely without importance as an additional resource.

Inter-ethnic Relations: Winner Takes All

Following the outbreak of war, direct contact between Knin and Zagreb ceased, and given the RSK leaders' determination for 'their' territory to remain separate from the Croatian state, the interplay that mattered was primarily of a military nature: what was the relative strength of the two sides? The lack of willingness to negotiate was reinforced by a false sense of security among the Serb leaders provided by the presence of UN forces.[100] However, Belgrade and Zagreb were still negotiating and this led to fears among the RSK leadership that they would be sold out in an agreement between the two states. The interplay between the Serb leaders and Zagreb was, therefore, affected by changing relations with the kin-state.

98. *Croatian International Relations Review*. 1999. 'Chronology 1993: April through June', 5(15/16), 131.
99. N. Stefanović. 1993. 'A Referendum by Candlelight', *Vreme NDA*, 28 June. From: http://www.scc.rutgers.edu/serbian_digest/.
100. Burg and Shoup, *The War in Bosnia-Herzegovina*, 92

The outbreak of war and the loss of Croatian territory had led to a marked drop in Tuđman's ratings. The HDZ was facing collapse and Tuđman found himself challenged by the extreme Croat Party of Right (Hrvatska stranka prava, HSP).[101] The Croatian president was desperate for the fighting to stop so that the army could be strengthened and the acceptance of the Vance Plan in early 1992 was, consequently, an easy choice. Prior to the signing of the Vance Plan, the Croatian parliament had conceded to international conditions for recognition and had passed the Constitutional Law on Human Rights and Freedoms.[102] Following recommendations from the Badinter Commission, this law was amended in May 1992 and autonomous status was granted to the regions of Knin and Glina.[103] This was more than the Croatian government had previously been willing to offer the Serbs but the RSK leaders were bent on their intransigent position and it did not make them more willing to consider a future as part of a Croatian state.

Despite this apparent stalemate and an unwillingness to compromise, negotiations between Zagreb and Knin gradually began in 1993. However, both sides were adamant about not making significant concessions and divisions within the HDZ affected the Croatian position as well as Serb perceptions of their 'opponent'. While the Serb leaders did not express any special alarm over the challenge from the HSP,[104] the hardliners within the HDZ were a greater cause for concern.

Negotiations despite Croatian Offensives

Paradoxically, the resumption of negotiations happened after an intensification of the military conflict when the Croatian army launched an offensive against the RSK in January 1993 and retook the strategic Maslenica Bridge.[105] The president of the RSK, Goran Hadžić, was in a weak position and in order to save his political life, he needed a success,

101. J. Lovrić. 1991. 'Opposition in Croatia', *Vreme NDA*, 25 November. From: http://www.scc.rutgers.edu/serbian_digest/.
102. I. Grdešić. 1997. 'Building the State: Actors and Agendas', in I. Šiber (ed.), *The 1990 and 1992/3 Sabor Elections in Croatia*, Berlin: Sigma, 120.
103. B. Vukas. 1999. 'The Legal Status of Minorities in Croatia', in S. Trifunovska (ed.) *Minorities in Europe: Croatia, Estonia and Slovakia*, The Hague: TMC Asser Press, 44. S. Trifunovska. 1999. 'Political and Security Aspects of Minorities in Croatia', in S. Trifunovska (ed.) *Minorities in Europe: Croatia, Estonia and Slovakia*, The Hague: TMC Asser Press, 28.
104. Hislope, 'Intra-ethnic Conflict,' 487.
105. F. Švarm. 1993. 'Clashes, Elections, Negotiations', *Vreme NDA*, 22 February. From: http://www.scc.rutgers.edu/serbian_digest/.

he needed to change the rules of the game. The conflict situation mattered insofar as Hadžić would be significantly weakened if the Croatian forces made additional gains; internal competition and increased isolation from Belgrade provided further incentives for negotiations. Changing relations with Belgrade could be said to have changed the structure of the interplay: an alliance between Belgrade and Zagreb became a possibility and this dampened the effect of the bipartisan structure. Fear of being marginalized gave the RSK leadership incentives for moderation.

The renewed Croatian offences indirectly affected the outcome of the RSK elections since they reinforced Babić's argument that agreeing to the Vance Plan had been a mistake.[106] While this argument was primarily targeted against Belgrade, it meant that the radical posturing of the Croatian side did influence the outcome of intra-Serb rivalry, even if it did not affect the position of the leadership. After the change in the RSK leadership, more substantial results were actually reached in the negotiations even though the new leadership appeared more hard line. The Croatian government maintained that it would not go beyond what had already been offered in the Constitution and the Constitutional Law,[107] but agreements on other areas were nevertheless reached. The RSK leaders still rejected the possibility of becoming part of a Croatian state and, therefore, one could argue that the position of the Croatian government mattered little for the positions they adopted. But the military position of the Serbs was weakening and while the RSK leadership proved very capable of ignoring this fact, a conciliatory position from the Croatian government might have made it easier for them to recognize the need for compromise.

Following the thaw in Zagreb-Knin relations, which culminated in the reopening of the Zagreb-Belgrade highway, intransigent positions again came to the fore. In January 1995, Tuđman, partly due to pressure from HDZ hardliners, announced that the mandate of the UN forces in Croatia would not be extended.[108] This was a clear provocation and resulted in predictable hard-line reactions in Knin where Martić stated that he was unwilling to negotiate as long as the Croatian government intended to terminate the mandate. Negotiations nevertheless continued and were apparently going well[109] but when the Z-4 Plan was tabled, Martić refused to even look at it. Lack of trust in the intentions of the Croatian

106. Author's interview with Filip Švarm.
107. B. Marković. 2002. 'Yugoslav Crisis and the World, 1994', *Balkan Repository Project*.
108. F. Švarm and D. Hedl. 1995. 'Bye, Bye Boys in Blue', *Vreme NDA*, 23 January. From: http://www.scc.rutgers.edu/serbian_digest/.
109. F. Švarm. 1995. 'We Are Not Backing Out', *Vreme NDA*, 6 February. From: http://www.scc.rutgers.edu/serbian_digest/.

government may, therefore, have been a factor adding to the failure of the plan. The Croatian government must have been aware that the cancellation of the UN mandate would weaken the more moderate elements of the RSK leadership, and the Croatian envoy, Hrvoje Šarinić, was even told so directly by Milošević.[110] One of the chief Croatian negotiators, Slavko Degoricija, had argued during previous negotiations that more moderate forces did exist in the RSK but that they needed to be given guarantees before they could accept reintegration with Croatia.[111] However, in early 1995, the Croatian government sensed that a negotiated solution was no longer necessary and the strengthening of extremists in the RSK was, therefore, not unhelpful. The extent to which the Croatian government's move added to the strength of the extremists should, however, not be exaggerated: Martić was already far stronger than Mikelić and had access to military resources which Mikelić lacked.

When a new arrangement for UN forces, UNCRO, was accepted in April 1995, the Z-4 Plan was already dead. Timing is crucial and by April 1995 positions on the Serb side had hardened. Whether the Croatian government was actually willing to compromise is, furthermore, questionable, and the RSK leaders certainly did not believe it. There was, therefore, an added risk associated with negotiations, in addition to internal backlash, namely the risk of being cheated. When the RSK leaders finally agreed at the eleventh hour to compromise, the Croatian government was clearly not interested and demanded what amounted to an unconditional surrender.[112] Due to the intransigent position of both sides, Owen describes it as a 'winner takes all stand-off', which Tuđman won;[113] no side was willing or able to veer significantly from their intransigent position and a compromise was, therefore, unfeasible. However, in late 1994 this did not seem so impossible: dynamics within the RSK were gradually changing, agreements were actually reached and trust was increasing among the negotiators. In this sense, the decision to cancel the UN mandate was crucial. The moderates in the RSK were not powerful enough to force a compromise through but Martić and Babić might have been able to persuade their followers – and especially military forces – of the need for compromise. Therefore, while intra-ethnic competition, kin-state relations and international pressure was crucial for willingness to negotiate,

110. *Croatian International Relations Review*. 2002. 'Chronology 1994/5: November 1994 through April 1995', 8(26/27), 80.
111. *Feral Tribune*, 14 December 1993, 8.
112. F. Švarm. 1995. 'The View from the Fort', *Vreme NDA*, 7 August. From: http://www.scc.rutgers.edu/serbian_digest/.
113. Owen, *Balkan Odyssey*, 327.

simultaneous moderation was necessary for an agreement. Such a situation did not, however, materialize and part of the reason is to be found in internal divisions within the HDZ and the Croatian government, which fuelled Croatian intransigence and Serb mistrust.

The Effect of Divisions on the Croatian Side

Throughout the war, Tuđman found himself pressured by the right wing of the ruling party, which urged him to take a much more radical course and specifically to refrain from any compromises with the Serbs. Internal politics played a crucial part in the president's decisions and Woodward argues that military adventures were used as a means for winning support: in January 1993, the military offensive took place three days before local elections and elections to the upper house of parliament. Similarly, in September of the same year, the Croatian army invaded the Medak area immediately prior to the HDZ congress.[114] In these instances, Tuđman was inclined to the right wing of his party.[115] After the signing of the Croat-Bosniak Washington Agreement for Bosnia, there was a greater level of optimism surrounding talks between Zagreb and Knin. Although both sides were still making uncompromising statements, it was felt that this was mostly meant for internal audiences.[116] Shortly afterwards, however, a serious rift emerged within the HDZ over the party's policy in Bosnia and several high-profile members chose to leave the party. Following this split, the hard-line faction of the HDZ became dominant and the disarray led to a postponement of negotiations on an economic agreement with the RSK and ultimately reactivated hostilities between Zagreb and Knin.[117]

Although the radicalization of Zagreb's position in 1993 paradoxically led to renewed negotiations, and later offences only caused temporary halts in talks, rifts within the HDZ did cause scepticism among the RSK leaders as to the implementation of the agreements reached.[118] The lack of cohesion of the Croatian side, therefore, increased the already rampant mistrust. Moreover, rightist pressure was one of the reasons for the

114. Woodward, *Balkan Tragedy*, 354.
115. F. Švarm. 1993. 'A Fragile Pontoon Link', *Vreme NDA*, 26 July. From: http://www.scc. rutgers.edu/serbian_digest/.
116. F. Švarm. 1994. 'The Start of the Trade-off', *Vreme NDA*, 28 March. From: http://www. scc.rutgers.edu/serbian_digest/.
117. Gagnon, *The Myth of Ethnic War*, 159. Woodward, *Balkan Tragedy*, 356. M. Pupovac. 1994. 'Moving Towards Peace in Krajina?' *War Report* (May), 8–9.
118. M. Jelovac. 1993. 'Brutal History', *Vreme NDA*, 6 September. From: http://www.scc. rutgers.edu/serbian_digest/.

cancellation of the UN mandate in early 1995 and this added to a new round of intransigence in the RSK, consolidating the zero-sum nature of the conflict. In general, however, intra-Serb competition during the war was less directly influenced by the actions and rhetoric of the Croatian leaders. The RSK's temporary willingness to negotiate was primarily caused by internal competition and pressure from Belgrade rather than being a reaction to the Croatian negotiating position. Instead, what mattered in terms of inter-ethnic relations was the relative military strength of the RSK, as well as the changing structure of relations, from bipartite to tripartite.

Fractionalization and Infighting in Wartime Croatia

The imperative of unity following the outbreak of war did not ensure cohesion for long and divisions soon re-emerged. However, emerging competition from other parties and independents was accompanied by different dynamics from the intra-party competition that had characterized the prewar period. Importantly, radicalization was not the preferred strategy in the face of outside competition. Rather, outflanking was attempted by rival parties and independents but incumbent leaders did not respond with a radicalization of their position: firstly, they frequently had other resources at their disposal to marginalize the opposition; and secondly, since the opposition also criticized them on other issues, political positioning on the issue of the war was not necessarily a winning strategy. The issue of the war was still salient, but competition was also based on regional and ideological cleavages and fuelled by charges of war profiteering and incompetence.

Thus, when Hadžić's government found itself in an increasingly untenable position, losing control and pressured from all sides, they chose to negotiate in an attempt to change the situation. Hadžić lost the battle, but the more moderate course – the willingness to negotiate – persisted under the new leadership that had previously criticized Hadžić for the same 'offence' and was itself faced with hard-line challengers. However, the importance of coercive resources did constrain the leaders and they refrained from accepting compromises on the future status of the RSK since they feared that this would cost them the support of hardliners, the people in control of various military and paramilitary forces. The leadership relied on these forces for their continued hold on power and could not simply suppress them. Furthermore, since these forces most often challenged the leadership due to its position on the war issue, adopting an extreme position could make the problem disappear. Competition from within the party or movement thereby resulted in radicalization of the dominant position and internal divisions, therefore, ultimately fuelled the intransigence of the Krajina leaders.

Parties as such were of limited importance; other sources of support were more important, as the ascent of Martić demonstrated. Of greater importance were links with the paramilitary, the economic and military support of Belgrade, and the possibility of establishing alliances with other parties or actors. The RSK parliament was, however, of some significance since support from parliament was used as a way of strengthening contested positions, and one of the strategies used by the leaders was to call sessions in their geographical strongholds. Negotiators always insisted on the need for acceptance by parliament, fearing that they would otherwise risk outbidding when returning to the RSK.[119] The existence of more moderate Serb voices outside of the RSK served to undermine the claim to homogeneity made by the radical RSK leaders but their impact on RSK politics was limited.

The wartime period saw an important change in relations with the kin-state, and towards the end of the war the Serbs in the RSK were all but ignored by the Serbian regime. A clear distinction was then made between Serbs in Serbia and Serbs outside, and, hence, between local and kin-state leaders. Such a distinction was made by Belgrade as well as by local leaders asserting their independence. At this point, Belgrade's support was no longer decisive for whether a local leader could maintain his position of power, whereas it had earlier been the sine qua non of political success in the RSK. The local elites had other resources at their disposal, could appeal to other audiences, and Belgrade had lost its credibility. This changed the dynamics and the borders of intra-ethnic competition and reinforced radicalism.

Political competition in this context of failed transition, ethnification and war took on a distinct character. Non-political resources, especially military resources, were of great importance; new politically salient issues, primarily valence issues, emerged; party competition increased but party structures as such were not important. Compared with the prewar period, the importance of popular attitudes and the position of the 'other side' was also reduced. The Serb leaders, nevertheless, continued to argue that they

---

119. Author's interview with Slavko Degoricija (Zagreb, 10 December 2003).

were acting according to the will of the people and it is interesting to note that Babić, in defence of his radicalism, said that he thought he was representing the views held by the majority of Serbs: 'I think that I was not an extremist but was simply performing my public duties, which implied reflecting public opinion'.[120] However, most of the leaders actually lacked a popular mandate until the holding of elections in late 1993. In these elections, the constraint posed by popular attitudes was also limited since the control of other resources could be used to manipulate their expression and the choice for the voters was, furthermore, highly restricted. The only issue on which candidates really differed was the issue of relations with Belgrade. This could, therefore, provide a possible basis for power, but even on this issue the general population was not the most important audience: rival elites were primarily vying for the support of paramilitary forces, political alliance partners in the RSK, the Serb Radicals and the Bosnian Serb leaders. Similarly, while referenda were used as a reserve resource in elite competition, it was only available to those who were already in a powerful position.

Finally, the importance of inter-ethnic relations was reduced compared to the prewar period. Radicalization was generally not reciprocated and other factors were more important for the direction of competition. The military balance of power was the most important aspect of the interplay, and the conflict situation rather than the position of the Croatian leadership, therefore, proved a decisive influence.

120. ICTY, 'Babić's testimony,' 13628.

CHAPTER SIX

Wartime Bosnia: Divided We Stand

In the previous chapter we saw how wartime intra-Serb competition in the Republic of Serb Krajina (RSK) was characterized by greater independence from Belgrade, by the emergence of competition from other ethnic parties, by the dominance of coercive resources and by the consequent great significance of (para)military forces. In prewar Bosnia, intra-Serb competition had been less intense than in Croatia but this gradually changed during the war, although the SDS retained its dominance throughout the period and the leadership remained intact.

When war broke out in Bosnia, the SDS leadership had already established the Serb Republic of Bosnia-Herzegovina (later renamed Republika Srpska, RS). The establishment of the statelet, therefore, did not provide for leadership challenges, as it had in Croatia, and the leadership had a much more unified party behind it than the Serbs on the other side of the border. There had been murmurings of regional divisions but not to the extent that it threatened the leadership of the SDS. One could expect that this stronger, more unified party would be better able than its Croatian counterpart to avoid debilitating fractionalization during the war. But even at their strongest, the SDS and the RS leadership were not monolithic. As in Croatia, Serb representatives were also found outside the RS; these had greater influence than the 'urban Serb' leaders in Croatia, due to the persistence of a non-ethnic option, but in the RS their influence was limited at best.

Internal divisions in the SDS were on the increase throughout the period and they gradually became important for the position of the RS leaders. Even more significant, however, were the increasingly strenuous relations between civilian and military leaders; the RS leaders were heavily dependent on the military, both to pursue their war aims and to hold on to power. As a further challenge to the power of the previously near-monolithic leaders, opposition parties also began to emerge. Finally, kin-state relations became progressively less cordial; they were significantly damaged by wrangling over the Vance-Owen Peace Plan and descended into open conflict following the RS rejection of the Contact Group Plan. Belgrade had played a less direct role in prewar Bosnia than in prewar Croatia, but this did not make it easier for Milošević to abandon the Bosnian Serbs. The Serbian president instead chose to pressure the leadership and tried to sow divisions, and Belgrade thereby became a very significant audience in the intra-Serb competition. The different oppositional forces were not unrelated and political dynamics in the RS underwent a change when they began to coalesce. They overlapped on a number of cleavages and issues which facilitated their cooperation: they shared similar positions on the issue of war, they overlapped on a regional and ideological cleavage, and all criticized the rampant war profiteering associated with the leadership. Their cooperation was, moreover, given further impetus by personal power ambitions, especially those of the RS army commander, Ratko Mladić. The oppositional challenge occurred at a time when the military balance was also changing which provided a further incentive for the leadership to adopt a different position. As in the Croatian case, this chapter will show that radicalization is not the only possible outcome of intra-ethnic rivalry – even in a situation of war and polarization – and also that competition was not decided by elites successfully playing the 'ethnic card'.

Increasing Fractionalization and Rifts with the Army

Shortly after the war broke out, the RS government issued a decree which froze the work of political parties 'in times of imminent threat of war and in a state of war'.[1] This decree meant that while the upper tiers of the SDS still functioned, other parts of the party ceased to have influence[2] and the decree   was, in effect, imposing a more authoritarian structure. It, moreover, served to dissuade competition from other political parties. The official reason for the decree was the need for unity in a time of war[3] but it also increased the control of the party leadership and one of the reasons for the decision was presumably a fear that the RS army would otherwise have too great an influence.[4] The civilian leadership crucially depended

---

1.   See, for example, ICTY. 2003. 'Judgement: Prosecutor vs. Blagoje Simić, Miroslav Tadić, Simo Zarić (IT-95-9-T)', 17 October, para 467.
2.   Author's interview with Đorđe Mikić, member of the SDS's political council (Banja Luka, 7 November 2003).
3.   Author's interview with Slobodan Nagradić.
4.   Author's interview with Đorđe Mikić.

on the army and its supply of coercive resources, but it did not trust the army completely and therefore sought to limit its influence.

However, in the spring of 1993 the SDS leadership reversed its position and decided to reactivate the work of the party. According to Vladimir Lukić, who was RS prime minister at the time, this was decided following pressure from SDS officials who felt their influence slipping.[5] But although the reactivation of the party certainly satisfied some party officials, it also resulted in increasing divisions within the party and it opened up possibilities for the organization of competing parties. Initially, the internal divisions were, however, not significant in the upper echelons of the RS, which was under the firm control of Radovan Karadžić. The RS constitution gave the president significant powers and the government had little independent authority on issues of importance; crucially, all military issues were solely under the president's authority.[6] The SDS as such did not play a significant role in the RS government: not all government ministers were SDS members and control of the government was in the hands of Karadžić rather than the party.[7] Rajko Kasagić, who became prime minister in 1995, argues that 'the prime minister de facto was Karadžić'.[8] During the war there were frequent prime ministerial changes: five prime ministers in a period of less than four years. These changes were formally decided by parliament but it served as a way for Karadžić to avoid criticism; the prime ministers proved to be useful scapegoats.[9]

The RS parliament was constituted of Serb deputies who had left the Bosnian parliament in April 1992 and it was able to play a more autonomous role than the government; Karadžić was elected by parliament and depended on its continued support. The RS parliament was, however, very much dominated by the SDS: apart from seven independent deputies, all members of parliament were also SDS members and a parliamentary opposition, therefore, did not exist. This did, nevertheless, not mean that parliament was devoid of importance. As in the RSK, the RS parliament was used to strengthen contested positions, especially if there was considerable pressure from Belgrade and/or international forces. Peace plans were, therefore, subject to parliamentary approval. The insistence on parliamentary approval proved particularly important in the rejection of the Vance-Owen Peace Plan in May 1993. Karadžić had, after intense pressure from Milošević and international

5. Author's interview with Vladimir Lukić.
6. RS constitution art. 80ff, in Kuzmanović, *Konstitutivni akti.*
7. Author's interview with Vladimir Lukić.
8. Author's interview with Rajko Kasagić.
9. Ibid.

mediators, finally agreed to the plan, under the provision that the RS parliament approved it. However, this acceptance did not have the support of the rest of the RS leadership, and Momčilo Krajišnik, the speaker of parliament and second in command of the SDS, was especially against it. Karadžić publicly stated that he hoped the deputies would accept the plan[10] but given the divisions within the leadership it is unsurprising that his support for the plan was half-hearted at best. Owen argues that following the predictable parliamentary rejection, Krajišnik became very influential and Karadžić consequently deemed it necessary to have his deputy on board at all times.[11]

When it came to the party leadership, the government and the parliament, Karadžić was, therefore, faced with few direct challenges to his leadership, but he was aware of the existing divisions and the dangers to his position if he alienated the rest of the SDS leadership. These divisions were primarily based on the issue of the war and, therefore, constrained the positions that Karadžić was able to adopt and the compromises that he was able to accept. They thereby reinforced his intransigence. Owen contends that Karadžić 'never allowed any difference to emerge between himself and Krajisnik, and often asked for solutions to be imposed on him [Karadžić]'.[12] Outside the leadership, divisions also existed but they were fairly muted. Kasagić recalls, 'it was possible to see that there was a lot of mistrust or dissatisfaction', while Lukić likewise asserts, 'the SDS was not a monolithic party during the war'.[13] Ensuring cohesion of the SDS, especially the leadership, was a priority for Karadžić and he was in large part successful. Lack of cohesion in the SDS, therefore, only becomes striking when one looks at regional factions in the party. When these factions began to converge with the army, with opposition parties and with Belgrade, they became a very serious threat to the RS leadership.

Regional Factions Grow in Importance

The most important of the regional factions, that of Bosnian Krajina, had already shown its desire for autonomy before the war, but during the war it became stronger and also began exerting influence over the RS leadership. In addition to this faction, there was an eastern Herzegovina

10. *Politika*, 4 May 1993, 1.
11. ICTY. 2003. 'Transcripts: Prosecutor vs. Slobodan Milošević (IT-02-54)', Transcripts from David Owen's testimony, 4 November, 28561.
12. Owen, *Balkan Odyssey*, 53.
13. Author's interviews with Rajko Kasagić and Vladimir Lukić.

lobby, led by Bozidar Vučurevic, and the RS leaders during the war lacked control of the town of Bijeljina, where Ljubisa 'Mauzer' Savić and his elite unit of the RS army, the Panthers, were in command.[14] The regional conflicts that underlay the divisions were exacerbated by a breakdown in communications and by the different impact of the war on various parts of the RS.[15]

Banja Luka versus the 'Village with a TV Station'

During the war, Serbs from Banja Luka became increasingly dissatisfied with their fate being decided by a 'village with a TV station', as they called Pale.[16] Banja Luka's looming dissatisfaction first came to a head in September 1993 when members of the 16th Banja Luka Brigade and some members of the 1st Krajina Corps rebelled. The rebellion was accompanied by demonstrations of discontent in a number of other army units and among the civilian population directed against 'war profiteers' and the leaders of the SDS.[17] Many of the rebels' demands centred on conditions for the army but significant political demands were also uttered: the government's resignation, the holding of elections and the forming of a new government with all regions proportionally represented.[18] The conflict was eventually solved through negotiations and the rebels gave up their political demands. However, the rebellion caused a rift in the SDS leadership since Biljana Plavšić, RS vice-president, openly supported the rebels,[19] and Predrag Radić, the wartime mayor of Banja Luka, argues that the rebellion marked the 'beginning of the end of SDS'.[20] It was at least the beginning of the end of monolithic SDS rule. The SDS in Banja Luka had been among the targets of the rebellion and it was, therefore, not a symptom of an internal SDS conflict, but it demonstrated the existence of a pool of dissatisfaction that the Krajina faction could feed into as well as the possibility of forging an alliance with the military.

14. Bougarel, 'Bosnia and Hercegovina,'105. F. Švarm. 1994. 'Knin Between Two Kingdoms', *Vreme NDA*, 15 August. From: http://www.scc.rutgers.edu/serbian_digest/.
15. Bougarel, 'Bosnia and Hercegovina,' 105, 107.
16. D. Anastasijević. 1994. 'The Left Bank', *Vreme NDA*, 29 August. From: http://www.scc.rutgers.edu/serbian_digest/.
17. Bougarel, 'Bosnia and Hercegovina,' 107.
18. U. Komlenović. 1993. 'Every Day is Tuesday', *Vreme NDA*, 20 September. From: http://www.scc.rutgers.edu/serbian_digest/.
19. D. Anastasijević. 1994. 'Biljana Plavsic, Vice-President Bosnian Serb Republic', *Vreme NDA*, 15 August. From: http://www.scc.rutgers.edu/serbian_digest/.
20. G. Gagula. 1999. 'Ask Novic About Red Van', *Nezavisne Novine*, 15 September. From: http://www.ex-yupress.com/neznov/neznov3.html.

Krajina proved a challenge to the RS leadership because, due to its geographical position, it could create a state of its own by joining the RSK in Croatia; the Krajina faction therefore had to be kept on board. When the Contact Group Plan was discussed in the summer of 1994, some political circles in Banja Luka began protesting and insisted on knowing the verdict of the RS parliament, since the plan would cede large parts of Bosnian Krajina.[21] Karadžić consequently decided to enrage Belgrade with yet another rejection rather than face potential rivals within the RS.[22] In late 1994, however, some SDS deputies from Banja Luka took a decisive step in a more moderate direction when they met Milošević along with several RS opposition forces. The Krajina leaders had not previously constituted more moderate rivals to the RS leadership and Krajina deputies had been among the most vociferous opponents of the Vance-Owen Peace Plan.[23] However, military losses posed an increasing threat for Krajina towards the end of the war. In addition to divisions over a settlement, there was criticism in Banja Luka of the sums of money spent by the negotiation teams and scandals over financial abuse, embezzlement, war profiteering and corruption further augmented the divisions.[24]

Karadžić reacted to the challenge by imposing strict censorship and for a while the conflict was fairly muted.[25] But it was left brewing and fear and mistrust became widespread following the fall of Croatian Krajina and the loss of western Bosnia; the Bosnian Krajina leaders feared that large parts of the Banja Luka region would be sacrificed by Pale. They argued that the insistence on Sarajevo had resulted in a loss of territory in Bosnian Krajina and they demanded a reversal of this strategy.[26] Consequently, in October 1995, various political parties and individuals, including high-ranking SDS members, formed the Krajina Patriotic Front (Krajina otadžbinski front). The Patriotic Front, which was supported by the RS army, finally challenged Pale directly and demanded Karadžić's resignation. Unable to counter this, Karadžić withdrew to the Sarajevo region where he managed to regain control of the army, but with Krajina slipping away from him and eastern Herzegovina also proclaiming its

21. *Vreme NDA*, 25 July 1994. M. Milošević, D. Reljić, D. Grujić, F. Švarm. 1994. 'Total Recall', *Vreme NDA*, 8 August. From: http://www.scc.rutgers.edu/serbian_digest/.
22. *Vreme NDA*, 25 July 1994. From: http://www.scc.rutgers.edu/serbian_digest/.
23. *Politika*, 6 May 1991, 1.
24. U. Komlenović. 1995. 'All Karadzic's Opponents', *Vreme NDA*, 10 April. From: http://www.scc.rutgers.edu/serbian_digest/.
25. F. Švarm. 1995. 'Karadzic vs. Everyone Else', *Vreme NDA*, 13 June. From: http://www.scc.rutgers.edu/serbian_digest/.
26. P. Vučinić. 1995. 'Capital's Watchtower', *Vreme NDA*, 2 October. From: http://www.scc.rutgers.edu/serbian_digest/.

autonomy from the Pale leadership.[27] In the RS parliament, twenty SDS
deputies from Krajina signed an initiative to overthrow the government
and form a government of national salvation under the leadership of
Anđelko Grahovac from Banja Luka, who had been expelled from the
SDS for 'pro-Serbia deviations'.[28] Following a meeting in the SDS
deputies' club, however, they agreed to abandon this demand and
Karadžić conceded by sacrificing four generals and one lieutenant
colonel, as well as the prime minister, arguing that they were responsible
for the territorial losses suffered. The demand for a Krajina prime minister
was accommodated by appointing Rajko Kasagić, who was president of
SAO Krajina.[29] This was a compromise since Kasagić was, at the time,
known as a 'hawk' and close to Karadžić, although Kasagić himself
argues that Karadžić 'knew that I would not obey him'.[30]

When the Krajina leaders became afraid that their region would be
sacrificed, they finally decided to challenge Karadžić's leadership; they
realized that without the leadership's willingness to cede territory outside
Krajina, Banja Luka could be sacrificed. Earlier in the war, disagreements
with Pale were mostly about the lack of autonomy for the region, criticism of
some of the more blatant cases of war profiteering, as well as Banja Luka's
insistence on an intransigent position. Also underlying these divisions,
however, were the different traditions of the regions: Banja Luka had a strong
Partisan tradition and hence felt closer to the army than the strongly anti-
communist Pale. Thus the conflict between Banja Luka and Pale overlapped
with the growing conflict between political and military leaders, which
constituted the most significant challenge to the RS leadership.

Military versus Civilian Leaders

The army was a double-edged sword for the civilian leaders: they needed
its support, since their power depended on control of coercive resources,
but they also feared the army's potential influence and what they regarded
as its communist tendencies. The RS army was a product of the
communist system and it expected to enjoy significant autonomy from
civilian authorities in wartime.[31] The SDS leaders, therefore, encouraged

---

27. Bougarel, 'Bosnia and Hercegovina,' 112.
28. P. Vučinić. 1995. 'The Final Round', *Vreme NDA*, 23 October. P. Vučinić. 1995.
    'Milosevic's New Karadzic', *Vreme NDA*, 25 December. From: http://www.scc.rutgers.edu/
    serbian_digest/.
29. Author's interview with Rajko Kasagić.
30. Ibid.
31. Author's interview with Slobodan Nagradić. M. Vasić. 1995. 'Predsednik ili general',
    Vreme, 14 August, 14–15.

a belief that the army could not be trusted.[32] The second cause of the conflict was the corruption, theft and war profiteering associated with the RS political leadership, which high-ranking officers of the army found damaging to the conduct of war.[33] Finally, the personal rivalry between Radovan Karadžić and Ratko Mladić over absolute power in the statelet also helped fuel the conflict.

The ambitions of Mladić to provide more than military leadership first became clear during the debate over the Vance-Owen Peace Plan in the spring of 1993. Mladić's vehement opposition and thirty-fine-minute-long impassioned speech against acceptance was one of the decisive factors in parliament's rejection of the plan and, hence, the radicalization of the dominant position.[34] Owen argues that, after this session, Mladić began to have a political constituency.[35] The looming conflict was next manifested in September of the same year in the above-mentioned army rebellion in Banja Luka. The brigades orchestrating the rebellion issued a communiqué in which they argued, 'while we were fighting … skilful manipulators, with the blessing of the existing authorities, increased their private empires', and they proceeded to arrest people whom they alleged were war profiteers.[36] During the conflict between Pale and Belgrade over the Contact Group Plan, Mladić long resisted openly saying if he would side with the RS leadership and this only served to heighten doubts about the army's loyalty.[37] Some army officers, moreover, insisted that the RS leadership should decide what territories it intended to cede so 'people don't have to die for nothing'.[38] The conflict further intensified following military defeats when Karadžić insisted on his role as supreme commander and began wearing a uniform and, moreover, chose to strengthen the police corps and reorganize it as a military organization,[39] since he needed military forces that he could fully control. In April 1995, Mladić once again addressed the RS parliament, but this time with bleak news. He criticized the civilian authorities for interfering with the line of

32. Author's interview with Rajko Kasagić.
33. Ibid. Author's interview with Slobodan Nagradić.
34. N. Stefanović. 1993. 'The Pugnacious Commander', *Vreme NDA*, 24 May. From: http://www.scc.rutgers.edu/serbian_digest/.
35. ICTY, 'Owen's testimony,' 28562.
36. M. Vasić. 1993. 'A State Without Bread', *Vreme NDA*, 20 September. http://www.scc.rutgers.edu/serbian_digest/.
37. F. Švarm. 1994. 'The Silence of the General', *Vreme NDA*, 22 August. From: http://www.scc.rutgers.edu/serbian_digest/.
38. *Vreme NDA*, 25 July 1994.
39. F. Švarm. 1995. 'Civilian-Military Games', *Vreme NDA*, 24 April. From: http://www.scc.rutgers.edu/serbian_digest/.

command, demanded control of all economic facilities and told parliament, 'if a political solution isn't found through negotiations, the war will be long and exhausting for the RS', and that the proclamation of a state of war would, therefore, be required. But the deputies did not accept his warning. On the contrary, Mladić's report was rejected as a political pamphlet and there were calls for his resignation.[40]

International mediators tried to take advantage of the growing conflict between Mladić and Karadžić and Carl Bildt recalls how they used Mladić to undermine Karadžić and chose to negotiate directly with the military commander behind Karadžić's back.[41] Finally, in August 1995, Mladić's autonomous role became too much for Karadžić and, behind closed doors, the RS parliament decided to remove him from his post under emergency war conditions declared a week earlier. The newspaper *Politika* speculated that Karadžić wanted to remove Mladić to prevent a military coup by the generals.[42] If such an initiative had been under way it was averted, but Karadžić had not yet won, since the next day Mladić's entire command signed a letter to the RS parliament rejecting Karadžić's announcement and declaring Mladić commander of the RS army.[43] Karadžić finally backed down and on 11 August 1995 he declared that the decision to remove Mladić had been annulled. Shortly thereafter he also backed down on the issue of negotiations and agreed to give Milošević the deciding vote in a joint Serb delegation. At this point, Karadžić controlled Pale and the majority of eastern RS and enjoyed the support of the RS special police, extreme nationalists in the RS and in Serbia, as well as SDS officials who feared Mladić's attack on war profiteers. But, by August 1995, this did not match Mladić's support and resources: the RS commander enjoyed the support of all the generals of the RS army, the Krajina faction of the SDS, the more moderate opposition parties and, finally, the Serbian regime which provided him with political, military and logistical support.[44]

The convergence between Mladić and the Krajina faction of the SDS was not only based on the issue of a settlement but also reflected a regional division of the RS and an ideological divide. Finally, both the army and the Krajina faction were attacking the rampant war profiteering

40. F. Švarm. 1995. 'Civilian-Military Games', *Vreme NDA*, 24 April. From: http://www.scc. rutgers.edu/serbian_digest/. Bougarel, 'Bosnia and Hercegovina,' 111–2.
41. C. Bildt. 1998. *Peace Journey: The Struggle for Peace in Bosnia*, London: Weidenfeld, 64.
42. *Croatian International Relations Review*. 2002. 'Chronology 1995: August 1 through August 31', 11(30/31), 54.
43. *Politika*, 7 August 1995, 1.
44. M. Vasić. 1995. 'Predsednik ili general', *Vreme*, 14 August, 14–15.

and corruption associated with the SDS leadership.[45] When the army and the Krajina faction began coalescing, they could effect a change away from centrifugal dynamics: Karadžić feared being removed by forces urging negotiations rather than by more radical forces.

Non-parliamentary Multipartyism

The most severe competition to the RS political leadership therefore came from within the party and from the army. On the other hand, competition from other parties was scarce though not non-existent, and the RS leadership even proudly described the statelet as a 'multiparty democracy'.[46] At the beginning of the war, competition to the SDS was, however, even more limited than in the prewar period since Serb representatives closed ranks behind the party. Almost all Serb representatives from non-ethnic parties joined the SDS after the outbreak of war, and there were only seven exceptions in the RS parliament. Thus, deputies who had been elected for the SDP, the Reformists or the DSS on a non-ethnic platform chose to join the explicitly Serb party. The non-ethnic parties ceased to operate in the territory under RS control and the only alternative to joining the SDS in this part of Bosnia, therefore, was to become an independent. One of the prime examples of this conversion was Dragan Kalinić, a former communist leader elected for the Reformists, who became powerful in the SDS. And if anyone in the party doubted Kalinić's nationalist credentials, his speech to the RS parliament in May 1992 proved them wrong: 'Among all the issues this assembly should decide on, the most important one is this: Have we chosen the option of war or the option of negotiations? ... I do not hesitate in selecting the first option, the option of war'.[47]

Despite this homogenization of Serb political representation, divisions soon began to emerge and alternative political initiatives were launched, especially after the ban on political parties was lifted in March 1993. The first party to be formed after the war began was the Liberal Party (Liberalna stranka, LS), which was founded in April 1992 before the work of parties was frozen. Not a nationalist party, the Liberals consisted of Banja Luka intellectuals who supported negotiations and an end to the war.[48] The party illustrated the continued existence of non-ethnic,

---

45. Ibid.
46. Kuzmanović, *Konstitutivni akti*, 60.
47. ICTY, 'Prosecutor vs. Radoslav Brdjanin,' 1171.
48. Author's interview with Miodrag Živanović (Banja Luka, 22 October 2003).

moderate voices in the RS but its influence was marginal. A party of much greater concern to the SDS was the Serb Radical Party (Srpska radikalna stranka, SRS), which, just before and during the war, increased its popularity significantly and represented an even more extreme position than the SDS. Apparently, some members of the SDS were simultaneously members of the SRS, thereby giving the leadership reasons to fear splits in the party: in 1992, Radoslav Brđanin, who was then president of the SAO Krajina crisis headquarters,[49] reportedly said on a radio show that he had an SRS membership card signed by Šešelj personally.[50]

The SRS started working in 1992 and was formally founded in Bosnia in March 1993 by Nikola Poplašen, a university professor. Poplašen lists two reasons for founding the party: firstly, in order to pursue the goal of uniting all Serbs in one state since the SRS felt that this goal was not sufficiently pursued by the SDS, and they argued that the party lacked autonomy in relation to Milošević who was seen as an obstacle; secondly, to break the SDS monopoly and fight the crime and authoritarianism associated with the party.[51] Finally, there was the Socialist Party of Republika Srpska (Socijalistička partija Republike Srpske, SPRS), which was founded in Banja Luka in June 1993 by Dragutin Ilić. Contrary to the SRS, the Socialist Party charged a more moderate course than the SDS and supported the different peace plans rejected by the RS leaders. The party established municipal organizations in most of the territory of the RS[52] but its most important organizational link was with Belgrade, and it was seen by the other opposition parties as little more than Milošević's mouthpiece.[53]

Consequently, by the second year of the war, the SDS was faced with competition from both more extreme and more moderate parties, and it was also challenged on issues other than the issue of war, with war profiteering and the regional divide being of particular importance. The challenge to the SDS's power was, however, limited since none of the parties were represented in parliament. Opposition activities, therefore, mostly consisted of public announcements while the parties were institutionalized.[54] But the RS leaders still feared the possible impact of

49. In effect, president of the regional government.
50. ICTY. 1996. 'Transcripts: Prosecutor vs. Duško Tadić (IT-94-I-T)', Transcript from testimony of anonymous witness, 30 May–4 June, 1807–8.
51. Author's interview with Nikola Poplašen.
52. Author's interview with Dragutin Ilić.
53. Author's interviews with Ognjen Tadić (Banja Luka, 7 November 2003) and Miodrag Živanović.
54. Author's interviews with Nikola Poplašen and Ognjen Tadić.

increased competition and, therefore, chose to harshly repress the opposition. Ognjen Tadić, from the SRS, argues that the treatment of the opposition included 'arrests, political liquidations, physical liquidations'.[55] The Liberal Party was similarly reduced by sending most of its members to the front line of the war.[56] The leader of the party, Miodrag Živanović, recalls that it had to function semi-legally: 'I was on the front, and I came to Banja Luka to make press conferences, and then I went back to the front, to save my life. Because it was safer there'.[57]

In parliament the only opposition to the SDS was made up by seven independent deputies. Following the rejection of the Contact Group Plan and the resulting clash between Belgrade and Pale, they constituted themselves as a group, the 'Club of Independent Deputies' under the leadership of Milorad Dodik, and began to act as an opposition to the SDS and Karadžić.[58] They issued a demand for a parliamentary session to achieve final peace and they blamed Karadžić and Krajišnik for the casualties in the period following the rejection of the Contact Group Plan.[59] Dodik coalesced with other opposition forces from Krajina and argued that the RS leadership's insistence on its right to Sarajevo 'has resulted in the loss of a large part of Bosnian Krajina'.[60] The club was taken very seriously by the SDS leadership and Krajišnik stated 'someone wants to break up the RS Parliament',[61] and announced greater discipline in the SDS.[62] The Club of Independents had no party apparatus behind them, nor formal structure, but they nevertheless began coordinating their stands and, for instance, voted against the dismissal of Mladić in August 1995, which parliament, at least according to SDS leaders, otherwise supported unanimously.[63]

The fear of being outflanked by the Serb Radicals was one of the reasons for the reactivation of the work of the SDS in 1993[64] and it,

55. Author's interview with Ognjen Tadić.
56. Author's interview with Miodrag Živanović.
57. Ibid.
58. Author's interview with Igor Radojičić, SNSD spokesman (Banja Luka, 1 December 2003). Milorad Dodik had been elected for the Reformists in 1990.
59. P. Vučinić and P. Rovac. 1995. 'Playing on the Reformists Ticket', Vreme NDA, 6 February. From: http://www.scc.rutgers.edu/serbian_digest/.
60. P. Vučinić. 1995. 'Capital's Watchtower', Vreme NDA, 2 October. From: http://www.scc.rutgers.edu/serbian_digest/.
61. P. Vučinić and P. Rovac. 1995. 'Playing on the Reformists Ticket', Vreme NDA, 6 February. From: http://www.scc.rutgers.edu/serbian_digest/.
62. F. Švarm and D. Dimović. 1995. 'Our Man in Pale', Vreme NDA, 16 January. From: http://www.scc.rutgers.edu/serbian_digest/.
63. Croatian International Relations Review, 'Chronology 1995,' 49.
64. Author's interview with Slobodan Nagradić.

thereby, indirectly affected the increasing lack of cohesion in the party. Moreover, the break of the SDS's monolithic status seems to have fostered or inspired divisions within the SDS itself, especially towards the end of the war when the Banja Luka faction cooperated with opposition parties in a bid to defeat the Pale leadership. The opposition, even if not a significant threat on its own, affected internal dynamics in the SDS as well as relations with the army and, thereby, eventually gave rise to more centripetal dynamics. The SDS leadership was aware of the potential dangers posed by competing parties, but the presence of rival parties did not lead the SDS to take a more extreme position. Clearly, the SDS had already adopted an extreme position but it is also of importance that the opposition did not just challenge the SDS on the issue of the war, and a more extreme position on this issue was, therefore, not necessarily the answer. Furthermore, the distribution of resources meant that the SDS could prevent the opposition parties from becoming a serious threat; they were repressed with harsh means and were, therefore, not able to effectively appeal to the audiences of importance for the SDS's hold on power. Consequently, the leadership did not have to compete through political positioning. However, when the opposition parties fostered an alliance with other oppositional forces, the RS leadership was eventually forced to change its position or face defeat. The direction of competition had changed.

Serbs outside the RS

Despite the strategy of national homogenization undertaken by the SDS, Serb representatives were still found outside the RS. These representatives challenged the conflation of Serb politics and RS politics.

In order to maintain the multi-ethnic nature of the Bosnian Presidency, replacements had to be found after the SDS deputies left the Bosnian institutions in April 1992. Following the constitution and electoral law, the posts were offered to the two runners-up from the 1990 Presidency election – Mirko Pejanović and Nenad Kecmanović – who were, respectively, leaders of the DSS and the Reformists. Their acceptance caused fury in Pale where Karadžić exclaimed that Pejanović and Kecmanović were 'the private Serbs of Alija Izetbegovic'.[65] Kecmanović quickly wilted under the pressure exerted on him by the RS and Belgrade and left Sarajevo in June 1992, when he was replaced by Tatjana Ljuić-

---

65. R. Ninčić. 1992, 'A New Breed of Serbs', *Vreme NDA*, 8 June. From: http://www. scc.rutgers.edu/serbian_digest/.

Mijatović of the SDP, and Mirko Lazović, also of the SDP, was appointed Speaker of Parliament.[66] The Serb members of the Bosnian Presidency took a radically different approach to the RS leaders: they stayed in Sarajevo and they spoke out against war and separation. In that way they can be seen as playing a similar role to Milan Đukić in Croatia: they were the 'loyal Serbs'. But there are also important differences: Pejanović, Ljuić-Mijatović and Lazović represented non-ethnic parties; they held their positions as ethnic Serbs but not as representatives of an ethnic party. A non-ethnic option still existed; ethnification was not complete. This is for example, illustrated by the not insignificant number of Serbs serving in the Bosnian army, including its deputy commander, Jovan Divjak. The Serb representatives insist that they had real influence on some important issues, while acknowledging that their most important role was perhaps to help keep alive the non-ethnic conception of Bosnia.[67]

In the RS, the influence of the 'Sarajevo Serbs' was very limited, although they had some links with more moderate opposition parties in the statelet.[68] The Liberal Party also attempted to develop contacts with non-ethnic parties in Sarajevo,[69] and Dodik's Club of Independents similarly had secret contacts with the Bosnian opposition. In May 1995, these contacts were made public when Dodik met Sejfudin Tokić, leader of the Union of Social Democrats, in the Italian city of Perugia and they declared their support for the Contact Group Plan.[70] In September of that year, opposition parties from across Bosnia again met in Perugia and issued a declaration in which they demanded an immediate stop to the war.[71] These meetings are significant: firstly, because engaging in cooperation across the ethnic divide was sure to give the RS opposition deputies the label 'traitors'; it was a very significant signal of moderation and attested to the emergence of new dynamics. Secondly, the presence of Serb opposition representatives from the RS as well as from Sarajevo strengthened the attempt to break the SDS's monopoly on representating the Bosnian Serbs. Even so, the contribution of the 'Sarajevo Serbs' to the changing dynamics in the RS was limited at best.

---

66. Pejanović, *Through Bosnian Eyes,* 103, 109.
67. Author's interviews with Miro Lazović (Sarajevo, 29 June 2004), Tatjana Ljujić-Mijatović (Sarajevo, 2 July 2004) and Mirko Pejanović (Sarajevo, 6 July 2004).
68. M. Milošević, D. Reljić, D. Grujić, F. Švarm. 1994. 'Total Recall', *Vreme NDA,* 8 August. From: http://www.scc.rutgers.edu/serbian_digest/. Author's interview with Mirko Pejanović.
69. Author's interview with Miodrag Živanović.
70. F. Švarm. 1995. 'Karadzic vs. Everyone Else', *Vreme NDA,* 13 June. From: http://www.scc.rutgers.edu/serbian_digest/.
71. D. Peranić. 1995. 'Gathering of Democratic Alternative Forum from the Whole of B&H', *AIM Press,* 2 October. From: http://www.aimpress.ch/.

As mentioned above, one decisive change in the wartime period was relations with the kin-state. But what influenced Belgrade's altered role in the RS and what effect did this change have?

Kin-state Involvement: A Divided RS Argues over Belgrade's Influence

Even though Milošević was initially uncontested in the RS, the Pale leaders soon followed the pattern established on the Croatian side of the border: relations became increasingly strenuous as Milošević distanced himself from the war and his former protégés began to assert their independence. Again mirroring events in the RSK, Belgrade utilized internal divisions to try to maintain control while local leaders sought cooperation with the Serbian opposition and with the RSK in an attempt to bolster their autonomy. The specific dynamics, however, differed from those in the RSK: Belgrade initially had greater difficulty influencing internal competition and the falling out with the local leaders was much more severe.

Increasing Divisions between Pale and Belgrade

Shortly after Milošević fell out with Babić in the RSK, there were speculations that he might also be looking for a replacement for Karadžić, for a leader more inclined to compromise and less inclined to power ambitions.[72] Karadžić had, for a while, been increasingly asserting his independence and making statements to the effect that he, and not Milošević, was the leader of the Serbs in Bosnia.[73] Milošević, therefore, had reason to fear that Karadžić might follow Babić's course and an attempt to engineer a leadership change became progressively more likely. This, however, never materialized and once it became clear that the ousting in Knin would not be followed by a similar one in Pale, Karadžić felt safe in his leadership position. Commentators argued that the war in Bosnia played an important part in Milošević's election victory in late 1992 and the Serbian president could not, therefore, afford to suddenly reverse his position.[74]

---

72. M. Čamo. 1992. 'Pucanje srpskog monolita', *Slobodna Bosna*, 16 January, 5.
73. Ibid.
74. S. Cerović. 1993. 'Geneva Ghosts', *Vreme NDA*, 18 January. From: http://www.scc. rutgers.edu/serbian_digest/.

This seeming coexistence and codependence was, however, shattered when the Vance-Owen Peace Plan was tabled in the spring of 1993. Although relations between Belgrade and the RS leaders had been fairly unproblematic during the first year of the war, Milošević was not completely trusted in Pale. In the RS parliament there was widespread belief that Karadžić had been forced to sign the agreement and this caused great resistance among the deputies.[75] Milošević was, furthermore, not aided by the vehement opposition of some SDS leaders to the plan, by Mladić's impassioned speech against it or by Karadžić's half-hearted support. Thus, even though Milošević appealed to Serb unity, he only managed to win two votes.[76] The humiliation greatly angered Milošević who made no effort to hide his resentment and described the behaviour of the RS leaders as that of 'drunk poker players'.[77] On a more formal level, Milošević, along with the Yugoslav and the Montenegrin presidents, issued a public letter to the RS parliament in which they stated, 'You have no right to endanger 10 million citizens of Yugoslavia'. But the parliament rejected the implied assertion that Milošević enjoyed a special position by responding, 'We allow ourselves the same right that you have to make decisions that are of importance to the Serbian people'.[78] Belgrade also resorted to more tangible measures than mere insults in an effort to discipline the 'drunk poker players'. The Serbian government imposed a blockade on the Drina, cutting off all supplies except food and medical supplies, and flavoured it with an attack on the 'luxurious lifestyle' the Pale leaders were enjoying in Belgrade 'while the people suffer'.[79]

After temporarily backtracking, Belgrade finally broke with the RS leadership in August 1994 following their rejection of the Contact Group Plan. Before the vote in the RS parliament, the Serbian president issued a letter in which he reminded the deputies that 'the Serbian people have only one president, chosen directly by the people and with a fully legitimate mandate'.[80] Once again the special position of Milošević was used to try to pressure the local Serb leaders. Some of the deputies acknowledged Milošević's special position but still insisted that the

75. Author's interview with Vladimir Lukić.
76. S. Cerović. 1993. 'Political Debauchery', *Vreme NDA*, 10 May. From: http://www.scc. rutgers.edu/serbian_digest/.
77. F. Švarm. 1994. 'Kidnappers and Hostages', *Vreme NDA*, 13 June. From: http://www.scc.rutgers.edu/serbian_digest/.
78. Ibid.
79. M. Vasić. 1993. 'Out of the Frying Pan into the Fire', *Vreme NDA*, 10 May. From: http://www.scc.rutgers.edu/serbian_digest/.
80. F. Švarm Filip. 1994. 'The President's Three Letters', *Vreme NDA*, 15 August. From: http://www.scc.rutgers.edu/serbian_digest/.

parliament had other considerations as well. Thus, Milanović stated: '[We] have never either with words or acts showed that we dismissed the fact that there is only one elected head of state of the Serbian people ... We have wanted him to be our president as well. [But] we are answerable to this people [the people of the RS]'. However, some deputies spoke out in clear defiance of Belgrade. Radoslav Brđanin, from the powerful Krajina faction, stated, 'Those playing the roles of puppets at crucial moments must be immediately recognized and removed, or the darkness will engulf us'.[81] Ultimately, Belgrade's persuasion and threats were to no avail and when the RS parliament decided to hold a referendum on the plan, thereby in effect rejecting it, Belgrade announced that they were breaking off all economic and political relations with the Pale leadership and banning all transport to the RS except of food, clothes and medicine.

Despite this break in relations, the RS leaders remained calm, convinced that Milošević would again be forced to change his position.[82] What they had not considered, however, was that divisions in the RS leadership were growing and this would increase Belgrade's influence in the RS. Furthermore, the Banja Luka faction of the SDS and the opposition parties based in the same city were growing in strength.

Belgrade and RS Elite Competition

Prior to the definitive break between Pale and Belgrade, the Serbian government did not make much use of internal divisions in the RS: the leadership was cohesive and the opposition weak. Consequently, Belgrade did not try to remove Karadžić when the Vance-Owen Peace Plan was rejected. With the formation of the Radicals in Bosnia in early 1993, relations with Belgrade, however, became a factor in elite competition in the RS[83] and the challenge from the SRS seems to have contributed to the SDS distancing itself from Milošević: the Pale leaders were vulnerable to rivals who accused them of being too close to Milošević and thereby of being too moderate. This kind of criticism also came from within the SDS's own ranks.

The distancing from Belgrade, therefore, ensured cohesion on the RS radical wing but the introduction of the economic embargo after the rejection of the Contact Group Plan destroyed the overall cohesion. In the RS parliament, Milorad Dodik formed his Club of Independent Deputies,

81. *Vreme NDA*, 8 August 1994. From: http://www.scc.rutgers.edu/serbian_digest/.
82. M. Milošević, D. Reljić, D. Grujić, F. Švarm. 1994. 'Total Recall', *Vreme NDA*, 8 August. From: http://www.scc.rutgers.edu/serbian_digest/.
83. Author's interview with Nikola Poplašen.

while the opposition parties stepped up their campaigns.[84] The clash between Belgrade and Pale started a process of rot among the Bosnian Serbs, which was precisely Milošević's goal. In order to further divisions in the RS, Milošević publicly blamed Karadžić for the military defeats suffered in western Bosnia.[85] Aside from the public slandering of the Pale leaders, Milošević also actively sought to increase his support in the RS parliament through contacts with disgruntled deputies, and in late 1994 SDS deputies from Banja Luka met the Serbian president in Belgrade. Following this meeting Karadžić admitted for the first time that divisions in parliament were growing, saying that fifteen out of eighty-two MPs were members of the 'Left' and close to the 'Left in Serbia', which is to say close to the opposition and to Milošević.[86] According to rumours at the time, Milošević was even more confident of his support in the RS parliament and said that he already had twenty-five out of the forty-two deputies necessary for a majority.[87] Belgrade also coalesced with the opposition parties and Milošević had a special relation with the Socialist Party (SPRS), which was formed shortly after the rejection of the Vance-Owen Peace Plan. The founder of the party, Dragutin Ilić, acknowledges that he received three kinds of assistance from the Serbian government: access to the media, material aid and physical protection.[88]

In addition to fostering political divisions, the Serbian authorities also sought to augment the already-existing conflict between the political and military leaderships in the RS. Milošević recognized the importance of the military for the civilian leadership and saw a deepening conflict as the best way to effect a change in the political position of the RS leadership. For this purpose, Milošević could utilize the close relationship between Mladić and the military leadership in Belgrade;[89] even when the embargo against the RS was imposed, Belgrade continued to have RS army officers on its payroll. Milošević did not want to engineer an RS military defeat; what he wanted was a change in the political position. The close link between Mladić and Belgrade persisted throughout the war and although the RS commander, after some initial hesitation, rejected the Contact

84. Bougarel, 'Bosnia and Hercegovina,' 111.
85. M. Vasić and F. Švarm. 1994. 'Storm over Bosnia', *Vreme NDA*, 7 November. From: http://www.scc.rutgers.edu/serbian_digest/.
86. N. Stefanović. 1994. 'Buying Time', *Vreme NDA*, 12 December. http://www.scc. rutgers.edu/serbian_digest/.
87. M. Vasić and F. Švarm. 1994. 'Storm over Bosnia', *Vreme NDA*, 7 November. From: http://www.scc.rutgers.edu/serbian_digest/.
88. Author's interview with Dragutin Ilić.
89. Gow, *The Serbian Project*, 180

Group Plan, he continued having secret contacts with Milošević.[90] Ultimately, Mladić chose to follow Milošević's lead, even though he reportedly rejected launching a coup against the political leadership.[91]

Belgrade's strategy was highly effective in augmenting divisions in the RS and thereby served to weaken Karadžić. However, Karadžić's initial reaction was to seek to strengthen his power base within the RS, consequently adopting an even more intransigent position. While the strategy was eventually successful, it took a long time for it to have the desired effect. Only in August 1995 were the RS leaders so weak that they gave in: they agreed to a joint Serb delegation in Dayton among which Milošević would have the deciding vote. During the Dayton negotiations, Milošević dismissed any objections from the RS delegates and boasted 'I'll make sure they accept the final agreement'.[92] And so they did, after Milošević had reportedly threatened Karadžić and the rest of the leadership with arrest.[93]

Attempting to Counter Belgrade

As was the case in the RSK, the Pale leadership did not just stand idly by when Milošević tried to undermine their power base. Instead, they sought alternative alliance partners, mainly in the Serbian opposition. Many of the Serbian opposition leaders, such as Šešelj and Đinđić, had roots in Bosnia and, moreover, they estimated that support for the Serbs in Bosnia could provide fertile ground for weakening Milošević. Thus, after Pale's break with Milošević over the Contact Group Plan, several Serbian opposition politicians paid visits to the RS.[94]

The RS leaders found one of their strongest supporters in the leader of the Serb Radicals. Šešelj was strongly opposed to the Vance-Owen Peace Plan and, following the RS rejection, he offered his support and attempted to create havoc in Belgrade. When Milošević introduced sanctions against the RS following the rejection of the Contact Group Plan, Šešelj described it as definite proof that Milošević had betrayed the interests of the Serb people.[95] But even though Karadžić needed the support, he was still

---

90. Thomas, *Serbia under Milošević*, 204.
91. Ibid., 240. Sell, *Milosevic and the Destruction of Yugoslavia*, 233.
92. Holbrooke, *To End a War*, 243.
93. Sell, *Milosevic and the Destruction of Yugoslavia* , 254.
94. F. Švarm and D. Dimović. 1995. 'Our Man in Pale', *Vreme NDA*, 16 January. From: http://www.scc.rutgers.edu/serbian_digest/.
95. M. Milošević, D. Reljić, D. Grujić, F. Švarm. 1994. 'Total Recall', *Vreme NDA*, 8 August. From: http://www.scc.rutgers.edu/serbian_digest/.

cautious not to let the Radicals become too strong in the RS. The Bosnian version of the SRS was closely linked with the party in Serbia and in order to avoid increased competition from the party, Karadžić chose to curtail its activities.[96] Internal competition in the RS thereby weakened the Pale leaders in their conflict with Milošević since they could not fully embrace cooperation with the Radicals.

In addition to the obvious support of the Radicals, the SDS was also wooing other forces in Belgrade. It had most success with Vojislav Koštunica's Democratic Party of Serbia (Demokratska stranka Srbije, DSS), with which the SDS had strong ideological affinity, including close links with the Serbian Orthodox Church. Throughout the conflict with Milošević, the DSS was to remain a staunch supporter of Pale and Koštunica dismissed all political attempts to divide the Serbs.[97] The position of the DS was more equivocal, but following the change in leadership and the coming to power of Zoran Đinđić, the party increasingly sought to make political capital of the Belgrade-Pale rift. The DS consequently came out against the Contact Group Plan.[98] The RS leaders, therefore, enjoyed the support of an almost united opposition following the Belgrade-Pale rift: they were backed by the SRS, the DSS, the DS, by the Serbian Orthodox Church and by a group of 'national intellectuals'.[99]

However, this support was of limited use to Karadžić as the Serbian opposition was too weak and disunited for Milošević to be seriously concerned.[100] Even the Serbian Orthodox Church was plagued by internal divisions: hardliners dominated at the time of the Contact Group Plan,[101] but the more moderately inclined Patriarch Pavle regained control and supported peace talks in 1995. Karadžić had counted on Milošević not being able to abandon the RS because of the Serbian opposition but he had overestimated its strength.[102] In 1993, when Milošević first decided to punish the Pale leaders, the situation had been somewhat different: the Radicals had created a huge spectacle in Serbia and the RS elite was still

---

96. F. Švarm and D. Dimović. 1995. 'Our Man in Pale', *Vreme NDA*, 16 January. From: http://www.scc.rutgers.edu/serbian_digest/.
97. Thomas, *Serbia under Milošević*, 222.
98. Ibid., 220.
99. M. Milošević. 1994. 'Public Vices, Secret Diplomacy', *Vreme NDA*, 17 October. From: http://www.scc.rutgers.edu/serbian_digest/.
100. F. Švarm and D. Dimović. 1995. 'Our Man in Pale', *Vreme NDA*, 16 January. From: http://www.scc.rutgers.edu/serbian_digest/.
101. M. Milošević and V. Brajović. 1994. 'Pictures from Pale', *Vreme NDA*, 15 August. From: http://www.scc.rutgers.edu/serbian_digest/.
102. M. Milošević, D. Reljić, D. Grujić, F. Švarm. 1994. 'Total Recall', *Vreme NDA*, 8 August. From: http://www.scc.rutgers.edu/serbian_digest/.

united. Eventually, Milošević backtracked. This furthered the intransigence of the RS leaders and, in 1994, they were convinced that Milošević would again reverse his position. But by then the situation was different: divisions, which Milošević could make use of, were appearing in the RS elite and the SRS was in a far weaker position. Milošević had concentrated his coercive force on the Radicals and Šešelj was, in September 1994, given a prison sentence for two violent attacks in the federal parliament. Thus amputated, the Radicals were unable to repeat the spectacles of 1993 and capitalize on their support for Pale.[103]

As relations between Belgrade and Pale became increasingly frosty, Milošević was no longer seen as the legitimate leader to whom the RS leaders owed their allegiance. This change in the borders of the intra-ethnic space was, as in the RSK, based on Milošević's political position rather than on an explicitly changed view of Serb identity. Again, the analysis pointed to the degree of internal divisions and the access to alternative resources as decisive for the influence that the kin-state leader could exert.

The General Population: Referenda and Civil Protests, but Limited Influence

In the prewar period, the impact of popular attitudes was reduced once the non-ethnic parties became marginalized. Party competition re-emerged during the war but the general population remained of limited importance, despite the leadership's rhetorical regard for popular opinion.

The RS parliament was constituted by Serb deputies elected to the Bosnian parliament in the 1990 elections. However, their mandates were problematic, even though they were popularly elected: firstly, they had been elected to a different parliament and usually on a more moderate basis; and secondly, a number of them were elected for non-ethnic parties but subsequently chose to join the SDS. Nevertheless, this popular mandate would often be pointed to in internal competition and Plavšić, for example, emphasized that contrary to Karadžić she had been elected by the Serb people.[104] The RS population was, however, not given a chance to renew this mandate during the war. No elections were held, despite the opposition's insistence and despite the fact that the mandates from 1990

103. F. Švarm and D. Dimović. 1995. 'Our Man in Pale', *Vreme NDA*, 16 January. From: http://www.scc.rutgers.edu/serbian_digest/.
104. D. Anastasijević. 1994. 'Biljana Plavsic, Vice-President Bosnian Serb Republic', *Vreme NDA*, 15 August. From: http://www.scc.rutgers.edu/serbian_digest/.

expired in 1994. Surveys were not conducted either, making it very difficult to assess popular opinion, and few channels were open for popular influence anyway.

Aside from the referenda held on peace agreements, the only way for the general population to register support or disagreement was through civil protest. However, the Serb Radicals argue that a local election was actually held in Jajce in 1993 but that the results were cancelled by the RS authorities when the Radicals emerged as the winner.[105] It has not been possible to confirm this event but it fits well with the SDS's pattern of suppressing the opposition. Referenda were, on the other hand, a popular instrument that was used when the RS leaders wanted to strengthen their defiant position. Consequently, referenda were held on the Vance-Owen Peace Plan and on the Contact Group Plan since the RS leaders could, thereby, argue that they were only following the will of the people. The official results in both referenda pointed to a massive turnout and overwhelming rejection of the proposed plans. Thus, in the referendum on the Vance-Owen Peace Plan in August 1993, turnout was reported to be around 90 per cent with well over 90 per cent of voters rejecting the agreement.[106] In the Contact Group Plan referendum, turnout was reported to be 91 per cent with 95 per cent rejecting the plan, despite a fierce campaign in its favour waged by the Belgrade media machine.[107] In a state of war, such high turnouts seem highly unlikely and the overwhelming rejection of the plan should be taken with a pinch of salt: these are official results from authorities not averse to bending the rules of democratic competition.

Regardless of the extent to which the referenda reflected actual popular opinion, they did not have a significant impact. Everyone knew in advance what the results would be, otherwise the RS leaders would never have called a referendum, and the political agenda had already moved on by the time they were held. In late 1995, the RS authorities organized a referendum on the Dayton Agreement in the Serb-controlled part of Sarajevo. The referendum was a desperate attempt to alter the agreement that had awarded all of Sarajevo to the Bosniak-Croat Federation and, therefore, would mean the loss of RS control of the suburbs. But despite an overwhelming rejection of the plan – 98.7 per cent of the approximately 80,000 people who voted were said to have voted against[108] – the

---

105. Author's interview with Ognjen Tadić.
106. S. Lalović. 1993. 'Nezvanični podaci: 'Ne' Vens-Ovenov Planu', *Politika*, 18 May, 1.
107. Silber and Little, *The Death of Yugoslavia*, 343. *Croatian International Relations Review*. 2001. 'Chronology 1994: May through August', 7(22/23), 48.
108. B. Lekić. 1995. 'Night Moves', *Vreme NDA*, 18 December. From: http://www.scc.rutgers.edu/serbian_digest/.

referendum failed to achieve any changes in the Dayton Agreement or in the political position of the Serb leadership. The RS leaders knew that popular support was not enough for them to retain power and they were too weak to make use of the result. Popular opinion, therefore, cannot be said to have been an important constraint on the position of leaders.

Popular resistance to the policies of the RS leadership was expressed on at least two occasions. When the RS parliament accepted the Owen-Stoltenberg Plan, this caused strong reactions in the territories that were to be ceded.[109] Of greater concern to the RS leadership, however, was the September 1993 rebellion in Banja Luka which was accompanied by civilian demonstrations.[110] Nevertheless, loss of popular support was not the main concern for the SDS leadership who feared growing divisions within its own ranks as well as an intensification of the conflict with the army. The SDS leadership worried about cooperation between its rivals and a possible coup. The SDS's rivals could conceivably have made use of popular discontent and, thereby, weakened the leadership but as long as the war was ongoing the possibilities for doing so were limited and other resources were of greater importance. Judah argues that by 1995 it was common for Serbs in Bosnia to privately whisper that Karadžić and the other leaders were 'all crooks'.[111] But even if this were true for the majority of the population, there were no channels through which it could affect the leadership and the opposition was unable to utilize such attitudes.

As in the case of Croatia, the impact of popular attitudes during the war was consequently very limited. Other resources were more effective in elite competition and they were widely available. Finally, the importance of inter-ethnic relations was, as in Croatia, largely based on the military balance.

Inter-ethnic Relations: Military Balance Decisive

Direct interaction between the leaders of the ethnic parties was reduced considerably once war broke out.[112] Moreover, due to the RS leadership's uncompromising insistence on a separate Serb territory, the positions of SDA and HDZ leaders were of limited importance: the Serb leaders were not interested in any proposals for coexistence. The relations that really mattered were of a military nature: had the military balance changed, and

---

109. Bougarel, 'Bosnia and Hercegovina,' 105.
110. Ibid., 107.
111. Judah, *The Serbs,* 296. See also Glenny, *The Fall of Yugoslavia,* 263.
112. It was limited to negotiations, usually under international auspices, where the opposing leaders might not even meet face to face.

was defeat becoming increasingly likely? This ultimately fostered a change in the Serb position, in combination with the changed dynamics of intra-ethnic competition and kin-state pressure.

Changing Alliances

After war broke out, the Pale leaders put some effort into breaking up the Bosniak-Croat alliance, realizing that this would significantly strengthen their military position. Unlike in the prewar period, the wooing was mostly reserved for the Croats, and the SDS's strategy was to get the Herzegovin faction of the HDZ to agree to a division of Bosnia. HDZ and SDS leaders met frequently, and Karadžić and Mate Boban agreed on dividing Bosnia between them at a meeting in Graz in May 1992. The Bosnian Croat leadership continued, however, to pursue two separate and contradictory policies: secret collusion with the Serbs and a formal alliance with the SDA and the Bosnian government.[113] But the latter alliance broke down in the spring of 1993 when war broke out between the Croat Defence Council (Hrvatsko vijeće odbrane, HVO) and the Bosnian army. This greatly strengthened the Serb military position and the RS leadership sought to build on the broken alliance by cooperating with the Bosniak Fikret Abdić, who had declared an autonomous province in northwest Bosnia and was now at war with the Sarajevo government.[114] With this move, the RS leaders hoped to strengthen their position in Krajina and weaken the Bosnian government. But by 1994, Pale's luck in terms of shifting alliances was changing: the Bosnian and the Croatian governments signed the Washington Agreement on a Bosniak-Croat Federation in March, and Abdić was defeated in August. Consequently, the RS was facing a more united front and the military balance began to change.

Negotiations and Stalemate

The frequency of negotiations was much higher in Bosnia than in Croatia where the RSK leaders refused to negotiate for prolonged periods of time. International mediators kept the negotiation process going but one crucial element was lacking: simultaneity. When one side was prepared to accept an agreement, the other side rejected it. The strategies chosen by the leaders were based on the proposals themselves, on the internal competition that they were faced with, as well as on an assessment of the

---

113. Silber and Little, *The Death of Yugoslavia*, 306–8.
114. Ibid., 306.

other side's position. If the others would reject the proposal anyway, then acceptance was a strategy for winning international favour. The strategic adoption of positions was explicitly acknowledged by Izetbegović when the Bosnian government only accepted the Contact Group Plan because they were certain that the Serbs would reject it.[115] It was, thus, a complex, nested game with many actors and many constraints.

A military stalemate had emerged in the beginning of 1994[116] but without this resulting in a willingness to compromise. The leaders were still constrained by internal forces, they did not want to show weakness and, furthermore, hoped for a future improvement in their situation. For the Serbs, however, things began to change with the fall of Kupres in the autumn of 1994, dubbed a betrayal by the HVO.[117] It was, thus, the first tangible effect of the re-launched Bosniak-Croat alliance. This event was followed by additional changes on the battlefield and a new form of stalemate arose: a mutually hurting stalemate in which 'all involved were constrained by the prospective cost of a return to armed hostilities'.[118] Following NATO bombings of Serb positions in August 1995, the Serb leadership were in fact facing the prospect of serious military defeat, and it was made clear that continued Serb radicalism would come at a price. The change in relative military strength deepened existing divisions in the RS and, combined with significant pressure from the kin-state and changed internal dynamics, it finally resulted in acceptance of a settlement.

Fractionalization and Infighting in Wartime Bosnia

From being a very unified party at the beginning of the war, the SDS in Bosnia became increasingly plagued by fractionalization and the RS leadership also had to deal with a growing rift with the military. Karadžić constantly feared being undermined from within and after his near defeat over the Vance-Owen Peace Plan, he took no steps without ensuring the backing of the rest of the leadership, and a more radical position resulted.

Competition from other parties grew in significance during the war and was affected by, and in turn affected, intra-party divisions. When the SDS was reactivated, it feared competition from the Radicals, but this move opened up for increasing competition from other parties and also helped

115. Silber and Little, *The Death of Yugoslavia*, 340.
116. J. Gow. 1997. *Triumph of the Lack of Will*, London: Hurst, 261.
117. M. Vasić. 1994. 'War without Declaration', *Vreme NDA*, 14 November. From: http://www.scc.rutgers.edu/serbian_digest/.
118. Gow, *Triumph of the Lack of Will*, 281.

foster divisions within the formerly cohesive SDS. Towards the end of the war, moderating dynamics finally emerged, whereas earlier the most serious challenges to the RS leadership had come from more extreme challengers. This was to a considerable extent the result of overlapping cleavages and issues: the oppositional forces found common ground on regional and ideological cleavages, on the issue of a settlement, on links with Belgrade and on the issue of war profiteering. The more extreme challengers had enjoyed the support of paramilitary forces, while the more moderate forces lacked this kind of resources until the army sided with the opposition and the Banja Luka faction of the SDS. This new alliance provided the opposition and the Banja Luka faction with needed military resources and it gave Mladić his first political base within the RS.[119] Responses to intra-ethnic challengers are, thus, affected by both the form of this competition, the resources available and the issues on which it is centred.

The Bosnian case again demonstrated the predominance of non-political resources in the wartime competition. Within the RS, the main audiences to the competition were intra-party forces and, even more decisively, paramilitary forces and various other military constellations. The general population was, on the other hand, not a significant audience during the war: there were no channels for influence, no elections were held and the opposition could not make use of its potential popular support. The only way to express support or resistance was through referenda or civil protest. However, referenda did not affect the position of the RS leaders and popular expressions of dissent, while of concern to the RS leadership, were not significant as long as the leaders controlled the non-political resources that were dominant in elite competition.

Although relations with the kin-state were increasingly strenuous, Belgrade had an important impact on competition in the RS. Contrary to what was the case in Croatia, however, Belgrade only became a significant influence on internal competition in 1994. The high degree of cohesion made it more difficult for Belgrade to affect elite positions by playing on internal divisions and Milošević had no desire for a leadership change until the rejection of the Vance-Owen Peace Plan in 1993. Growing divisions in the statelet increased the potential for kin-state influence but the intransigence of the RS leadership was remarkably resilient. The Pale leaders had access to alternative resources and alliance partners and, furthermore, found themselves challenged on the issue of relations with Belgrade by forces within their own party and by the Serb Radicals. The intransigent position of the RS leadership, finally, meant

119. D. Anastasijević. 1995. 'Crucial Defence of Power', *Vreme NDA, Digest* 23 October. From: http://www.scc.rutgers.edu/serbian_digest/.

that Croat and Bosniak elite positions were of limited influence. What mattered was the relative military strength but this only led to a change in position when combined with changed dynamics of intra-ethnic competition and kin-state pressure.

Wartime Intra-ethnic Rivalry

Following the outbreak of war, ethnification was no longer an issue, and even the 'urban Serb' leaders defined themselves – and were, especially, defined by others – as specifically Serb representatives. In the initial period after the outbreak of war, there was a closing of ranks behind the dominant Serb party, but this only provided a brief respite from disunity which, in a context of ethnification, returned even more forcefully. Thus, in both cases, intra-ethnic rivalry intensified despite a situation of extreme insecurity.

Democracy was still used as a legitimizing concept and political competition formally took the form of competition between political parties in a parliamentary system. However, the parties were dominated by their leaders and party structures were strikingly weak. Competition between parties, therefore, did not take the form of competition between two party organizations but was rather a competition between leaders who had different levels of political and especially non-political resources at their disposal. It was about individual leaders and the resources they controlled.

Throughout the war, military and paramilitary forces played a crucial role, in alliance or in competition with civilian leaders. The civilian leaders lacked full control of military forces, but they depended on their resources. This left the civilian leaders constrained and civilian-military links were decisive for the outcome of the intra-Serb competition. Thus, the resources of importance in the political competition were often far from 'conventional' democratic resources: links with Belgrade, support from (para)military forces as well as the bending of political rules to take advantage of regional differences in parliamentary support. Popular attitudes were of limited importance: changes in the dynamics of competition were not led by popular demands and, even when elections or referenda were held, these reflected the balance of power in terms of the resources that really mattered – economic resources and, above all, military resources. The elections in the RSK and the salience of the 'Belgrade issue' are, therefore, only a partial exception to the lack of significance of popular attitudes. Persistent Serb intransigence greatly reduced the impact of actions and the rhetoric of other ethnic leaders, and what mattered in both cases was the military balance. Military strength and the risk of defeat directly affect future prospects for elites, not only the general population.

Radicalization was still the dominant dynamic when leaders were met with challenges from within their own party or from related paramilitary forces. If they had been contemplating moderation under such circumstances, they were forced to reverse their position or face defeat. However, radicalization was not the chosen response to competition if it came from outside the party or movement, regardless of whether the challengers were more moderate or more extreme. In the RSK, leaders chose to negotiate with the Croatian government despite severe challenges from other parties and independents. When faced with opposition parties, the RS leadership primarily tried to suppress them with the coercive resources that the war and the SDS-dominated regime made so readily available. However, towards the end of the war – when the opposition parties, the SDS Krajina faction and the army coalesced – the RS leadership lacked the strength to continue its intransigent position and was forced to reverse it: radicalization would not save the leadership and its relative strength was not sufficient to marginalize rivals. This also illustrates the effect of more moderate challenges from within: in such a situation, radicalization will not provide a solution and the choice is consequently to either marginalize the challengers or accommodate them by adopting a more moderate position. Towards the end of the war, Karadžić had to choose the latter option.

There therefore seems to be an interesting difference in the dynamics of *intra*-party and *inter*-party rivalry. Leaders relied on resources emanating from within the party or movement and they were, therefore, less likely to be able to merely suppress any challenges. In both cases even the strongest leaders were constrained by other leaders in the party and by paramilitary forces. Another difference between the two kinds of competition was that challenges from within the party were often focused on the issue of the war, and radicalization, therefore, provided a sufficient response. In the opposition from other parties, other issues were often also prominent, thereby preventing radicalization from pre-empting the attacks. And it is indeed interesting, and somewhat surprising, that other politically salient issues could emerge despite the situation of war. Before the war, competition had been mainly based on the issue of the inter-ethnic conflict, even though regional and ideological cleavages had also played a role. During the war, these cleavages increased in importance, but the real change was the importance of valence issues, especially the issue of war profiteering. These cleavages and issues fostered the creation of new alliances and altered the strategies open to beleaguered leaders.

The issues on which the intra-ethnic rivalry is based have an important impact on the resulting dynamics.

These divisions also influenced relations with the kin-state and one general trend clearly emerged from both cases: Belgrade fell out with almost all leaders of the local Serbs, with Babić, Martić and Karadžić. Milošević changed his strategy and goals following military failures and international pressure, but he had difficulties taking the local Serb leaders along: the Serbian president was no longer always able to dictate developments in the two statelets. These changed relations brought about a considerable change in rhetoric. In the prewar phase, the unity of the Serbs and the special position of Milošević as 'the President of all Serbs' was emphasized by most actors, but as the conflict deepened, the distinct nature of the Serbs in Serbia and the Serbs outside Serbia was increasingly stressed by both sides. When his position became questioned, Milošević sought to influence elite competition in the two statelets in order to retain control. Belgrade thereby became a very strong, but largely external, influence on the local competition. There was, thus, a change in the form of influence: from being at least partly based on shared ethnicity to being almost exclusively based on the need for Belgrade's resources.

Milošević's attempt to engineer more moderate dynamics was, however, not always successful. In the RSK it worked in the conflict with Babić but failed when, towards the end of the war, Babić and Martić decided to go against Milošević's man, Mikelić. In the RS, the strategy was slow-working and only in 1995 did more centripetal dynamics emerge. One of the factors limiting Milošević's success in engineering moderating dynamics was that the link with Belgrade increasingly became a disputed issue among local elites. While the elites did not change their position on the issue of the war, they could score political points by vowing to assert their independence and not take orders from Belgrade. The ability to take a more independent position was affected by the involvement of the opposition parties from Serbia, which functioned as an alternative audience that gave the leaders hope of being able to continue their intransigent positioning. Moreover, the leaders had access to alternative paramilitary resources that could be used in the internal competition. The detachment of the Serbian regime was relative and it retained strong links with the military, but its ability to influence developments was reduced.

When Pale and Belgrade fell out, the resulting conflict was much more intense than the one between Belgrade and various Knin leaders. In the RSK, Milošević never used the military and economic powers he possessed and, furthermore, he did not actively push for an agreement with Croatia.[120] Milošević had generally been able to influence the RSK leadership without resorting to sanctions but, by 1995, this ability to control elite competition in the RSK had diminished whereas it was on the rise in the RS, possibly due to the sanctions imposed. In the RSK, kin-state influence was reduced towards the end of the war by the high degree of fractionalization, the frequently changing alliances and access to paramilitary resources. An additional reason for Milošević's more forceful reaction may have been the greater sway of the Pale leaders in Serbia. Milošević would have been more concerned about a prolonged conflict with Pale, since the RS leaders had a greater chance of undermining his position. Milošević himself professed that the reason was that he could not afford another intra-Serb conflict.[121] Finally, from a strategic perspective, Milošević knew, in 1995, that Tuđman would not accept an agreement and the only thing Belgrade could hope for was for the situation to remain frozen.

Conflict context	Decisive audiences	Outcome
• Authoritarian statelets • Intense violence • Complete ethnification	• Military and paramilitary forces • Kin-state (decreasing) • Party structures, incl. parliament	*Competition within parties* • Radicalization *Competition between parties* • Radicalization • No response • Relative moderation

Figure 6.1 Wartime Intra-Serb Rivalry

120. Sell, *Milosevic and the Destruction of Yugoslavia*, 239.
121. Cohen, *Broken Bonds*, 243.

CHAPTER SEVEN

Warlords, Spoilers and Moderates

Notwithstanding the imperative of unity in the face of severe conflict, as famously called for in the motto 'only unity saves the Serbs', disunity prevailed throughout the conflict and war. Rivalry was unrelenting and even the 'President of all Serbs', Slobodan Milošević, was unable to always dictate Serb politics in Croatia and Bosnia. The need for guarding the position of the nation was clearly not enough to prevent divisions. Horowitz's thesis that intra-ethnic competition will be limited by a concern for weakening the position of the group was not, therefore, supported by the two cases. On the contrary, when military fortunes were reversing, disunity became even more pronounced. Thus, divisions intensified despite a situation of extreme insecurity. There are, however, some factors that seemed to cause greater unity and, therefore, serve as exceptions to the overall tendency of increased disunity in times of crisis. Firstly, when ethnification was still part of the political struggle and non-ethnic rivals were yet to be marginalized, intra-ethnic competition was limited to fairly low-intensity competition within ethnic parties. Secondly, the risk of being outvoted and, more importantly, the outbreak of war caused a temporary homogenization of the Serb community. It is, however, important to realize that this unity was in large part enforced, and the overall picture was one of disunity.

The persistence of leadership rivalry was not only a question of 'parasitic criminal elements'[1] using the impunity offered by war to fight over lucrative war profiteering. Power struggles certainly played a role but divisions were also based on different views of strategies and goals in the conflict and on regional and ideological cleavages.[2] Ethnic groups are, contrary to the intra-group cohesion implied in concepts such as 'ethnic

---

1. W.A. Kemp. 2004. 'The Business of Ethnic Conflict', *Security Dialogue* 35(1), 45. Kemp is referring to factors that sustain a conflict
2. See also Caspersen, "Intragroup Divisions in Ethnic Conflicts.'

conflict', not homogeneous and internal divisions are the norm. This lack of homogeneity is important since intra-ethnic competition impacts on the possibility for conflict resolution, it influences the factors that drive a conflict, and it undermines nationalist claims to popular legitimacy.

A number of interesting findings have emerged from the analysis, findings that contradict or add to existing theorizing. Radicalization was, contrary to what is argued in most theoretical literature, not the only possible outcome of intra-ethnic competition, and when radicalization did result it was most often not based on appeals to popular attitudes. Other resources were more available and effective in the competition, which was consequently not driven by popular demands. The lack of success in playing the ethnic card also meant that the ethnification of politics was part of the political struggle; it was not an automatic process based on the overwhelming power of ethnicity. In terms of relations with 'opposing' ethnic leaders, this was found to be of great importance for the ethnification of politics, but radicalization or moderation was not necessarily reciprocated; other factors were often more significant for the direction of competition. Finally, kin-state relations proved highly fluid; the longevity of ethnic solidarity was limited and the ability of the kin-state to control local developments varied greatly.

The assumption of outbidding based on 'playing the ethnic card' and appealing to extreme mass sentiments is, thus, far too simplified. Intra-ethnic rivalry does not necessarily lead to radicalization and other audiences or support bases, in particular 'men with guns', can be far more important than the general population. Much of this analysis is, however, based on a highly intense conflict situation, and if violence predominates it is perhaps unsurprising that popular demands do not drive the conflict. Moreover, would similar dynamics have been observed if the international presence had been stronger, if there had been a direct attempt to alter the dynamics of intra-ethnic rivalry? To analyse the effect of a different context – a non-violent context with a strong international presence – the following section will briefly track postwar developments in the two cases. What are the changes and what are the continuities?

Serb Rivalry in Postwar Croatia and Bosnia

The end of the war left the Serbs in significantly different positions in the two cases. Whereas the Serbs in Croatia were, in Owen's words, 'the biggest losers',[3] the Serb leaders in Bosnia had been more successful in

---

3. Owen, *Balkan Odyssey*, 387.

pursuing their nationalist goals. In Croatia, almost no Serbs were left in Krajina and the leaders in Eastern Slavonia had to settle for the Erdut Agreement, which was all but silent on the political arrangements that would be implemented following the reintegration of the region. In Republika Srpska, the leaders could look to the continued existence of their statelet, albeit within a Bosnian state and with the added risk of indictment by the Hague Tribunal. The flight of the radicals from Krajina altered the dynamics of competition in Croatia, while elections were finally held in Bosnia thereby allowing the opposition to gain an institutional foothold. An important change in the postwar phase was the introduction of an important international dimension: in Bosnia and in Eastern Slavonia, international administrators became an important audience to intra-Serb competition. The international community had also earlier influenced the dynamics of Serbs politics, but in the postwar period the influence of international authorities was much more direct: they influenced the distribution of resources between moderates and extremists and reduced the availability and effectiveness of coercive resources. The role of the kin-state was reduced significantly in this phase and the Serbs in Croatia and Bosnia were all but ignored by Belgrade. The importance of political resources located within Croatia and Bosnia increased and kin-state influence was reduced accordingly. Despite these changes brought about by the end of the war, the immediate postwar dynamics were, to a considerable extent, built on wartime divisions.

Croatia: Moderating Dynamics Gradually Become Dominant

The Croatian offensive in Krajina brought with it a significant change in the Serb leadership. Hitherto dominating actors such as Babić and Martić fled Krajina and found themselves in Belgrade without any influence on the continued unfolding of events. The remaining Serb political elites were, therefore, the Eastern Slavonian leaders and the leaders of the 'urban Serbs'. Moderating dynamics gradually became dominant but they were, despite the change in the conflict situation, initially not driven by popular demand.

Competition for Positions in the Remnants of the SDS

According to the Erdut Agreement, Eastern Slavonia was to be under UN administration for a transitional period of one year, with the possibility of a one-year extension should either side request it. The UN's administrator,

Jacques Klein, was consequently the highest authority in the region and he exerted a very tangible influence on intra-Serb rivalry by choosing to circumvent the president of SAO Slavonia, Goran Hadžić, and instead work with the more moderate Vojislav Stanimirović, who was president of the Eastern Slavonia executive council.[4] Hadžić was, however, still waiting in the wings and demanded a referendum on the 'integrity' of Eastern Slavonia; insisting that it should be reintegrated as a single unit instead of being split between two counties.[5] The outcome of the leadership struggle in the remnants of the SDS, therefore, was crucial for the dominant Serb position and for the peaceful reintegration of the region.

Contrary to the wartime dynamics, the more moderate position this time prevailed, but it was a narrow victory. Although Hadžić lacked influence among the transitional authorities, his authority in the SDS was still considerable and Stanimirović had to resort to arguing that Croatian citizenship, which Hadžić had not acquired, was a precondition for a party leader in a reintegrated Eastern Slavonia. This earned him only a slender victory in the main board (nineteen votes to fourteen) and Hadžić's supporters allegedly commented that it 'could be settled in the streets too'.[6] However, coercive resources no longer decided political outcomes: the international presence was a significant influence, which supported the moderate option, but the victorious leader still had to resort to less than democratic methods. Hadžić could previously have relied on Belgrade's support but the Serbian regime now played a very limited role; the Serb minority in Croatia was largely ignored, not only by Milošević but also by the Serbian opposition. Belgrade reportedly made clear to Hadžić that it supported the terms of reintegration and, therefore, he had no one else to turn to.[7] A referendum was organized in April 1997 and the result pointed to overwhelming popular support for preserving the 'integrity' of the region and hence for Hadžić's stand.[8] But it was all to no avail: Hadžić lost the battle over the party leadership and the region was reintegrated as planned. Public opinion was not allowed to impact the outcome of elite competition in the region.

4. Author's interview with Vojislav Stanimirović (Vukovar, 25 September 2003).
5. D. Hedl. 1997. 'Elections as the Only Choice' *AIM Press*, 12 March. From: http://www.aimpress.ch/.
6. Ibid.
7. M. Čulić. 1997. 'Pakleno Podunavlje', *Feral Tribune*, 10 February, 7–8.
8. F. Švarm. 1997. 'Following Orders From Belgrade', *Vreme NDA*, 12 April. From: http://www.scc.rutgers.edu/serbian_digest/.

Centripetal Dynamics after Merger

Changing dynamics also affected the 'urban Serb' representatives but the main fault line between Milorad Pupovac and Milan Đukić persisted. During the war, Đukić was accused of being a puppet of the Croatian government but he now gradually began inhabiting the more extreme position. In March 1997, Pupovac's Independent Serb Party (Samostalna srpska stranka, SSS) merged with the remnants of the SDS under the name of the Independent Democratic Serb Party (Samostalna demokratska srpska stranka, SDSS). With this move, the main Serb political forces in Croatia had chosen a conciliatory course and the party showed itself more willing than Đukić's SNS to cooperate with the Croatian government.[9]

In local elections held shortly after the formation of the SDSS, the party established a stronghold in Eastern Slavonia where it won majorities in eleven out of twenty-eight municipalities.[10] But in the election for the Croatian upper house, the Serb parties were less fortunate: none of them succeeded in getting a candidate elected and the SDSS only gained two seats through President Tuđman's personal appointments. Prior to the elections, the Serb leaders in Eastern Slavonia had managed to weaken their own position considerably: they hesitated until forty-eight hours before the elections to recommend that the population go to the polls and a similar hesitation over the issue of Croatian identity papers left many prospective Serb voters without adequate documents on election day.[11] In the remaining territory of what had been the RSK, there were only a few Serbs left and potential Serb candidates were reluctant to run for office due to the considerable risks involved.[12] Although these elections were relatively free and fair, and undemocratic resources played a far less important role, voter attitudes were still not clearly reflected in the outcome: through their hesitation, the Serb leaders had limited the participation of Serb voters, intimidation was a concern and Serb representation in the upper house of parliament was based on the will of the Croatian authorities rather than the preference of Serb voters. In the continued competition between the two Serb parties, Đukić's SNS pursued a strategy of outbidding and even accused Pupovac of being a

9. B. Rašeta. 1997. 'Interview Milorad Pupovac', *Vreme NDA*, 10 May. From: http://www.scc.rutgers.edu/serbian_digest/.
10. N. Zakošek. 1997. 'Pregled rezultata izbora za domove Sabora Republike Hravtske i za županijske skupštine', *Politička Misao* 34(2).
11. D. Hedl. 1997. 'Two Bridges and Three Serb Auto-goals', *AIM Press* 20 April. From: http://www.aimpress.ch/.
12. A. Anić. 1997. 'Elections in Western Slavonia', *AIM Press* 25 March. From: http://www.aimpress.ch/.

traitor.[13] This strategy was successful in the 2000 elections for the lower house of parliament, when the SNS won the only Serb mandate, but gradually its backing decreased and in the 2003 elections it failed to win parliamentary representation. While this would seem to reflect more moderate popular attitudes, it undoubtedly also reflects the far better party organization built up by the SDSS.

Serb Rivalry in Postwar Croatia

Competition among Serb elites in Croatia was, after the end of the war, marked by the weak position of the Serbs as well as the by the departure of the Knin hardliners. In Eastern Slavonia, the hardliners were marginalized due to pressure and actions taken by the international authorities as well as due to the 'political trickery' of intra-party rivals. The support of the international authorities was an important resource in elite competition in Eastern Slavonia and the presence of international forces also meant that the threat of Hadžić's supporters taking the intra-party struggle to 'the streets' did not prove decisive. But despite this change in the resources of importance, strategies not clearly democratic in nature were still used to settle leadership struggles. Notwithstanding the end of violence, popular attitudes do not appear to have been decisive for the initial centripetal dynamics in the postwar period. But despite the temporary support for a more radical SNS, popular attitudes mattered for the persistence of the centripetal dynamics since elections were held and other resources had become less important.

Bosnia: Hardliner Moderates and SDS Splits

Similar developments can be observed in the Bosnian case: relative moderation ensued but it was driven by power ambitions and international pressure rather than by popular demand. The end of the war did not initially bring about any changes in the RS leadership, although indictment for war crimes eventually forced Karadžić to exert his power from behind the scenes. Ethnification was still dominant: political competition was confined to intra-ethnic competition and even within this separate party system socio-economic cleavages were insignificant.[14] But this did not prevent intra-Serb competition from becoming even more

13. Author's interview with Milan Đukić.
14. Bose, *Bosnia after Dayton*, 210.

fragmented and the dynamics of competition were now heavily influenced by the international presence.

The SDS, and especially Karadžić, had been significantly weakened by the signing of the Dayton Agreement, which constituted a humiliating defeat for the war-bent leaders who were left completely without influence during the negotiations. However, when Karadžić re-emerged on the political scene, his position was one of strict non-cooperation and, in the spring of 1996, he stated: 'the international community is wasting its time looking for Serbs with moderate stands'.[15] Within the SDS, Karadžić made sure that this statement would hold true and he ousted the RS prime minister, Rajko Kasagić, for being too moderate, for being too willing to cooperate with the international authorities.[16]

The holding of elections in September 1996 gave a stimulus for SDS factions to establish themselves as parties. This resulted in the creation of a number of smaller parties that joined forces in the Democratic Patriotic Bloc (Demokratski patriotski blok, DPB). The DPB criticized individuals in the SDS and the concentration of power in Pale but did not argue for greater moderation on the issue of inter-ethnic relations: 'Our common goal is to preserve what was won and defended with blood'.[17] The elections also gave the wartime opposition parties a chance to test their strength against the SDS. The Left was united in the People's Union for Peace – Union for Peace and Progress (Narodni savez za slobodan mir – Savez za mir i progres). This coalition was made up of the Socialist Party, the Liberal Party, the Yugoslav United Left (JUL) and the newly formed Alliance of Independent Social Democrats (Saves nezavisnih socijaldemokrata, SNSD), which was created on the basis of Dodik's Club of Independent Deputies. Karadžić feared this coalition and already in February 1996 he had stated, 'the new enemies are people with left-wing ideas that are alien to the Serbian people'.[18] Finally, the SDS was faced with the Serb Radicals who ran with a programme almost indistinguishable from that of the SDS.[19] Thus, the SDS was met with opposition from both sides, although the moderation of the more moderate forces should not be exaggerated: apart from the only 'civic' party – the

15. F. Švarm. 1996. 'Kasagic Fired', *Vreme NDA*, 2 April. From: http://www.scc .rutgers.edu/serbian_digest/.
16. *Evropski Novisti*, 18 May 1996. From: http://www.ex-yupress.com/evnovosti/evnovosti5.html
17. The leader of the DPB, Predrag Radić, quoted in D. Todorović. 1996. 'I Won't Keep Quiet', *Vreme NDA*, 29 June. From: http://www.scc.rutgers.edu/serbian_digest/.
18. J. Pomfret. 1996. 'Bosnia's Serb's Leader Stages Show of Defiance', *Washington Post*, 10 February, 1.
19. P. Vučinić. 1996. 'Conflicting Forces', *Vreme NDA*, 17 August. From: http://www.scc .rutgers.edu/serbian_digest/.

Liberal Party– most parties maintained that unification with Serbia was a priority, although the imagined time frame for this unification differed significantly between the parties.[20]

If the international authorities had been hoping for a moderate groundswell, then the results of the 1996 elections left them disappointed. The SDS did experience a considerable decrease in its support compared with the 1990 elections, but with 52 per cent of the votes the party still held an absolute majority in the RS assembly. Karadžić had, before the elections, gradually been losing support,[21] but the SDS regained much of its strength following run-ins with the international authorities and the forcing of Karadžić from the political scene.[22]

Table 7.1 Elections to the RS National Assembly, 1996

SDS	SRS	DPB	Union for Peace and Progress	SDA
52 pct (45)	7 pct (6)	3 pct (2)	12 pct (10)	16 pct (14)

Vote percentage and number of mandates won. Source: Z. Tomić and N. Herceg. 1998. *Izbori u Bosni i Hercegovini*, Mostar: Centar za studije novinarstva.

What does the election result tell us about popular opinion? The voters did face an actual choice with a range of different parties to choose between, but the distribution of resources was greatly skewed in the SDS's favour and the party benefited in particular from its control of the media.[23] There were, moreover, many reports of irregularities.[24] Even so, there is nothing that indicates a landslide of moderate opinion. In a poll from 1997, 91 per cent of Serb respondents were opposed to a unified Bosnian state[25] and the attitudes of the population and their elected leaders do not, therefore, seem far removed. Bildt argues that the immediate postwar climate was marked by increased radicalization of both the SDA and the HDZ[26] and this radicalization arguably helped the SDS regain some of its lost ground as

20. D. Stavljanin. 1996. 'Belgrade or Pale', *Vreme NDA*, 12 February. From: http://www.scc. rutgers.edu/serbian_digest/.
21. L. Smajlović. 1996. 'Svi Miloševićevi ljudi', *Vreme*, 25 May, 14–15.
22. Bildt, *Peace Journey*, 189, 229.
23. OSCE. 1996. 'Preliminary Statement of the Co-ordinator for International Monitoring.' M.Vidović. 1996. 'Controlled by Pale and Belgrade', *AIM Press*, 5 August. From: http://www.aimpress.ch/.
24. The International Crisis Group argued that the voter participation amounted to a 103 per cent turnout! P. Shoup. 1997. 'The Elections in Bosnia and Herzegovina: The End of an Illusion', *Problems of Post-Communism* 44(1), 10.
25. Bose, *Bosnia after Dayton*, 2.
26. Bildt, *Peace Journey*, 189.

it could argue that, despite problems of corruption, war profiteering and the setback in Dayton, there was still a need for the SDS's policies and its established nationalist credentials. Further ammunition for the SDS's position was provided by the exodus of Serbs from Sarajevo, which strengthened the argument for ethnic separation.[27] Popular support had become much more significant in intra-ethnic elite competition and the general population seemed susceptible to arguments of continued threat and the need for protection.

The Emergence of New Dynamics

Immediately after the 1996 elections, the SDS leadership appeared to be united with Karadžić ruling from behind the scenes. Karadžić had chosen Biljana Plavšić as his replacement and with this choice of a hard-line loyalist his continued control seemed ensured.[28] This was, however, only until Plavšić started asserting herself; strongly pressured by international authorities, she came to the conclusion that greater pragmatism was the best way to preserve the RS. However, this view was not shared by Karadžić and others and the conflict rapidly intensified and left the RS sharply divided: each side had part of the media, police and even army loyal to them.[29]

The competing centres of power became formalized when Plavšić was expelled from the SDS and subsequently formed the Serb National Alliance (Srpski narodni savez, SNS). As with the other SDS splinter parties, differences between the SDS and SNS were limited: their political programmes were very similar and the vice-president of the SNS, Ostoja Knežević, stated that they had left the SDS 'because the program of the SDS was not implemented in practice although it is good'.[30] The ability of Plavšić to retain her post as president despite having fallen out with the SDS leadership depended crucially on the presence of international forces: Pale's inability to solve the conflict through coercive means owed more to the presence of NATO's Stabilisation Force (SFOR) than the end of the war. The local military was now an ineffective source of power since it was faced with the much stronger SFOR. Moreover, given its new parliamentary basis, the opposition was able to exert significant influence

27. Ibid., 198.
28. P. Vučinić. 1996. 'The Man in the High Castle', *Vreme NDA*, 28 May. From: http://www.scc.rutgers.edu/serbian_digest/.
29. T. Topić. 1997. 'Twilight Zone in Republika Srpska', *Vreme NDA*, 23 August. From: http://www.scc.rutgers.edu/serbian_digest/.
30. D. Novaković. 1997. 'Party against "Position" and "Opposition"', *AIM Press*, 30 October. From: http://www.aimpress.ch/.

on the rivalry between the Pale leadership and Plavšić; except for the Serb Radicals and the Liberal Party, the opposition parties eventually chose to support Plavšić.

The first elections held after this conflict boiled over were the September 1997 local elections. As expected, the SDS was further weakened but, contrary to expectations, the result was a great triumph for the Serb Radicals, who won over 20 per cent of the vote with almost no election campaigning. This support for the ultra-nationalist option again made clear that a new era of moderation was not sweeping over the RS.[31]

Table 7.2 Elections to the RS National Assembly, 1997

SDS	SRS	SNS	SPRS	SNSD	KCD (SDA)
26 pct (24)	16 pct (15)	16 pct (15)	10 pct (9)	3 pct (2)	17 pct (16)

Vote percentage and number of mandates won. Source: Tomić and Herceg, *Izbori u Bosni*.

The results of extraordinary elections for the RS assembly, held two months later, further eroded the SDS's support but, again, it did not give a landslide victory to the more moderate parties: the SDS's support fell to 26 per cent but a considerable part of the loss was picked up by the Radicals with 16 per cent of the vote. The rest of the SDS's former votes went to Plavšić's SNS, also with 16 per cent, while the remainder of the opposition did not make any inroads. In this election, the SDS could not make use of state resources to strengthen its position, to the same extent as it previously had, and the media was now actually biased in Plavšić's favour following SFOR's seizure of the Pale TV transmitters.[32] There is, therefore, no basis for arguing that the results significantly overestimated the support enjoyed by the nationalist parties.

Plavšić's supporters did not secure a majority in the RS assembly and a new prime minister would, therefore, have to rely on support from Bosniak and Croat deputies. This proved to be difficult to swallow for many leaders[33] and Plavšić was therefore faced with a narrow range of options, in the end appointing Dodik, leader of the SNSD, who accepted the nomination. Dodik's government was finally elected at a dramatic assembly session after SDS and SRS deputies had adjourned for the

31. B. Perić. 1997. 'Rise of the Radicals, Decline of the Socialists', *AIM Press*, 16 September. From: http://www.aimpress.ch/.
32. OSCE/ODIHR. 1997. 'Republika Srpska National Assembly Elections, 22–23 November 1997'.
33. Author's interview with Igor Radojičić.

night.[34] Intra-ethnic rivalry, therefore, eventually resulted in a moderation of the dominant position, but this was not a voter-driven process. Given pressure from the international authorities, moderation was one way of gaining an advantage in the competition: the international authorities had been very eager for a split in the SDS to emerge and were highly instrumental in the events.

The moderation entailed by the SDS losing power should not, however, be exaggerated. Plavšić's coalition also included parties that were anything but moderate and some opposition politicians question the significance of the split. Miodrag Živanović, of the Liberal Party, argues: 'it was a constructed conflict ... [the SNS] was a clone of the SDS'.[35] The SDS was, in any case, far from defeated and made a strong comeback in the 2000 elections but the growth of party pluralism had by then forced the party to moderate its position.[36]

Serb Rivalry in Postwar Bosnia

Unlike the Serb leaders in Croatia, the RS leaders were not forced to admit defeat: they could claim to have successfully defended their statelet, despite the humiliation in Dayton. The main part of the leadership was still in place, ethnification was still characteristic of politics and the continuation of wartime dynamics of division and competition was the dominant trend. However, not everything was continuous: international authorities now played a decisive role in intra-Serb rivalry and in the emergence of more moderating dynamics.

Even though the more centripetal dynamics that were emerging do not appear to have been voter-led, the holding of elections meant that the population of the RS could no longer be ignored and the foothold gained by the opposition as a consequence was of great importance for the changing dynamics of competition. Popular support mattered, even though the emergence of centripetal dynamics did not reflect a change in popular attitudes. As a consequence, the positions of other ethnic leaders mattered more and radical posturing prevented other issues from becoming salient, helping the SDS retain its dominance in the first election.

Similar dynamics were found, therefore, in the immediate postwar period, despite the end of violence. Radicalization was not the only possible outcome of intra-ethnic rivalry, in fact relative moderation ensued, and popular attitudes were not the primary driving force. Additionally,

34. D. Chandler. 2000. *Faking Democracy after Dayton*, London: Pluto, 127.
35. Author's interview with Miodrag Živanović.
36. Bose, *Bosnia after Dayton*, 211.

international authorities were shown to be able to exert significant influence on the rivalry, even if the effect was not always as intended.

Intra-ethnic Rivalry in Three Conflict Phases

The analysis of intra-Serb rivalry in three phases of conflict has uncovered some interesting, and somewhat surprising, dynamics. These findings relate to the direction of competition, the audiences to which the elites appeal, the ethnification of politics and kin-state relations. They have implications for conflict analysis and will be used to suggest an alternative approach to analysing intra-ethnic leadership rivalry.

The Dynamics of Competition

One of the most important findings was, as already mentioned, that intra-ethnic competition did not necessarily result in radicalization, even in a situation of war and polarization. Intra-ethnic challengers were often suppressed by the incumbent leaders and no change in position therefore resulted. This was most notably the case for most of the wartime period in both the RSK and the RS, when the leadership met challenges from other parties with repression rather than political manoeuvring. But the analysis also found instances of intra-ethnic competition leading to relative moderation. Examples of this include competition over the Vance Plan in the RSK, when support for the plan provided a quick route to power. Also during the war, Hadžić began to negotiate despite being fiercely attacked by hardliners and these same hardliners continued on this course when they won power, despite also being attacked from the flanks. But the most durable example, during the war, was the change in dynamics in the RS towards the end of the war, when opposition parties, the army and SDS factions coalesced. Centripetal dynamics were, finally, dominant in the postwar period in both cases, despite the persistence of intense intra-ethnic competition. Intra-ethnic rivalry is, therefore, not necessarily detrimental to reaching a settlement even in the context of an intense, violent conflict. This is contrary to Kaufmann's argument that large-scale violence and atrocities provide hardliners with an 'unanswerable argument' and that conciliation is therefore 'easy to denounce as dangerous to group security or as actually traitorous'.[37] Although this form of outbidding certainly takes place, its success is not the only possible outcome of internal rivalry.

---

37. Kaufmann, 'Possible and Impossible Solutions', 142–3.

For the impact of intra-ethnic rivalry, it matters what kind of challengers the leaders are faced with. An important difference was found between challenges from within the party or movement and challenges from other parties, with the former most often causing radicalization. This difference can be explained in terms of politically relevant resources and the issues on which the challenge was based. Especially during the war, positions of power relied on resources emanating from within the party and the movement at large, paramilitary support in particular. This made it more difficult to merely suppress challengers. Furthermore, these internal divisions were mostly over the issue of the war, and by radicalizing the leader could, therefore, ensure continued control of the necessary resources. In case of competition from other parties, the leader could often choose to suppress the opposition rather than change position. Moreover, the opposition parties would frequently also challenge the incumbent leader on other issues than the war, and radicalization on this issue, therefore, would not pre-empt them. Hence when Hadžić was not only facing outbidding on the issue of negotiations but was also being accused of war profiteering and incompetence, he did not have many options since he did not have the necessary resources to suppress his rivals. Instead he sought a more drastic change by initiating negotiations with the Croatian government. Finally, more moderate opposition forces were in some instances able to force a change in the dominant position but alliances were needed in order for this to succeed. This was what happened when more moderate factions of the SDS had the opportunity to coalesce with opposition parties, with the army, with Belgrade and/or with international authorities. The incumbent leaders could then choose between changing their position or face defeat.

The issues underlying competition are, thus, important for the effect of such internal rivalry. But to what extent can other issues become salient in a situation of violence? After all, Gagnon argues that violence has the effect of rendering all other issues politically insignificant.[38] However, if all significant actors take the same position on the national issue, then political competition will likely be focused on other issues, including valence issues such as war profiteering and corruption. In both cases, such issues were salient despite the situation of war and polarization. Moreover, ideological and regional cleavages were also of great importance for the dynamics of competition.

Internal rivalry was significantly affected by the transitional context in which it was played out. Political parties were, in general, leader-

---

38. Gagnon, 'Ethnic Conflict as an Intra-group Phenomenon,' 89.

dominated, their organization was weak and they resembled political movements rather than structured parties. As a consequence, cohesion was often limited, central party structures were of negligible importance, and other resources became important in intra-party struggles. This resulted in more intense intra-party competition and greater risk of radicalization. In the competition between parties, there was a great degree of fluctuation in political positions, parties were not organized around a consolidated programme and today's moderate could be tomorrow's hardliner. The transitional situation served to reduce the impact of popular attitudes and this was compounded by the outbreak of war. Popular attitudes, therefore, became of limited importance for intra-Serb rivalry.

Elite Competition and Popular Attitudes

In the theoretical literature on intra-ethnic elite competition, outbidding is held to be about mass responsiveness to playing the ethnic card, the idea being that elites will refrain from moderating since they fear that more extreme rivals can successfully outflank them by appealing to mass sentiments. But the two cases showed that popular support can, in some circumstances, be of far less importance than other resources used in intra-ethnic rivalry: radicalization was not driven by popular demand; it was not about elites successfully playing the ethnic card. This does not mean that popular attitudes had no importance at all. Rather, they mattered for the ethnification of politics in the prewar period and became of increasing importance in the postwar period when outbidding was at times an effective strategy. However, intra-Serb rivalry was not driven by popular attitudes. The general population lacked alternatives and could be taken along, but popular attitudes were not the driving force behind radicalization or, for that matter, moderation. Other resources were more important, especially during the war when coercive resources were crucial for the direction and outcome of intra-Serb rivalry. Thus 'men with guns' were often the decisive audience.

One could argue that the limited impact of popular attitudes, in a situation of postcommunist transition and increasingly tense conflict, is hardly a surprising conclusion. However, it does depart from existing theorizing on intra-ethnic elite competition. Moreover, the holding of elections and referenda as well as elites claiming to represent the 'will of the people' would lead one to expect greater popular influence on the position of leaders. Even in non-violent phases of the conflict, the impact of popular attitudes was often limited and violence, therefore, is not the only variable of importance.

The Ethnification of Politics

The ethnification of politics, and the subsequent marginalization of non-ethnic rivals, was necessary for the SDS to become dominant in the Serb community. But ethnification was part of the political struggle and should be analysed in terms of political competition. While being aided by outside events, the ability to make an ethnic cleavage dominant also depends on the distribution of resources between the ethnic and non-ethnic parities. An ethnic party system did not automatically emerge due to some overwhelming power of ethnicity. In Bosnia, the SDS benefited from the weak leadership of the SK-SDP, the problems the Reformists had in organizing themselves, internal competition between the non-ethnic parties, and the stronger organization that the party had established compared with its counterpart in Croatia. Serb voters consequently closed ranks behind the party. The SDS in Croatia also achieved dominance, despite its poor showing in the elections. This process of ethnification was strengthened by the Croatian government recognizing the party as the legitimate Serb representative, increasing divisions within the SKH-SDP, improved organization of the party, and the use of non-democratic methods to force out non-SDS officials.

The gradual ethnification, and the continued existence of non-ethnic rivals, made it instrumental to adopt a vague position. Competition was not only about mobilizing the faithful, since the faithful might be the minority, and potential supporters could be discouraged by extreme rhetoric. It was, thus, a symptom of the lack of success in playing the ethnic card: the power of ethnicity was not enough in itself to ensure the ethnic parties' dominance. From a vague position the Serb parties could, moreover, engage in negotiations or even cooperation with Croat and Bosniak parties, which served to strengthen the ethnification of politics. One of the consequences of this vague position, however, was that the leadership became vulnerable to outbidding. While ethnification when complete will generally lead to radicalization, since incentives for vagueness disappears, a more gradual process of ethnification can, therefore, paradoxically also foster radicalization.

The Effect of Inter-ethnic Relations

As a corrective to the idea that radical nationalism feeds on other radical nationalisms, the analysis found that radicalism was not necessarily reciprocated and that the process of radicalization, although aided by Croat or Bosniak radicalization, was frequently more the result of other factors, especially intra-party challenges and kin-state pressure. Changes in intra-ethnic elite rivalry – radicalization or moderation – need not be a response to changed rhetoric or actions of the 'other side'. Consequently, one can question the benefit of analysing conflicts predominantly in terms of reactive frameworks.

This does not mean that the interplay was not at times of great significance for Serb rivalry. In Croatia, in the prewar period, it delivered ammunition to the extremists, while the cancellation of the UN mandate during the war heightened mistrust and strengthened the hardliners. In Bosnia, in the prewar period, the possibility for shifting alliances put a dampener on radicalization and the change in alliance patterns significantly affected Serb positioning. During the war the prospect of serious defeat combined with internal Serb dynamics to finally cause willingness to compromise; and in the postwar period, the radicalism of the HDZ and the SDA helped the SDS reclaim some of its lost ground. However, in none of the above instances did inter-ethnic interplay alone account for the dynamics of intra-Serb competition.

The effect of the interplay was greatest when ethnification was still an issue, when the other ethnic leaders could help impose the ethnic cleavage as the dominant cleavage and hence marginalize non-ethnic rivals. In this phase, the same paradox was found in both cases: the initially relative moderate position of the ethnic parties and the resulting willingness to have contacts actually helped reinforce ethnification. During the war, the intransigence related to the choice of the war option greatly reduced the impact of actions and rhetoric of the other ethnic leaders because what mattered was relative military strength. It was, however, the perception of military strength that was important and its effect still depended on the dynamics of internal competition. As Marieke Kleibor points out, 'ripeness' for conflict settlement thereby becomes a function of internal politics.[39] The resulting imperfect simultaneity of moderation causes problems for reaching settlements; both the intra-ethnic competition and the inter-ethnic interplay, including the military balance, have to be right and the question of timing is therefore crucial. A stalemate or a suitable configuration of intra-ethnic rivalry may persist for a long time without producing negotiation results.

Kin-state Involvement in Intra-ethnic Elite Competition

The potential influence of a kin-state on intra-ethnic elite competition can be derived from two sources. Firstly, from it being a *kin*-state that, due to

39. M. Kleibor. 1994. 'Ripeness of Conflict: A Fruitful Notion?' *Journal of Peace Research* 31(1), 114.

shared ethnicity, is given authority to become involved in local political competition. Secondly, influence can be primarily due to it being a state, with the kin-state leader having access to resources that local leaders lack.

As Milošević fell out with the local leaders, the demarcation of intra-ethnic dynamics changed. To begin with, Milošević was part of the intra-ethnic dynamics, although not part of the intra-ethnic competition, but when Milošević's position became increasingly questioned he sought to influence elite competition in the two statelets in order to retain control. Kin-state dynamics and 'local' intra-ethnic dynamics are not necessarily distinct: the definition of ethnic identity is flexible and local elites can seek to exclude or include the kin-state, thereby rejecting or accepting the authority of the kin-state leader. Brubaker's 'relational fields' – the nationalizing state, the minority and the kin-state – may therefore also overlap, which adds further fluidity to a theory that already insists on the instability of the triadic relationship. It is, moreover, useful to make a distinction between different forms of kin-state influence, since acceptance of the special authority of the kin-state leader is likely to vary in different phases. In the two cases, it was greatest in the prewar phase, when ethnification was yet incomplete and it was important to demonstrate the unity of all Serbs. In the wartime phase and in the postwar phase ethnification was a reality and the authority of the kin-state leader was increasingly downplayed: although political competition was ethnicized, local leaders defined the space of legitimate leadership as being limited by borders, not by ethnicity.

The effect of kin-state involvement was initially to strengthen radicalization through support for the most uncompromising factions. Later on, following intense international pressure and military failures in Croatia, Milošević attempted to engineer more moderate dynamics but this strategy was not always successful since the local leaders enjoyed support from the Serbian opposition and controlled their own paramilitary forces. Relations with Belgrade had, moreover, become a salient issue in the local competition: rival elites could score political points by vowing to assert their independence and not take orders from Belgrade. The degree of internal competition, furthermore, affected the extent to which the kin-state could exert its influence.

The preceding analysis has highlighted the importance of intra-Serb rivalry in the Yugoslav conflict and war. Intra-ethnic competition is the norm in ethnic conflicts, and elite rhetoric alleging unity, the protection of national interests and popular legitimacy should not be accepted at face value. Consequently, intra-ethnic leadership rivalry ought to constitute an integral part of conflict analysis, but it is important to move beyond conventional theoretical expectations: radicalization is not the only possible outcome of such rivalry and popular attitudes can be of limited importance. Intra-ethnic competition should not, therefore, be reduced to outflanking elites successfully playing the ethnic card.

Implications for Conflict Analysis

The lack of internal homogeneity and the resulting fluidity, even in a context of violence, has a number of important implications for conflict analysis. Even though internal leadership rivalry may not translate into alliances across the ethnic divide, it still matters for the development of a conflict and for possible ways out.

In terms of settlement negotiations, the analysis allows us to further refine well-known concepts such as 'spoilers' and conflict 'ripeness'. According to Zartman, a conflict's ripeness for resolution depends on the existence of a 'mutually hurting stalemate' and a 'way out'.[40] However, these concepts are difficult to define, apart from ex post, and will often depend on perceptions as much as on the actual conflict situation. Is a stalemate perceived as hurting and is a way out perceived to be possible? Moreover, whether a stalemate is hurting or not is likely to depend more on internal politics than on the military balance.[41] In Republika Srpska, a military stalemate existed for over a year without this resulting in a perception of a 'hurting stalemate'. Willingness to negotiate, meanwhile, necessitated a further change in the military balance and in the dynamics of internal competition. A similar example can be found in the case of Israel/Palestine: when the PLO began to perceive the existence of a hurting stalemate in the early 1990s, this had much to do with their increasing isolation in Tunis and fear that the Intifada would allow Hamas to become dominant in the Palestinian community.[42] A focus on intra-ethnic rivalry allows for greater sophistication, and accuracy, when ascertaining the existence of a ripe moment for conflict resolution. Such a focus should recognize the different sources of division – from challenges based on greed to those based on different views of what is best for the

---

40. The theory originally also contained a third component: a valid spokesperson. This is even more clearly linked to internal politics. I.W. Zartman. 2003. 'The Timing of Peace Initiatives: Hurting Stalemates and Ripe Moments', in J. Darby and R. MacGinty (eds), *Contemporary Peacemaking: Conflict, Violence and Peace Processes*, Houndsmills: Palgrave Macmillan, 22
41. See also Kleibor, 'Ripeness of Conflict.'
42. See, for example, G. Usher. 1999. *Dispathes from Palestine*, London: Pluto.

ethnic group – as well as the politically relevant audiences. Internal politics need not be driven by popular demands.

The idea of a ripe moment for peace is closely linked to the concept of 'spoilers'.[43] If an accommodative leader is faced with significant spoiler behaviour, then this will either lead to unwillingness to commit to peace in the first place or to an unsustainable peace. Walter Kemp contends that, 'marginalizing the potential deal breakers necessitates, at a minimum, a hurting stalemate',[44] but this really is only a minimum. Spoilers can be driven by other motives and be constrained by forces that are not primarily interested in the military balance. A mutually hurting stalemate depends on perceptions and constraints facing the individual leader and is therefore not likely to be uniformly felt. Stedman's concept of 'spoilers' is largely based on their commitment to goals and the extent of these goals. What is missing from this is a focus on capacity. This is rectified to some extent by Kelly M. Greenhill and Solomon Mayor who, in their capabilities-based model, focus on opportunity-structure rather than intentions when explaining spoiler behaviour.[45] Greenhill and Mayor highlight the importance of military and economic resources, but their framework does not include an analysis of 'domestic political incentives' even though they acknowledge their crucial importance.[46] It therefore does not provide fully satisfactory answers to questions such as: does the spoiler constitute a threat to a leader who is willing to negotiate, will the leader have to change position or face defeat, and what is the basis of the spoiler's power? To answer these questions, one must look at the dynamics of internal competition. Audiences, and the resources they supply, are key to the spoiler's impact: who are the politically relevant audiences, whom do they back, what is the resulting distribution of resources? Thus, when Milan Babić challenged Jovan Rašković on his greater willingness to negotiate, he could rely on support from Belgrade and consequently came to control crucial coercive resources. Rašković enjoyed greater popular support, but in a climate of intensifying conflict this proved insufficient as the general population was not the most relevant audience. However, not all spoilers are successful, not all attempts at outbidding are successful. For example, the 'Real IRA', an IRA splinter group, failed to wreck the Northern Irish peace process in

43. Stedman, 'Spoiler Problems.'
44. W. Kemp. 2005. 'Selfish Determination: The Questionable Ownership of Autonomy Movements', *Ethnopolitics* 4(1), 91
45. K.M. Greenhill and S. Major. 2006. 'The Perils of Profiling: Civil War Spoilers and the Collapse of Intrastate Peace Accords', *International Security* 31(3).
46. Ibid., 13

1998 because, although they had access to coercive resources, they lacked support in the wider nationalist community. The politically relevant audiences differed as did the distribution of resources. Outbidding or the existence of spoilers need therefore not breed radicalization; some spoilers can be ignored, some can be marginalized.

By analysing potential spoiler behaviour this way, it is also possible to decide with greater certainty what constitutes 'sufficient inclusion' in a peace process; who are the veto players that need to be included.[47] This not only depends on their expected popular support but also on their control of such things as the paramilitary. It will, therefore, often be necessary to negotiate with unpleasant characters – a coalition of moderates will likely prove insufficient – although with a change in politically relevant audiences and resources, they can possibly be marginalized in a postwar context.   International involvement can potentially play a significant role, in changing the resources of importance and in affecting their distribution. However, affecting the outcome of internal competition requires detailed knowledge of its dynamics, especially since interference can lead to a backlash, as has been seen in the case of Bosnia where international attempts to strengthen the moderates have often failed spectacularly. What seems to have worked is to target the powerbase of the radical forces. For example, in 2001, access to funds in Hercegovačka Banka was blocked with the purpose of undercutting the financing of Croat extremism. By focusing on the powerbase of competing leaders, on audiences and on resources, one can analyse the nexus of greed and grievance.[48] What is the basis of a leaders' power? Are they constrained by popular demand or by 'men with guns' or 'men with money'? This will impact on possible solutions to the conflict: should we address greed or grievances, or both?

Thus, conflict analysts should recognize the importance of intra-ethnic leadership rivalry and should analyse the basis of such divisions and the resources of the competing leaders, while also being aware of the fluidity of such divisions, of positions, alliances and the distribution of resources. Such complexity is lost if ethnic homogeneity is assumed and ethnic solidarities are viewed as static.

47. Darby and MacGinty, 'Conclusion', 267
48. For arguments on the importance of this nexus, see e.g. Kemp, 'Selfish Determination.' M. Berdal. 2005. 'Beyond Greed and Grievance – And Not Too Soon', *Review of International Studies* 31.

Analysing Contested Nationalism

Intra-ethnic rivalry, consequently, has important implications for conflict analysis. The impact of such internal divisions, be it in the form of spoilers or more moderate voices trying to have a say, depends on the particular configuration of this competition and the context in which it is played out. I am therefore suggesting a framework that goes beyond an automatic assumption of outflanking based on extreme popular sentiments; an approach which holds that the key to the impact of such rivalry is the different audiences to which competing elites appeal.

The existence of more than one politically relevant audience means that intra-ethnic elite competition can be seen as a form of 'nested games' in which elites must consider the effect of their positions in more than one arena.[49] In most conflicts, elites will need to seek support from the general population and from their own party/movement, including the military. But other audiences can be added to this list. In the case of Croatia and Bosnia, the kin-state was a very significant audience, providing military and economic resources and even interfering directly in the local rivalry. In the postwar period, international actors became an important audience. These audiences are important to elites because they provide them with the resources needed if they are to be victorious in intra-ethnic rivalry. The attitudes found among the audiences of significance will, therefore, decisively influence the impact of intra-ethnic competition: what will be the best strategy to ensure the support of the audience that provides the most effective resources? Resources from one arena can, to some extent, substitute for resources from another and autonomy from audiences such as the kin-state is, therefore, strongly influenced by the existence of other bases of support. However, the effectiveness and availability of resources emanating from different audiences will change in the course of a conflict. For example, coercive resources were, during the war, more important than democratic ones, such as popular support, and the latter could not substitute for the former; having links with military forces was more important than reflecting popular attitudes. Finally, the institutional framework –such as the regime type – will serve as an additional influence on the relative importance of different resources as well as on their distribution.

In addition to the distribution of resources, one of the factors influencing the chosen response to intra-ethnic challenges is the issues on which this challenge is based. If issues other than the conflict are included

---

49. The term 'nested games' describes a situation in which actors have to act simultaneously in several arenas and the different constraints found in these arenas may lead them to pursue seemingly irrational behaviour. Tsebelis, *Nested Games.*

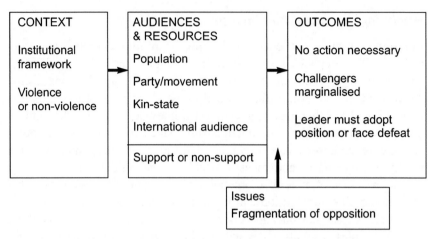

Figure 7.1 Intra-ethnic Elite Rivalry: A Framework for Analysis

then radicalization is a less effective pre-emptive strategy. Other strategies, therefore, are likely to be tried and relative moderation on the conflict issue can even be a way of trying to change the rules of the game for a cornered leader. A final variable of importance was shown to be the configuration of competition, especially the fragmentation of the opposition: is it cohesive enough to constitute a challenge?

This framework emphasizes the importance of identifying politically relevant audiences, which is done by analysing the context in which competition is played out: the phase of the conflict and the regime type. The next step is then to uncover the attitudes held by politically relevant audiences and the resulting distribution of resources. Attitudes will be influenced by the inter-ethnic conflict but not solely by this; the kin-state and 'men with guns and/or money' may, for example, be driven by interests other than the common good. Finally, issues of salience in the competition and the fragmentation of the opposition should be considered since these factors will also influence the direction and outcome of intra-ethnic rivalry.

Corresponding to the outcomes found in the two cases, there are three possible outcomes if a leader is faced with challenges:

1) no action is necessary;
2) the challengers are marginalized and no change in position ensues;
3) the incumbent leader must adopt the opposition's position or face defeat.

Only the latter option corresponds with the theory of outbidding, but note that this need not be based on popular attitudes nor does the change in position necessarily take a radical direction. In a context of war, popular attitudes are likely to prove to be of limited importance and leaders are likely constrained by 'men with guns' rather than the general population. This is not to say, however, that warlords do not enjoy popular backing and that they would be replaced automatically by fluffy liberals if free and fair elections were held, something which seems to have been the more or less implicit hope in Bosnia and Afghanistan, for example. But it does mean that a postwar situation is likely to be associated with a different set of politically relevant audiences and resources and this could change the outcome of leadership contests.

Some may question the generalizability of these findings and counter that the framework has been developed based on two transitional cases. Although ethnic conflicts frequently occur in such settings,[50] they are also found in other political contexts: conflicts in clearly authoritarian settings, such as Sudan, or in more democratic settings, such as in the Basque Country. A transitional situation affects the structures of emerging parties and makes fractionalization more likely. Moreover, the impact of popular sentiments is likely to be reduced and non-democratic resources increase in importance. Additional differences between the Yugoslav cases and other cases of conflict could similarly be pointed to – for example, the availability of natural resources and the degree of international involvement. Such contextual variables are important since they significantly impact on the dynamics of intra-communal rivalry. The above-mentioned differences will, for example, influence the relative importance of different audiences and the resources they are able to supply. However, these differences can be encompassed by the framework; it is a flexible approach to analysing intra-ethnic competition not a fully-fledged theory.

A few examples of both successful and unsuccessful outbidding will serve to illustrate, in brief, the usefulness of focusing on politically relevant audiences and resources. In Northern Ireland, the Ulster Unionist Party (UUP) chose to support the Good Friday Agreement in 1998 despite fierce outbidding from Ian Paisley's Democratic Unionist Party (DUP). Earlier in the peace process, the UUP had embarked on a consultation exercise to canvas opinion in the Unionist community and came to the conclusion that it could expect popular support, which was narrowly borne out by the result of the agreement referendum in May 1998. Further impetus for its position was provided by the decision of militant loyalists to enter the political mainstream, which reduced the numbers of spoilers that the UUP had to concern itself with. Moreover, David Trimble, the

---

50. See, for example, E.D. Mansfield and J. Snyder. 2005. *Electing to fight: Why Emerging Democracies Go to War*, Cambridge, MA: MIT Press.

UUP leader, was pressured by the British government to compromise, and his hard-line credentials finally made it easier for him to bring the rest of the party along, even if it remained divided on the issue.[51]

A case of successful outbidding is found in Armenia, over the issue of Nagorno Karabakh. In 1998, Levon Ter-Petrosian was replaced as president by Robert Kocharian who criticized Ter-Petrosian's willingness to accept a phased approach to settlement negotiations. Kocharian enjoyed the support of the powerful Minister of the Interior and National Security, the Armenian military, much of the intelligentsia, the leaders of Nagorno Karabakh and the diaspora, while Ter-Petrosian had seen his support base reduced.[52] Outbidding was, however, unsuccessful a year later in Nagorno Karabakh (NK) itself when the defence minister, Samvel Babayan, accused the president, Arkady Ghukasian, of selling out and betraying NK's interests. However, the NK president's power was in the ascendancy. His popularity ratings were improving, he was supported by Armenia and he managed to win over the army while his challenger was tainted with allegations of war profiteering and corruption. Babayan was consequently dismissed and later imprisoned for an alleged assassination attempt against the president.[53]

Another example of unsuccessful outbidding is found in the Basque Country where ETA's ability to constrain more mainstream Basque parties has been considerably reduced because they have lost popular support, been weakened by successful police operations, discredited by association with crime, and have lost international backing following 9/11. ETA, moreover, became politically isolated in 1988 when all constitutional Basque parties put their differences behind them and committed to a pact against ETA and in favour of the autonomy status.[54]

Finally, one of the most well-known cases of successful spoiler behaviour is the assassination of President Juvenal Habyarimana of Rwanda following the signing of the Arusha Accords.[55] When Hutu

---

51. See, for example, J. Darby and R. MacGinty. 2000. 'Northern Ireland: Long Cold Peace', in J. Darby and R. MacGinty (eds), *The Management of Peace Processes*, Houndsmills: Macmillan.
52. M. Croissant. 1998. *The Armenia-Azerbaijan Conflict: Causes and Implications*, Westport, CT: Praeger, 123. D. Laitin and R.G. Suny. 1999. 'Armenia and Azerbaijan: Thinking a Way out of Karabakh', *Middle East Policy* 7(1), 155–6.
53. See, for example, De Waal, *Black Garden*, 241–5.
54. See, for example, L. Meer. 2001. 'The Basque Peace Process', in J. Darby and R. MacGinty (eds), *The Management of Peace Processes*, Houndsmills: Macmillan. F.J. Llera, J.M. Mata and C. Irvin. 1993. 'ETA: From Secret Army to Social Movement', *Terrorism and Political Violence* 5.
55. If this was indeed committed by Hutu extremists and not by the Tutsi-controlled Rwandan Patriotic Front.

extremists gained control of coercive resources, there was no sufficient international presence to stop them and more moderate challengers were ruthlessly murdered. Consequently, expressions of potential popular support for more a more moderate course were prevented.[56]

This is not a complicated framework for analysing contested nationalism, but it emphasizes the fluidity of intra-ethnic – and by implication inter-ethnic – relations; it focuses on audiences and resources and includes the possibility of limited popular influence and the emergence of salient issues other than the issue of war. In the conflict literature, and especially in the media, there is still a widespread tendency to understand ethnic groups as entities and cast them as actors.[57] This is an unhelpful and distorting simplification and this study calls for bringing 'the political' into the study of ethnic conflicts, rather than assuming unitary actors and static ethno-national ties.

56. See, for example, G. Prunier. 1995. *The Rwandan Crisis: History of a Genocide*, New York: Columbia University Press.
57. R. Brubaker. 2004. *Ethnicity without Groups*, Cambridge, MA: Harvard University Press, 9.

CHAPTER EIGHT

Conclusion: Contested Nationalism

Despite trying to make appearances to the contrary, unity was far from characteristic of the Serb leaders in Croatia and Bosnia in the 1990s. Serb politics was marked by great divisions, initially over the ethnic definition of politics and later by divisions between leaders who all gladly accepted the label 'Serb leader' and professed to be protecting the interests of the Serb nation. Such claims to a homogeneous national interest were clearly an illusion and divisions and rivalry persisted throughout the prewar and wartime periods and continued into the postwar period. This rivalry was fuelled by differing views of the inter-ethnic conflict, ideological and regional cleavages, valence issues and personal power ambitions.

Intra-Serb rivalry constitutes an underdeveloped aspect of the Yugoslav disintegration and war, an aspect which significantly impacted on the dominant Serb position in Croatia and Bosnia and which is, therefore, important to understanding the intensification of the conflict, the outbreak of war and the persistent difficulty in reaching a peace settlement. Through an in-depth analysis, involving dozens of interviews with actors directly involved in intra-Serb competition, this book has sought to throw some light on these dynamics of competition and on the variables affecting its impact. Theoretically, intra-ethnic elite competition is also underanalysed and almost limited to a theory of outbidding based on elite appeals to mass extremism. This study aimed to fill this gap in the literature and some interesting findings emerged from the empirical analysis. These findings were used to suggest a new framework for analysing contested nationalism, one which emphasizes that intra-ethnic competition should be analysed in terms of political competition with a focus on politically relevant audiences and resources, and which urges analysts to move beyond the assumption of ethnic outbidding. This holds some important lessons for conflict analysis and for the impact of intra-ethnic leadership rivalry.

The radicalization of the Serb position in Croatia and Bosnia owed much to internal rivalry but the outcome was by no means inevitable. Contrary to what is often argued in existing literature on the Yugoslav disintegration and war,[1] the dominance of the Serb hardliners was not based on elites successfully playing the ethnic card and mobilizing the population[2] but was instead especially contingent on coercive resources and support from Belgrade. Milošević was, however, not always able to dictate the direction of internal politics in the two Serb statelets. Local Serb leaders consequently enjoyed a certain level of autonomy, and this influenced the political position they adopted and hence the development of the war. This constitutes an important addition to existing literature on Serb politics in the 1990s.

Serb Disunity in Croatia and Bosnia

The dominance of the ethnic cleavage was not an automatic result of the formation of ethnic parties in Croatia and Bosnia. The ability of the ethnic or nationalist parties to ensure the dominance of this cleavage, and hence the marginalization of non-ethnic rivals, depended heavily on their control of political and non-political resources as well as on the interplay and even the cooperation between the ethnic parties. This ethnification of politics was, furthermore, aided by the transitional situation and by the associated weakly developed socio-economic linkages between political parties and the general population.

The position of the Serb leaders was significantly influenced by intra-Serb rivalry, and the lack of unity therefore had a decisive impact on the development of the conflict and the war. Intra-Serb competition greatly affected the decision by leaders to radicalize or moderate, and to reject or accept proposed settlements. This competition was characterized by a great flux in positions – today's hardliners could be tomorrow's moderates, and vice versa. Radicalization was most often the chosen response in cases of intra-party challenges but the emergence of an external opposition did not have the same effect. Moreover, when other issues were salient and/or the opposition could coalesce with (para)military forces or international authorities, moderating dynamics also ensued. Overall, however, intra-Serb competition was characterized

1. See, for example, Judah, *The Serbs*; Silber and Little, *The Death of Yugoslavia;* and many others.
2. For a detailed argument on the lack of success in popular mobilization, see Gagnon, *The Myth of Ethnic War*.

by the dominance of hardliners. How were the hardliners able to win the intra-Serb competition? How did they marginalize the moderates? Popular attitudes as well as the position of other ethnic leaders often had remarkably little influence on the dynamics of competition and its outcome. Outbidding was thus not about mass responsiveness to extreme rhetoric nor was it determined by missed opportunities for concessions to Serb demands. Generally, access to economic and coercive resources, in large part supplied by Belgrade, was much more decisive, and the dominance of the hardliners was contingent on these factors. The increased importance of non-political resources in the prewar period greatly aided the extremists and made possible the marginalization of moderates. Timing was crucial and the outcome was by no means predetermined.

Belgrade's involvement and support for the hardliners played a crucial role, though the Serb leaders in Croatia and Bosnia should not be regarded as mere puppets of the Serbian president. The leadership in the RSK and the RS played an increasingly independent role vis-à-vis Belgrade and the cooling of relations between Belgrade, Knin and Pale significantly affected the dynamics of elite competition in the two statelets. Finally, international involvement added a new audience of importance in the postwar period. This altered the incentives facing the elites and radicalization became a problematic strategy in the intra-ethnic rivalry: the international authorities influenced the distribution of resources which benefited less extreme forces.

When analysing the Yugoslav conflict, it would, therefore, be a serious simplification to regard the Serbs as monolithic. The dominance of hard-line Serb leaders in Croatia and Bosnia in the prewar period was an important factor in the Yugoslav disintegration. It strengthened Belgrade's position and made a peaceful solution increasingly unlikely. To fully understand the Yugoslav disintegration, it is therefore important to know how this dominance came about and on what it was based. During the war, intra-Serb rivalry increased in intensity and, at first, this served to entrench the radicalism of the leaders and made significant concessions and compromises impossible. Milošević's grip on Serb politics in the statelets gradually decreased but hard-line dominance persisted. However, the dynamics of competition could also give rise to centripetal dynamics, and a complete analysis of the end of the war must include an analysis of intra-Serb rivalry – to fully explain the increased willingness to negotiate in Bosnia and to explain the lack of such willingness in Croatia and Krajina's eventual downfall. Finally, the gradual moderation and increased stability of the postwar period cannot be understood without analysing the dynamics of intra-Serb competition. This is not to say that intra-Serb competition provides a complete explanation of the Yugoslav disintegration and war. Rather, an analysis of the intra-Serb competition is part of what is needed when explaining the Yugoslav disintegration and war – it is not sufficient but it is necessary. Intra-Serb competition in Croatia and Bosnia was strongly influenced by the inter-ethnic conflict, by international involvement and by kin-state involvement, but it was not merely an epiphenomenon of these factors. It is an independent dynamic which is particularly crucial when analysing the timing of political change, of radicalization or moderation.

Steven Burg and Paul Shoup argue, in their book *The War in Bosnia-Herzegovina*, that Western policymakers failed to respond to changes in the Serbian position.[3] If the dynamics of intra-Serb competition had been better understood it would arguably have aided international attempts to engineer a peaceful solution. In the prewar period, Serb claims of unity were largely accepted at face value and attempts were not made to support more moderate voices – for example, through the supply of resources or at least through recognition of their legitimacy. During the war, an understanding of the importance of Serb internal politics gradually developed, at least in the Bosnian case, and mediators tried to foster further divisions between Belgrade and Pale and between civilian and military leaders. International sanctions were instrumental in creating the rift between Belgrade and the local Serb leaders, but the resulting divisions were only utilized to a limited extent by mediators. A quicker result, an earlier emergence of centripetal dynamics, could conceivably have resulted from a clearer targeting of the resources on which the extremists relied or from a deliberate fostering of more moderate alliances.

The Impact of Intra-ethnic Leadership Rivalry

The analysis also has more general implications for conflict analysis, or can be used to refine existing concepts. The empirical findings are at odds with the dominant theoretical assumption of outbidding which holds that intra-ethnic competition will lead to radicalization based on elites playing on extreme mass sentiments. Contrary to this argument, intra-ethnic competition and the position of Serb leaders were only influenced to a limited extent by popular attitudes and radicalization was not the only response to challengers. The elites were generally not constrained by the general population; they had a high level of autonomy, and victory in intra-

3.   Burg and Shoup, *The War in Bosnia-Herzegovina*, 90.

Serb rivalry depended on resources other than popular support. Popular attitudes played a limited role, even though elections and referenda were held and the rhetoric of popular legitimacy and authenticity was given priority by competing elites. Crucial periods of radicalization can fall between elections and, even when elections and referenda are held, popular attitudes need not be the primary factor driving elite competition. Paradoxically, a claim to national self-determination can be an authoritarian claim. The lack of importance of popular attitudes was especially pronounced during the war but, even in the prewar and immediate postwar periods, popular sentiments were not determining changes in the position of leaders: neither radicalization nor moderation appear to have been driven by popular demands. The theory of outbidding also holds that radicalization will be the preferred response to intra-ethnic challenges. However, the analysis presented here shows that centrifugal dynamics did not automatically ensue. In fact, competition between parties led in some instances to relative moderation. According to existing theories, such moderation is based on the possibility or necessity of cross-ethnic alliances, and in the case of Horowitz's Alternative Vote system it is ultimately voter-led.[4] But the moderating dynamics that were uncovered in the analysis were not based on cross-ethnic cleavages and it was elite-led; it was a moderation that took place in spite of elite dominance and ethnicized political competition.

These findings can be used to refine well-known concepts such as 'spoilers' and conflict 'ripeness' which are more or less explicitly concerned with intra-ethnic divisions. The 'ripe moment' for a settlement, despite the primacy given to the existence of a military stalemate, is strongly influenced by internal politics. Is a stalemate perceived as hurting? Can a negotiated 'way out' be coupled with the leader's continued political and even physical survival? Similarly, the capacity of spoilers to undermine a peace process and to force the leadership to radicalize is a function of internal politics: the attitudes of politically relevant audiences, the resulting distribution of resources, the issues underlying the spoiler's challenge and the fragmentation of the competition. Based on these factors, it is possible to ascertain with greater certainty

1) if the spoiler is a veto player that needs to be included, or co-opted, in the process;
2) if, and how, the spoiler can be marginalized; or
3) if the spoiler is of negligible importance and can largely be ignored.

---

4. Sisk, *Power Sharing and International Mediation,* 16. Horowitz, *Ethnic Groups in Conflict,* 359–60.

Such a framework for analysing contested nationalism can also be used to explore the nexus of greed and grievance and the locus of constraint. Is a conflict sustained by the interest of 'men with guns', by the persistence of popular grievances or by some combination of the two?

Contested nationalism is the norm rather than the exception in situations of ethnic and national conflict. However, this will not always lead to radicalization and hence be detrimental to attempts to find a solution. The lack of homogeneity implies that these conflicts are not as static or as natural as is often assumed; alternative views and alternative interpretations exist, even if they are often marginalized and suppressed. Although there are numerous examples of successful outbidding – such as in Israel/Palestine, Rwanda and Armenia – there are probably as many examples of unsuccessful challenges, though these receive less attention. In addition to examples from the two Yugoslav cases, this analysis has mentioned failed flanking attempts by the Real IRA, by ETA and by the powerful defence minister in the case of Nagorno Karabakh. Intra-ethnic leadership rivalry should be analysed in terms of political competition, with a focus on politically relevant audiences and resources in the competition, and not be clouded by propaganda claims of national unity and the protection of national interests. Unity did not save the Serbs, but the reality of disunity was not destined to lead to extreme violence. If 'the political' is brought into the study of ethnic conflict, it becomes possible to better understand the complexities of intra-ethnic rivalry and possibly avoid, or at least limit, its negative manifestations.

REFERENCES

Books, Chapters in Books, Journal Articles and Unpublished Papers

Andjelić, N. 2003. *Bosnia-Herzegovina: The End of a Legacy*, London: Frank Cass.

Arnautović, S. 1996. *Izbori u Bosni i Hercegovini '90: Analiza izbornog procesa*, Sarajevo: Promocult.

Banac, I. 1984. *The National Question in Yugoslavia: Origins, History, Politics,* Ithaca, NY: Cornell University Press.

———. 1992. 'The Fearful Asymmetry of War: The Causes and Consequences of Yugoslavia's Demise', *Daedalus* 121(2): 141–74.

———. 1996. 'Foreword: The Politics of Cultural Diversity in Former Yugoslavia', in S.P. Ramet. *Balkan Babel*, Boulder, CO: Westview.

Barker, R. 1990. *Political Legitimacy and the State*, Oxford: Clarendon.

Barry, B. 1975. 'Review Article: Political Accommodation and Consociational Democracy', *British Journal of Political Science* 5(4): 477–505.

Beetham, D. 1991. *The Legitimation of Power*, London: MacMillan.

Berdal, M. 2005. 'Beyond Greed and Grievance – and Not Too Soon', *Review of International Studies* 31: 687–98.

Bildt, C. 1998. *Peace Journey: The Struggle for Peace in Bosnia*, London: Weidenfeld.

Bose, S. 2002. *Bosnia after Dayton*, London: Hurst.

Bougarel, X. 1996. 'Bosnia and Hercegovina: State and Communitarianism', in D. Dyker and I. Vejvoda (eds), *Yugoslavia and After*, London: Longman.

Brubaker, R. 1996. *Nationalism Reframed: Nationhood and the National Question in the New Europe,* Cambridge: Cambridge University Press.

———. 2004. *Ethnicity without Groups,* Cambridge, MA: Harvard University Press.

Burg, S.L and P.S. Shoup. 1999. *The War in Bosnia-Herzegovina: Ethnic Conflict and International Intervention*, Armonk, NY: M.E. Sharpe.

Caspersen, N. 2003. 'The Thorny Issue of Ethnic Autonomy in Croatia', *Journal of Ethnopolitics and Minority Issues in Europe* 3: 1–27.

———. 2006. 'Contingent Nationalist Dominance: Intra-Serb Challenges to the Serb Democratic Party', *Nationalities Papers* 34(1): 51–69.

———. 2007. 'Belgrade, Pale, Knin: Kin-state Control over Rebellious Puppets?' *Europe-Asia Studies* 59 (4): 619–39.

———. 2008 .'Between Puppets and Independent Actors: Kin-state Involvement in the Conflicts in Bosnia, Croatia and Nagorno Karabakh', *Ethnopolitics* 7(4): 357–72.

———. 2008. 'Intragroup Divisions in Ethnic Conflicts: From Popular Grievances to Power Struggles', *Nationalism and Ethnic Politics* 14(2): 239–65.

Chandler, D. 2000. *Faking Democracy after Dayton*, London: Pluto.

Cochrane, F. 1997. *Unionist Politics*, Cork: Cork University Press.

Cohen, L. 1995. *Broken Bonds: The Disintegration of Yugoslavia*, Boulder, CO: Westview.

——. 2002. *Serpent in the Bosom: The Rise and Fall of Slobodan Milošević*, Boulder, CO: Westview.

Collier, P. 2000. 'Doing Well out of War'. In M. Berdal & D. Malone (eds), *Greed and Grievance: Economic Agendas in Civil Wars*. Boulder, CO: Lynne Rienner.

Croatian International Relations Review, 1999. 'Chronology 1993: April through June', 5(15/16).

——. 2000. 'Chronology 1993, October through December', 6(18/19).

——. 2001. 'Chronology 1994: May through August', 7(22/23).

——. 2002. 'Chronology 1994/5: November 1994 through April 1995', 8(26/27).

——. 2002. 'Chronology 1995: August 1 through August 31', 11(30/31).

Croissant, M. 1998. *The Armenia-Azerbaijan Conflict: Causes and Implications*, Westport, CT: Praeger.

Dakić, M. 1994. *The Serbian Krayina: Historical Roots and Its Birth*, Knin: Iskra.

——. 2001. *Krajina kroz Vijekove*, Belgrade: Vedes.

Darby, J. and R. MacGinty. 2000. 'Conclusion: The Management of Peace', in J. Darby and R. MacGinty (eds), *The Management of Peace Processes*, Houndsmills: Macmillan.

——. 2000. 'Northern Ireland: Long Cold Peace', in J. Darby and R. MacGinty (eds), *The Management of Peace Processes*, Houndsmills: Macmillan.

——. 2003. 'Conclusion: Peace Processes, Present and Future', in J. Darby and R. MacGinty (eds), *Contemporary Peacemaking: Conflict, Violence and Peace Processes*, Houndsmills: Palgrave Macmillan.

De Waal, T. 2003. *Black Garden: Armenia and Azerbaijan through Peace and War*, New York: New York University Press.

Dević, A. 1997. 'Anti-War Initiatives and the Un-Making of Civic Identities in the Former Yugoslav Republics', *Journal of Historical Sociology* 10(2): 127–56.

Djokić, D. 2003. '(Dis)integrating Yugoslavia: King Alexander and Inter-war Yugoslavism', in D. Djokić (ed.) *Yugoslavism*, London: Hurst.

Dragović-Soso, J. 2002. *Saviours of the Nation: Serbia's Intellectual Opposition and the Revival of Nationalism*, London: Hurst

Esman, M.J. 1994. *Ethnic Politics*, Ithaca, NY: Cornell University Press.

——. 2000. 'Ethnic Pluralism: Strategies for Conflict Management', Paper presented at the conference 'Facing Ethnic Conflicts', Center for Development Research, Bonn, 14–16 December.

Evans, G. and M. Duffy. 1997. 'Beyond the Sectarian Divide: The Social Bases and Political Consequences of Nationalist and Unionist Party Competition in Northern Ireland', *British Journal of Political Science* 27(1): 47–81.

Fearon, J.D. and D.D. Laitin. 2000. 'Violence and the Social Construction of Ethnic Identity', *International Organization* 54(4): 845–77.

——. 2003. 'Ethnicity, Insurgency, and Civil War', *American Political Science Review* 97(1): 75–90.

Gagnon Jr., V.P. 1995. 'Ethnic Conflict as an Intra-group Phenomenon: A Preliminary Framework', *Revija za sociologiju* 26(1/2): 81–90.

——. 2004. *The Myth of Ethnic War: Serbia and Croatia in the 1990s*, Ithaca, NY: Cornell University Press.

Glenny, M. 1996. *The Fall of Yugoslavia*, London: Penguin.

Goldstein, I. 1999. *Croatia: A History*, London: Hurst.

Golubović, Z. 1996. 'The Causes of Ethno-Mobilization in the Former Yugoslavia', in S. Bianchini and D. Janjić (eds), *Ethnicity in Postcommunism*, Belgrade: Institute of Social Sciences.

Gordy, E. 1999. *The Culture of Power in Serbia*, University Park: Pennsylvania State University Press.

Gow, J. 1997. *Triumph of the Lack of Will*, London: Hurst

———. 2003. *The Serbian Project and Its Adversaries: A Strategy of War Crimes,* London: Hurst.

Grdešić, I. 1997. 'Building the State: Actors and Agendas', in I. Šiber (ed.) *The 1990 and 1992/3 Sabor Elections in Croatia*, Berlin: Sigma.

Grdešić, I., M. Kasapović, I. Šiber and N. Zakošek. 1991. *Hrvatska u izborima*, Zagreb: Naprijed.

Greenhill, K.M. and S. Major. 2006. 'The Perils of Profiling: Civil War Spoilers and the Collapse of Intrastate Peace Accords', *International Security* 31(3): 7–40.

Gurr, T.R. 1993. *Minorities at Risk: A Global View of Ethnopolitical Conflicts*, Washington DC: United States Institute of Peace.

Hislope, R. 1997. 'Intra-ethnic Conflict in Croatia and Serbia: Flanking and the Consequences for Democracy', *East European Quarterly* 30(4): 471–94.

———. 1998. 'The Generosity Moment: Ethnic Politics, Democratic Consolidation and the State in Yugoslavia (Croatia), South Africa and Czechoslovakia', *Democratization* 3(1): 64–89.

Holbrooke, R. 1999. *To End a War*, New York: Modern Library.

Horowitz, D. 1985. *Ethnic Groups in Conflict*, Berkeley: University of California Press.

———. 1990. 'Ethnic Conflict Management for Policy-Makers' in J.V. Montville (ed.) *Conflict and Peacemaking in Multiethnic Societies*, Toronto: Lexington.

———. 1991. *A Democratic South Africa? Constitutional Engineering in a Divided Society*, Berkeley: University of California Press.

———. 1997. 'Self-determination: Politics, Philosophy, and Law', in I. Shapiro and W. Kymlicka (eds), *Ethnicity and Group Rights*, New York: New York University Press.

———. 2000. 'Some Realism about Peacemaking', Paper presented at the conference 'Facing Ethnic Conflicts', Center for Development Research, Bonn, 14–16 December.

Isaković, Z. 2000. *Identity and Security in the Former Yugoslavia,* Aldershot: Ashgate.

Jović, D. 2003. 'Yugoslavism and Yugoslav Communism: From Tito to Kardelj', in D. Djokić (ed.) *Yugoslavism*, London: Hurst.

Judah, T. 2000. *The Serbs: History, Myth and the Destruction of Yugoslavia*, New Haven, CT: Yale University Press.

Kaldor, M. 1993. 'Yugoslavia and the New Nationalism', *New Left Review* 197: 96–112.

Kasapović, M. 1992. 'The Structure and Dynamics of the Yugoslav Political Environment and Elections in Croatia', in J. Seroka and V. Pavlović (eds), *The Tragedy of Yugoslavia*, Armonk, NY: M.E. Sharpe.

———. 1997. 'Parliamentary Elections in Croatia: Electoral Models and their Effects', in I. Šiber (ed.) *The 1990 and the 1992/93 Sabor Elections in Croatia,* Berlin: Sigma.

Kasapović, M. and N. Zakošek. 1997. 'Democratic Transition in Croatia: Between Democracy, Sovereignty and War', in I. Šiber (ed.) *The 1990 and the 1992/93 Sabor Elections in Croatia,* Berlin: Sigma.

Kaufmann, C. 1996. 'Possible and Impossible Solutions to Ethnic Wars', *International Security* 20(4): 136–75.

Kemp, W.A. 2004. 'The Business of Ethnic Conflict', *Security Dialogue* 35(1): 43–59.

———. 2005. 'Selfish Determination: The Questionable Ownership of Autonomy Movements', *Ethnopolitics* 4(1): 85–93.

Kitschelt, H., Z. Mansfeldova, R. Markowski and G. Tóka. 1999. *Post-Communist Party Systems*, New York: Cambridge University Press.

Kleibor, M. 1994. 'Ripeness of Conflict: A Fruitful Notion?' *Journal of Peace Research* 31(1): 109–16.

Kovačević, D. 2003. *Kavez: Krajina u dogovorenom ratu*, Belgrade: Srpski Demokratski Forum.

Kurspahić, K. 2003. *Prime Time Crime: Balkan Media in War and Peace*, Washington DC: United States Institute of Peace.

Kuzmanović, R. 1994. *Konstitutivni akti Republike Srpske*, Glas Srpski: Banja Luka.

Laitin, D. and R.G. Suny. 1999. 'Armenia and Azerbaijan: Thinking a Way out of Karabakh', *Middle East Policy* 7(1): 145–76.

Laver, M. 1975. 'Strategic Campaign Behaviour for Electors and Parties: The Northern Ireland Assembly Election of 1973', *European Journal of Political Research* 3: 21–45.

Lijphart, A. 1971. 'Comparative Politics and the Comparative Method', *American Political Science Review* 65(3): 682–93.

———. 1977. *Democracy in Plural Societies*, New Haven, CT: Yale University Press.

Llera, F.J., J. Mata and C.L. Irvin. 1993. 'ETA: From Secret Army to Social Movement', *Terrorism and Political Violence* 5: 106–34.

Malešević, S. 2000. 'Ethnicity and Federalism in Communist Yugoslavia and Its Successor States', in Y. Ghai (ed.) *Autonomy and Ethnicity*, Cambridge: Cambridge University Press.

Mansfield, E.D. and J. Snyder. 2005. *Electing to Fight: Why Emerging Democracies Go to War*, Cambridge, MA: MIT Press.

Marković, B. 2002. 'Yugoslav Crisis and the World, 1994', *Balkan Repository Project.* From: >http://www.balkan-archive.org.yu/politics/chronology/chron94.html<

Marković, V. 1996. 'Three Misconceptions of Nationalism as Revealed through Empirical Experience', in S. Bianchini and D. Janjić (eds), *Ethnicity in Postcommunism*, Belgrade: Institute of Social Sciences.

Meer, L. 2001. 'The Basque Peace Process', in J. Darby and R. MacGinty (eds), *The Management of Peace Processes*, Houndsmills: Macmillan.

Mitchell, P. 1995. 'Competition in an Ethnic Dual Party System', *Ethnic and Racial Studies* 18(4): 773–96.

Mueller, J. 2000. 'The Banality of "Ethnic" War', *International Security* 25 (1): 42–70.

Nordlinger, E. 1972. *Conflict Regulation in Divided Societies*, Cambridge. MA: Center for International Affairs, Harvard University.

O'Leary, B. 1989. 'The Limits to Coercive Consociationalism in Northern Ireland', *Political Studies* 18(4): 562–88.

OSCE. 1996. 'Preliminary Statement of the Co-ordinator for International Monitoring', From: http://www.osce.org/documents/odihr/1996/10/1195_en.pdf.

OSCE/ODIHR, 1997. 'Republika Srpska National Assembly Elections, 22–23 November 1997', From : http://www.osce.org/documents/odihr/1997/12/1200_en.pdf.

Owen, D. 1995. *Balkan Odyssey,* San Diego, CA: Harvest Book.

Panossian, R. 2002. 'The Irony of Nagorno-Karabakh: Formal Institutions versus Informal Politics', in J. Hughes and G. Sasse (eds), *Ethnicity and Territory in the Former Soviet Union,* London: Frank Cass.

Pappalardo, A. 1981. 'The Conditions for Consociational Democracy: A Logical and Empirical Critique', *European Journal of Political Research* 9(4): 365–90.

Pavlowitch, S.K. 2003. 'Serbia, Montenegro and Yugoslavia', in D. Djokić (ed.) *Yugoslavism*, London: Hurst.

Pejanović, M. 2002. *Through Bosnian Eyes: The Political Memories of a Bosnian Serb,* Sarajevo: TKD Šahinpašić.

Plećaš, D. (ed.) *Deset godine Socijaldemokratske partije Hrvatske* 1990–2000, Zagreb: SDP.

Prstojević, M. (ed.). 1990. *BiH Izbori '90*, Sarajevo: Oslobođenje public.

Prunier, G. 1995. *The Rwandan Crisis: History of a Genocide*, New York: Columbia University Press.

Putnam, R. D. 1976. *The Comparative Study of Political Elites*, Englewood Cliffs: Prentice Hall.

Rabushka, A. and K. Shepsle. 1972. *Politics in Plural Societies: A Theory of Democratic Instability*, Columbus: Merrill.

Radošević, S. 1996. 'The Collapse of Yugoslavia: Between Chance and Necessity, 'in D. Dyker and I. Vejvoda (eds), *Yugoslavia and After*, London: Longman.

Ramet, S. P. 1992. *Nationalism and Federalism in Yugoslavia 1963–1983*, Bloomington: Indiana University Press.

Rašković, J. 1990. *Luda Zemlja*, Belgrade: Akvarijus.

Reilly, B. 2001. *Democracy in Divided Societies: Electoral Engineering for Conflict Management*, Cambridge: Cambridge University Press.

Sabol, Ž. (ed.). 1992. *Sabor Republike Hrvatske 1990–1992*, Zagreb: Hrvatski Sabor.

Sartori, G. 1976. *Parties and Party Systems*, Cambridge: Cambridge University Press.

Sell, L. 2002. *Milosevic and the Destruction of Yugoslavia*, Durham: Duke University Press.

Shoup, P. 1997. 'The Elections in Bosnia and Herzegovina: The End of an Illusion', *Problems of Post-Communism* 44(1): 3–15.

Šiber, I. and C. Wenzel. 1997. 'Electoral Behaviour in Croatia', in I. Šiber (ed.), *The 1990 and 1992/3 Sabor Elections in Croatia*, Berlin: Sigma.

Silber, L. and A. Little. 1996. *The Death of Yugoslavia*, London: Penguin.

Sisk, T. 1996. *Power Sharing and International Mediation in Ethnic Conflicts*, Washington DC: United States Institute of Peace.

Sjöblom, G. 1968. *Party Strategies in a Multiparty System*, Lund: Studentlitteratur.

Stedman, S. J. 1997. 'Spoiler Problems in Peace Processes', *International Security*, 22(2): 5-53.

Tatalović, S. 1996. 'Peaceful Solution of Conflicts in Croatia: Case study of Gorski Kotar', *Peace and the Sciences* XXVII (June): 38–46.

Thomas, R. 1999. *Serbia under Milošević*, London: Hurst.

Thompson, M. 1992. *A Paper House: The Ending of Yugoslavia*, London: Vintage.

Tomanović, V. 1996. 'Nationalism, Transition and Democracy', in S. Bianchini and D. Janjić (eds.), *Ethnicity in Postcommunism*, Belgrade: Institute of Social Sciences.

Tomić, Z. and N. Herceg. 1998. *Izbori u Bosni i Hercegovini*, Mostar: Centar za studije novinarstva.

Trifunovska, S. 1999. 'Political and Security Aspects of Minorities in Croatia', in her (ed.), *Minorities in Europe: Croatia, Estonia and Slovakia*, The Hague: TMC Asser Press.

Tsebelis, G. 1990. *Nested Games: Rational Choice in Comparative Politics*, Berkeley: University of California Press.

Usher, G. 1999. *Dispathes from Palestine*, London: Pluto.

Van Biezen, I. 2003. *Political Parties in New Democracies*, Basingstoke: Palgrave MacMillan.

Vejvoda, I. 1996. 'Yugoslavia 1945-91: From Decentralization without Democracy to Dissolution', in D. Dyker and I. Vejvoda (eds), *Yugoslavia and After*, London: Longman.

Vukas, B. 1999. 'The Legal Status of Minorities in Croatia', in S. Trifunovska (ed.) *Minorities in Europe: Croatia, Estonia and Slovakia*, The Hague: TMC Asser Press.

Woodward, S. 1995. *Balkan Tragedy: Chaos and Dissolution after the Cold War*, Washington, DC: Brookings Institution.

Zakošek, N. 1997. 'Political Parties and the Party System in Croatia', in I. Šiber (ed.) *The 1990 and 1992/3 Sabor Election in Croatia*, Berlin: Sigma.

------. 1997. 'Pregled rezultata izbora za domove Sabora Republike Hravtske i za županijske skupštine', *Politička Misao* 34(2): 129–43.

Zartman, I. 1995. 'Dynamics and Constraints in Negotiations in Internal Conflicts', in I. Zartman (ed.) *Elusive Peace: Negotiating an End to Civil War,* Washington, DC: Brookings Institution.

------. 1997. 'Explaining Oslo', *International Negotiation* 2: 195–215.

------. 2003. 'The Timing of Peace Initiatives: Hurting Stalemates and Ripe Moments', in J. Darby and R. MacGinty (eds), *Contemporary Peacemaking: Conflict, Violence and Peace Processes*, Houndsmills: Palgrave Macmillan

Zulfikarpašić, A. 1998. *The Bosniak*, London: Hurst.

Interviews

Croatian Case

Bakić, Ranko. Former President of the Social Democratic Party of Krajina. Banja Luka, 23 October 2003.

Dakić, Mile. Former President of the JSDS. Belgrade, 29 August 2003.

Degoricija, Slavko. Chief negotiator for the Croatian government, 1990–1994. Zagreb, 10 December 2003.

Đukić, Milan. President of the SNS. Zagreb, 30 July 2003.

Džakula, Veljko. Current President of the SDF; former president of SAO Western Slavonia; deputy prime minister in the RSK. Zagreb, 12 August 2003.

Ećimović, Dušan. RSK information minister, 1992–1993. Belgrade, 29 August 2003.

Hadžić, Goran. RSK president, 1992–1994. Belgrade, 30 October 2003.

Hedl, Drago. Journalist, *Feral Tribune*. Osijek, 11 September 2003.

Kovačević, Dragan. RSK information minister, 1995. Belgrade, 17 September 2004.

Leskovac, Rade. Former President of the SRS in Croatia. Vukovar, 26 September 2003.

Letica, Slaven. Franjo Tuđman's chief adviser, 1990–1991. Zagreb, 18 September 2003.

Ležajić, Rajko. Speaker of the RSK parliament, 1994–1995. Belgrade, 17 September 2004.

Lubovac, Branko. Minister in RSK government, 1993–1994. Belgrade, 28 October 2003.

Plećaš, Dušan. Secretary of the SDP's council, 1990 onwards. Zagreb, 26 March 2004.

Pupovac, Milorad. First President of the SDF; founder of the SSS; co-founder of the SDSS. Zagreb, 11 August 2003.

Rajić, Simo. Deputy Speaker of Parliament and MP for the SKH-SDP, 1990–1991. Zagreb, 19 March 2004.

Stanimirović, Vojislav. President of the SDSS; former president of Eastern Slavonia's executive council. Vukovar, 25 September 2003.

Švarm, Filip. Journalist, *Vreme*. Belgrade, 13 September 2004.

Višnjić, Ćedomir. President of *Prosvjeta*. Zagreb, 18 March 2004.

Vukćević, Vojislav. SDS vice-president, 1990–1991, and one of the party's founders. Belgrade, 7 August 2003.

Bosnian Case

Ilić, Dragutin. Founder of the SPRS. Banja Luka, 23 October 2003.

Kasagić, Rajko. RS prime minister, 1995–1996. Banja Luka, 11 November 2003.

Lazarević, Predrag. Founder of the Serb Party of Krajina; member of SDS's political council before the war. Banja Luka, 12 November 2003.

Lazović, Miro. Speaker of the Bosnian parliament during the war. Sarajevo, 29 June 2004.

Ljujić-Mijatović, Tatjana. Serb member of the wartime Bosnian presidency. Sarajevo, 2 July 2004.

Lukić, Vladimir. RS prime minister 1993–1994. Banja Luka, 2 December 2003.
Mikić, Đorđe. Member of the SDS's political council in 1990. Banja Luka, 7 November 2003.
Nagradić, Slobodan. Professor, Faculty of Political Science, University of Banja Luka. Sarajevo, 19 November 2003.
Pejanović, Mirko. Serb member of the Bosnian wartime presidency; President of the SGV. Sarajevo, 6 July 2004.
Poplašen, Nikola. Founder of the SRS in Bosnia. Banja Luka, 3 December 2003.
Radojičić, Igor. Spokesman for the SNSD; former spokesman for the SPRS. Banja Luka, 1 December 2003.
Tadić, Ognjen. Secretary General of the SRS. Banja Luka, 7 November 2003.
Živanović, Miodrag. Founder of the Liberal Party. Banja Luka, 22 October 2003.

Election Programmes

Jugoslavenska samostalna demokratska stranka. 1990. 'Politički program – deklaracija', *Naše Teme* 34(3/4): 747–51.
Prstojević, M. (ed.). 1990. *BiH Izbori '90*, Sarajevo: Oslobođenje public (Election programmes from the 1990 Bosnian elections).
Savez komunista Hrvatske: Stranka demokratskih promjena. 1990.'Za miran, sretan život u suverenoj i demokratskoj Hrvatskoj', *Naše Teme* 34(3/4): 622–47.
Srpska demokratska stranka. 1990. 'Programski ciljevi', *Naše Teme* 34(3/44): 774–81.

Transcripts from the International Criminal Tribunal on Yugoslavia

ICTY. 1996. 'Transcripts: Prosecutor vs Duško Tadić (IT–94–I–T)', Transcripts from testimony of anonymous witness, 30 May–4 June.
——. 2002. 'Transcripts: Prosecutor vs. Radoslav Brdjanin and Stojan Zupljanin (IT–99–36)', Transcripts from Robert Donia's testimony, 29–31 January.
——. 2002. 'Transcripts: Prosecutor vs Slobodan Milošević (IT–02–54)', Transcripts from Milan Babić's testimony, 18 November–9 December.
——. 2003. 'Judgement: Prosecutor vs. Blagoje Simić, Miroslav Tadić, Simo Zarić (IT–95–9–T)'. 17 October.
——. 2003 'Transcripts: Prosecutor vs Slobodan Milošević (IT–02–54)', Transcripts from David Owen's testimony, 3–4 November.

Newspapers and Magazines Consulted

AIM Press
Armenia Daily Digest
Borba
Danas
Dani
Evropski Novosti
Feral Tribune
Financial Times
Nezavisne Novine

Oslobođenje
Pečat
Politika
RFE/RL
Slobodna Bosna
Vjesnik
Vreme
Vreme NDA
War Report
Washington Post

INDEX